ROUTLEDGE LIBRARY EDITIONS: COLONIALISM AND IMPERIALISM

Volume 44

THE STRUGGLE FOR ASIA
1828–1914

THE STRUGGLE FOR ASIA
1828–1914

A Study in British and Russian Imperialism

DAVID GILLARD

LONDON AND NEW YORK

First published in 1977 by Methuen & Co. Ltd

This edition first published in 2023
by Routledge
4 Park Square, Milton Park, Abingdon, Oxon OX14 4RN

and by Routledge
605 Third Avenue, New York, NY 10158

Routledge is an imprint of the Taylor & Francis Group, an informa business

© 1977 David Gillard

All rights reserved. No part of this book may be reprinted or reproduced or utilised in any form or by any electronic, mechanical, or other means, now known or hereafter invented, including photocopying and recording, or in any information storage or retrieval system, without permission in writing from the publishers.

Trademark notice: Product or corporate names may be trademarks or registered trademarks, and are used only for identification and explanation without intent to infringe.

British Library Cataloguing in Publication Data
A catalogue record for this book is available from the British Library

ISBN: 978-1-032-41054-8 (Set)
ISBN: 978-1-032-44639-4 (Volume 44) (hbk)
ISBN: 978-1-032-44641-7 (Volume 44) (pbk)
ISBN: 978-1-003-37315-5 (Volume 44) (ebk)

DOI: 10.4324/9781003373155

Publisher's Note
The publisher has gone to great lengths to ensure the quality of this reprint but points out that some imperfections in the original copies may be apparent.

Disclaimer
The publisher has made every effort to trace copyright holders and would welcome correspondence from those they have been unable to trace.

The Struggle for Asia
1828-1914
A study in British and Russian imperialism

David Gillard

Methuen & Co Ltd
LONDON

*First published in 1977 by
Methuen & Co. Ltd
11 New Fetter Lane, London EC4P 4EE
First published as a University Paperback in 1980*

© *1977 David Gillard*

*Printed in Great Britain by
Butler & Tanner Ltd, Frome and London*

ISBN 0 416 13250 2 (hardback edition)
ISBN 0 416 74040 5 (paperback edition)

*All rights reserved. No part
of this book may be reprinted
or reproduced or utilized in any form
or by any electronic, mechanical or other means,
now known or hereafter invented, including photocopying and recording, or in any information
storage or retrieval system, without permission in writing from the publishers.*

British Library Cataloguing in Publication Data

Gillard, David
   The struggle for Asia, 1828–1914. –
   (University paperbacks; 708).
   1. Eastern question
   2. Great Britain – Foreign relations – Russia
   3. Russia – Foreign relations – Great Britain
   I. Title   II. Series
   950   D376.G7

ISBN 0 416 74040 5

Contents

	Preface	vii
	Introduction	1
Chapter 1	The rise of Russian and British power in Eurasia	7
Chapter 2	British leaders take alarm, 1828–33	18
Chapter 3	Palmerston's counter-offensive, 1833–41	43
Chapter 4	The British and the Russians lose control, 1841–53	68
Chapter 5	Russian leaders take alarm, 1853–60	92
Chapter 6	Alexander II's counter-offensive, 1860–78	115
Chapter 7	The Russians and the British lose confidence, 1878–94	134
Chapter 8	The end of the Great Game, 1894–1908	153
	Conclusion	179
	Further reading	186
	Index	199

Preface

Russo-British rivalry has been the subject of numerous books and articles, which have dealt in detail with its manifestation at different times and in various parts of Eurasia, but there has been no general survey for the continent as a whole, giving equal prominence to both Russian and British policies. I have tried to supply this in the present volume.

This book, like so many other works on international history, was inspired by the teaching and writings of Professor W. N. Medlicott, and I am most grateful for his guidance over the years. My thanks are also due to Mr Peter Wait of Methuen, whose patient and good-humoured assumption, in face of all evidence to the contrary, that one day I would actually complete the book, made it impossible to disappoint him; and to Joan, Penny and Nicholas Gillard, both for their help and for their equally beneficial distraction.

David R. Gillard
September 1974

NOTE ON SPELLING

I have, in general, followed the *Cambridge History of Islam* for the spelling of names in Islamic Asia.

D.R.G.

Introduction

International politics are commonly regarded as irrational and unprincipled. Political leaders of great states, who in private life and in domestic politics may be sane, intelligent, peaceable and morally earnest, are seen to use their power abroad in a violent and ruthless manner for reasons which can appear ludicrous to posterity and even to many of their contemporaries. They are obsessed with improbable dangers. They itch to control the destinies of weaker states. They may even commit thousands of their countrymen to shoot, stab, blast and burn other human beings and to risk the same fate in their turn. When those who criticize them for this come into office, they are apt to behave in the same way. The spectacle fascinates some observers and repels others. It is the current fashion to be repelled. From this viewpoint, the celebrated rivalry between the Russians and the British in Asia in the nineteenth century would seem to be a classic case of futility, mutual misunderstanding and the arrogance of power.

A hundred years ago most politically conscious people in Great Britain and Russia regarded the other's government with fear and mistrust. A great political game seemed to be in progress. The prize would be political ascendancy in Asia; the losing empire would go into permanent decline. There was only one war, the Crimean, in which their armies were directly engaged against one another, but they fought or intimidated most of the peoples of Asia who lived precariously between their two empires. Even when the cause of these local conflicts seemed remote from the 'Great Game', the outcome usually marked a crucial shift in the distribution of power and influence on which the 'Game' turned. And these conflicts were watched anxiously in the other capitals of Europe as well as in London and St Petersburg. For about eighty years, roughly from 1828 to 1908, the ever-growing Asian empires of Russia and Great Britain and the recurring tension between them were central to international politics on the whole Eurasian land mass.

What follows is a survey and a tentative explanation. That the Russians and the British built empires in Asia and that their empire-building brought conflict between them does not in itself, of course, clamour for explanation. Empire-building and the conflict of neighbouring empires have been normal ever since the emergence of political units powerful enough for the purpose. But why this should be so remains debatable. The case of the Russians and the British in Asia is significant to this debate for two reasons in particular. First, the character of a government's policies abroad is often supposed to be governed in some way by the country's institutions and its 'stage of historical development'. The contrast between the Russian and British political, social and economic systems was considerable throughout the nineteenth century, yet as 'imperialists' their motivations and conduct do not appear to be very different. The reasons for this may contribute to the search for a general explanation of 'imperialism'. Secondly, there was in both countries a good deal of hesitation as to whether the trend towards empire and conflict in Asia should be allowed to continue. Russian and British leaders alike were often slow or reluctant to engage in further empire-building, and their rivalry was spasmodic and not always whole-hearted. Yet the predominant tendency of their policies over the period as a whole was expansionist and their relationship hostile. By and large, they conformed to type, feeling, perhaps, as did Prince Gorchakov in 1864, that they were being 'irresistibly forced, less by ambition than by imperious necessity, into this onward movement where the greatest difficulty is to know where to stop'. It is not uncommon for policy-makers to feel in the grip of 'forces' beyond their control when they work in an international context. It is always worth looking for a rational explanation.

If their activities can be made intelligible at all, it will be by viewing Russo-British relations as a whole, as they were viewed at the time once each nation had identified the other as a major threat. Given the wide range of their interests, this means looking at Europe and Asia as a single continent. Until the nineteenth century it made sense to distinguish between the states system of Europe and the empires and principalities of Asia. It ceased to make sense when two members of the European states system were also the two most powerful states in Asia. It was during the first two decades of the nineteenth century that Great Britain and Russia became the most formidable powers on the whole Eurasian land mass. Only then did they begin to frighten one another. Between 1828 and 1833 there appeared to the British to have been a major shift of power in Russia's favour. By 1860 the British had spectacularly reversed this. After 1860 the balance tipped gradually in favour of the Russians. By 1908 both governments had become more concerned with the prospect of the Germans threatening them in Europe and in Asia. It is these shifts in the distribution of power and the responses made to them on the Eurasian continent which have to be explained. They constitute the story of what the British called the 'Great Game'.

It was a matter for dispute among commentators at the time whether the policies of the Russians or the British or both amounted to a bid for hegemony in Asia. The issue is still debated. Was there a Russian threat to India? Was there a British threat to central Asia? Did acting, even prematurely, on the assumption that there was a threat serve to remove temptation from the minds of the other government? Or did it cause such alarm as to create the very threat it was intended to frustrate? These questions are, of course, of a kind familiar in international history. It is endlessly debated, at any rate in France, whether Napoleon I's conquests were provoked by the hostility of neighbours who wrongly assumed the worst about his intentions, or whether they understood his intentions only too well. It is endlessly debated, especially in Germany, whether the Germans went to war in 1914 as the only way of ensuring their security against a hostile coalition, or whether the war showed that the partners in the coalition had correctly anticipated Germany's expansionist aims. In the same year that this latter controversy was given a new lease of life by Fritz Fischer, A. J. P. Taylor started another when he questioned whether the war of 1939 was part of a Nazi design for conquest, and explained it rather in terms of blundering attempts to anticipate such a threat. The Pacific war raised similar questions. Did the Americans and the British over-react to a limited programme of empire-building by the Japanese, thereby provoking their bid in 1941 for an empire vast enough for them to feel secure from western hostility? Or would forceful handling of the earlier Manchurian crisis have been a deterrent to any empire-building at all? The cold war between the communist and the non-communist worlds has given rise to comparable disputes. Were the communist powers responding defensively to a threat from the United States and western Europe, or was it the other way round? In this case, the rivalry and mutual suspicion of the Russians and the British in the nineteenth century have been called upon to prove either the continuity of Russian expansionism, or else the dangerous absurdity of harbouring fears about it.

These controversies persist despite ample evidence as to the thoughts and actions of the people involved. This is not because some historians are more skilled at reading the record than others, nor because they have some professional interest in keeping controversies alive. It is because there is, as yet, no consensus among them as to when a sequence of international events and the behaviour of the participants can be classified as aggressive, defensive, purposive, opportunistic and so on. Each historian must resolve the problem according to assumptions about human behaviour and the origin of events suggested by his own reading, observation and introspection. The assumptions will continue to vary, and so will the interpretation of major international developments, until biologists and psychologists can offer more definite guidance. The present interpretation of the Great Game rests upon a number of such assumptions, and, as they are only assumptions, it is right to spell them out in advance.

The participants in the history of international politics are taken to be all those who have seen themselves in a context wider than their own society, but particularly those who have the power to represent their society, officially or otherwise, in the world beyond its frontiers as politicians, soldiers, diplomats, traders, journalists, financiers and the like. Understanding international history means understanding their behaviour. It will be assumed that they are as other men and women in at least three important respects. First, they crave, like the rest of us, for a sense of understanding and control over their 'world', in their case the world of international politics. Secondly, they share with the rest of us the capacity not merely to perceive and interpret situations in their world offering danger or opportunity, but also to imagine possible dangers and opportunities which have not yet occurred, and to anticipate them by systematic and cooperative action. Thirdly, like everyone else, they exercise this capacity not only by speculating as to how their world works, but also by speculating how it might come to work in the future. These speculations provide the sense of understanding and control for which they crave, and are the prerequisites for anticipating danger and creating opportunity.

International history will be taken, therefore, as no different from any other kind in so far as it studies the behaviour of people endowed with an inherent urge to understand and feel in control of their particular environment, and an inherent capacity for the work of perception, imagination and cooperation necessary to achieve this. Their 'world' is a particularly wide and complex one. To understand it makes exceptional calls on their imagination, and to feel in control of it requires a high

Introduction

degree of sensitive anticipation and organized response to what they see as possible threats and opportunities. Politicians responsible for handling international problems are nearer than their fellow citizens, at any rate those in a stable social and political order, to the original human condition in which the capacity to imagine and anticipate danger or opportunity was constantly a matter of life or death. As with our remote ancestors, failure to guess correctly under such demanding circumstances is frequent, the costs of failure can be disastrous, and knowledge that the stakes are so high lends an air of drama to the proceedings of even a minor crisis. These politicians, too, have at their disposal abnormal power in the form of wealth and organization to produce weapons and to order their use if they sense that it is necessary. But, however the distinctiveness of their speculations and the exceptional nature of their power add to their interest as historical figures, their resulting behaviour does not call for an enquiry different in kind from that required to explain more humdrum human activities. Much of the explanation will be found in the speculative framework used to identify the dangers and opportunities they must deal with if their sense of understanding and control is to be sustained.

In trying to explain the behaviour of the international statesmen who conducted the Great Game, a good deal of emphasis will be placed, therefore, on the speculative frameworks which served them as a rough guide to action. Not many such working hypotheses about world politics tend to be current at any one time – some governments try to ensure that there is only one – and they are all likely to include answers to the same basic questions: how is power distributed among the world's peoples? which might threaten us? how and why should they do so? and how can our own power and influence be increased so as to make the world more safe, convenient and agreeable for us to live in? Writers and other publicists excited by such questions supply a steady stream of explicit and often conflicting answers, whose chance of wide acceptance depends on their advocates' skill in showing that they make better sense of world politics than any of their rivals. Acceptance by the policy-makers themselves of a new hypothesis or of one they have hitherto found unconvincing seems most likely to occur when their sense of understanding and control of international problems has been shaken by a dramatic sequence of events, bewildering in terms of the established hypothesis; it is especially likely if the unexpected events coincide with a change of political leadership. Using this approach to the Great Game, the erratic behaviour of its participants can be made to look intelligible enough. The situation created by Russian and British territorial expansion in the first two decades of the nineteenth century was full of the uncertainties, of the potential openings and hazards which it is human nature to try to imagine and anticipate. The resulting imaginative efforts of the people involved offer the historian a possible framework within which to describe and interpret the course of Russo-British rivalry in nineteenth-century Eurasia. The failure rate in imaginative anticipation will be seen as high, as it always is, but not abnormally so; the consequences were disturbing, as they usually are, but not catastrophic, as they might well have been. An explanation on these lines may leave international politics looking what most people would call irrational and unprincipled. It may also help to suggest why in this case, and perhaps most others, they could hardly have been otherwise.

I

The rise of Russian and British power in Eurasia

In 1800 China and France were the most imposing states in Eurasia. Nothing had yet happened to disturb the age-old Chinese belief that their empire was the centre of the world around which were grouped their political and cultural inferiors. The eighteenth century had witnessed a new peak of prosperity and peace for China, whose accomplishments in the art of civilization were widely admired by European commentators critical of their own societies. China's empire, always vast, now embraced more of the Asian mainland than ever before. There were something like three hundred million Chinese, about ten times the number of Europe's most populous states, Russia and France. By 1850 the figure had perhaps risen to four hundred and thirty millions. But already at the end of the eighteenth century this rapidly rising population was dangerously straining China's resources and threatening its internal peace. Moreover, since China's rulers took their supremacy in Asia for granted, they allowed the army and navy to fall into decay. The Chinese Empire, though as yet unchallenged, was more vulnerable than it appeared.

So was that of the French. Five thousand miles away they dominated western Europe as surely as the Chinese dominated east Asia. French armies controlled the Italian peninsula and the Low Countries, and had since 1793 repeatedly proved their superiority over the forces of Austria and Prussia in defence of the French Revolution. Within six years both these countries were to be reduced to near satellites of Napoleon's French Empire, which came to include practically the whole mainland of Europe outside Russia. But while the Chinese Empire was becoming vulnerable because its emperors were unaware of any impending challenge and were thus doing nothing to meet it, the French emperor had impatiently provoked a greater challenge than his armed forces were able to withstand.

His opponents, who felt too much threatened by Napoleon's growing empire to countenance its survival, were the rulers of Great Britain and Russia, and theirs was the principal challenge which China, too, would have to meet for very different reasons. In 1800 this was by no means apparent. Both Russia and Great Britain had emerged as formidable centres of power in the wars of the eighteenth century, but their exploits looked a good deal less solidly based than the sustained achievements of France and China. In terms of population, Russia had recently just overtaken France, but the spectacular increase in numbers which gave rise to the fear of Russia's millions swamping the armies of her European enemies was a later nineteenth-century phenomenon. Russian territory was, of course, already considerably more extensive than that of any other European state – even Russia west of the Urals was about seven times the area of the Habsburg Empire, second in size to Russia – but poor communications and general economic backwardness meant that the land gave forth only a fraction of the wealth of which it was capable. It was significant that the remarkable succession of Russian military victories had been gained, often very laboriously, at the expense of the declining Swedish, Turkish and Polish states and of a Prussia hard-pressed by several enemies in the Seven Years War. In 1799 Suvorov's brief contribution to the Second Coalition's campaigns against the French in Italy and Switzerland was brilliantly successful at first, but it was cut short when the Russian emperor Paul quarrelled with his allies and left the war. Russia's armies had still to prove that they could overcome any of the acknowledged 'Great Powers' of Europe.

In Asia Russia played a subdued role after the initial advance across Siberia in the sixteenth and seventeenth centuries. The famous clash with Chinese border forces in 1685–6 was an isolated incident. Instead of precipitating a clash of empires it served as an incentive for the amicable negotiation of better defined frontiers and regulated commerce. The treaties of Nerchinsk (1689) and Kyakhta (1727) set a peaceful pattern for Russia's relations with the Chinese Empire until the middle of the nineteenth century. Although both governments were actively consolidating their empires in east Asia during the eighteenth century, the inevitable border disputes were painlessly enough resolved. The Russian government's main concern was to preserve a valuable trading link and a major source of customs revenue. This meant adaptation to the Chinese point of view because the link was less important to the Chinese than to the Russians, and because the Chinese had local military

The rise of Russian and British power in Eurasia

superiority. The Russians had a profitable Asian empire of impressive dimensions, but their power and influence in relation to the Chinese still seemed slender to them as well as to the Chinese.

If it was uncertain how far Russia would continue to rise in the ranks of the world's powers, Great Britain, for all its remarkable innovations in industry, looked in 1800 like a state in decline. British power and prestige seemed to have reached their peak at the end of the Seven Years War. Over half a century of growing wealth and internal stability, together with two remarkable bursts of successful military and naval activity between 1703 and 1710 and between 1757 and 1759, had made for a rapid and spectacular accumulation of power in Europe, Asia and America. But by the end of the century the British had experienced growing difficulties and failures. Talk of reform or revolution, mutinies in the navy, insurrection in Ireland signalled a new mood of restlessness and impatience among many groups of the population. A substantial slice of empire had been lost when the British army failed to subdue a revolution on the part of American colonists. The British could not prevent the domination of western and central Europe by their most dangerous enemies, the French. The new French ruler, Napoleon Bonaparte, had also served notice of his ambition to supplant British power in Asia, and he had not been deterred by the defeat of his first attempt in 1798–9. The British navy had remained strong enough to secure the home islands and the overseas empire against French attack, but there was even a question mark over its continued ability to do this. If the French stabilized their now extensive control over Europe's resources and coastline, they might be able to amass sufficient naval power to overwhelm British defences throughout the world. At best, it seemed, the British could hope to hold what they had already won. Their chances of expanding their power appeared small.

Yet in less than twenty years the distribution of power on the Eurasian continent had been transformed to the advantage of Russia and Great Britain. They replaced France and China as the most imposing states, and no other states throughout the nineteenth century were to acquire such wide-ranging power to initiate or frustrate changes beyond their own frontiers. Even Napoleon III and William II, whose armies at one time outclassed those of either Great Britain or Russia, were irritably aware of how localized their power and influence were compared with the two huge Eurasian empires.

This striking change in the distribution of power was accomplished in three stages. During the first stage, between 1798 and 1806, both the British and the Russians made what were to prove crucial additions to their Asian empires at a time when they were signally failing to check the French advance in Europe. The second stage, between 1807 and 1812, was consolidatory: the British remained largely on the defensive in Europe and Asia alike in face of a Franco-Russian alliance against them, while the Russians fought to strengthen the position they had won at the expense of the Ottoman and Persian empires. These developments were preparatory to the final dramatic stage between 1813 and 1818, during which the French Empire in Europe was overthrown, primarily by British and Russian efforts, and the British secured effective control of India. It was in these years that the foundations were laid for nearly a century of Russo-British rivalry in Eurasia.

By coincidence, the Russians and the British took comparably decisive steps to develop their Asian empires within the space of the same few years, 1798–1806. The Russians at long last established themselves in strength on the southern side of the Caucasian mountain barrier, and came face to face with the declining Persian Empire. Beyond Persia lay India. There, the British, after equal hesitation, initiated a drive against rival centres of power which was soon to bring them mastery of the subcontinent.

Since the fading of Mongol power in the fifteenth and sixteenth centuries, Russia's international orientation had been European rather than Asian. Neighbouring European states, notably Sweden and Poland, provided the Russians with challenges to withstand and opportunities to exploit. Until well into the eighteenth century Asia offered neither to anything like the same degree. In east Asia the Chinese picture of the world depicted the Russians as simply one of many barbarian groups which could be kept in their place without undue effort. Nor did it lead them to covet Russia's Siberian lands as long as they were unquestionably outside the bounds of the Chinese Empire itself. For their part, the Russians were aware of the massive diversion of resources which would be needed to challenge the power of China. In the centre of Russia's southern flank the immediate neighbours were nomadic peoples of the steppe, whose fighting capacity and remoteness made their subjugation difficult while their raids on Russian territory were not damaging enough to make it an urgent task. In western Asia the Russians had reached the natural barrier of the Caucasus mountain chain. The problems and prospects encountered by Russians in Asia lacked the immediacy of those thrust upon Russian governments by the constantly changing pattern of European politics.

It was conflict with the Ottoman Empire, itself as much Asian as European, which drew the Russians to intervene more actively in Asian politics and to revive time-honoured visions of oriental empire. Ottoman power was derived from control of the Black Sea, the Balkan peninsula, and much of western Asia. Russians and Turks had become neighbours in 1676 when the frontier of the Ottoman Empire was advanced at the expense of Poland. During most of the following century the Russians had little to show for their periodic wars with the sultan's forces, but they did more than enough to alarm the government in Constantinople. By the 1760s its most influential elements believed that only a major military effort could permanently discourage the Russians from any further bid against the territorial bastions of the Empire. Between 1768 and 1774 and again between 1787 and 1792 the Turks waged war with this hope. Each time they failed. The result was Russian domination of the fertile steppe lands north of the Black Sea and of its coasts from the Dniester to the Kuban.

During the first of these wars a Russian force crossed the Caucasus range and loosened the Turkish hold on some of the mountain peoples to the south. A permanent road was built along one of the two possible military routes, and in 1783 Catherine assumed a protectorate over eastern Georgia. The Georgians were a Christian people, whose kingdom had broken up in the fifteenth century, leaving them at the mercy of the Ottoman and Persian empires. The latter's rivalry and wars usually left the Georgians to the west of the Suram range, a ridge thrown off at right angles from the main chain of the Caucasus mountains, under Turkish control, and those to the east under Persia. The presence of powerful fellow Christians across the mountains had long encouraged the Georgians to see the Russians as a liberating force. Russian protection, when it came, was nominal. Its assertion merely exposed the Georgians to retaliation from the Persians, who sacked Tbilisi (Tiflis) in 1795 and massacred the population. Over the next few years Russian policies in Transcaucasia were highly erratic, ranging from grandiose schemes of conquest to total withdrawal, but Georgia was finally annexed to the Russian Empire in 1801 and the process of incorporating other principalities and tribes in the region got under way. Russia's armies were at last over the Caucasus barrier on a permanent basis, and from now on could present a constant threat to the vulnerable Asian frontiers of the Turks and the Persians.

The British had no natural frontiers in Asia comparable to the mountains and deserts which the Russians had reached. But in India they had, by the end of the eighteenth century, secured a position so powerful that they had open to them the same kind of choice as was offered to the Russians by the line of the Caucasus – whether to rest content with holding it, or whether to use it as a base from which to expand still farther. Like the Russians they eventually became committed to the latter course, by fits and starts, around the turn of the century.

The English East India Company, like that of the Dutch, had been founded at the beginning of the seventeenth century to try and break the Portuguese monopoly of maritime trade with India and south-east Asia. Both companies were successful, and became very profitable concerns, with the Dutch concentrating on south-east Asia and the English on India. Since the sixteenth century the Mughal Empire had united India, and was second only to China as an Asian power. Its goodwill and its stable political framework allowed the English company to flourish. This stability disappeared during the eighteenth century with the breakup of the Mughal Empire into separate warring states. The company had to fight for the survival of its bases against hostile neighbouring princes and against the French, whose own East India Company had been a relative failure and who hoped by intervening in the conflicts among the Indian states to create political conditions favourable to their own commercial operations and inimical to their British competitors. With remarkable adaptation to new circumstances the English East India Company not only survived but in the space of a few years changed itself from an essentially commercial concern into one of the leading powers of India.

There were two other powers in India formidable enough to count as possible threats to the British. In the south was Mysore, made formidable by the talents and ambition of the Muslim adventurer, Ḥaydar ʿAlī, and of his son, Tīpū Sulṭān, who succeeded him in 1782. In the west and centre were the Marathas, the Hindu confederacy of military chiefs, whose empire was in decline but still had great reserves of strength and vitality. Mysore, the Marathas and the Company had all been in conflict with one another. The French, no longer direct contenders since their defeats in the mid-eighteenth century, maintained links with Mysore and the Marathas, and the presence of French weapons and of even freelance French military advisers could contribute to the world-wide war in which the French and British were currently engaged. The Company itself ruled Bengal and important bases at Madras and Bombay. Its troops had proved that the Company's territories could be held against even a coalition of its rivals, and until the end of the eighteenth century successive governors-general were largely content with the secure position they had won. A spectacular extension of British control occurred during Lord Wellesley's term as governor-general between 1798 and 1805. Wellesley's policy was a bid for hegemony over the whole of India. To this end territories belonging to helpless neighbours were annexed; the Niẓām of Ḥaydarābād and the weaker Maratha chiefs were persuaded to sign away their right to an independent foreign policy through 'subsidiary treaties', by which they paid for Company troops to protect them against their internal and external enemies; and war was waged against Mysore and the Marathas. In 1799 Tīpū Sulṭān was killed defending his capital, and a puppet ruler was installed in his place. British domination in southern India was assured. The war launched against the Marathas in 1803 brought dramatic victories, but was more difficult to bring to a swift conclusion. Wellesley's methods were deemed too costly. The Maratha war was wound up and he was recalled, but British military ascendancy had been clearly demonstrated to the Indian princes. It now seemed a question of how soon and how directly the British would seek to unify India under their rule.

The Russian crossing of the Caucasus and the British advances in India were to have momentous long-term consequences, but at the time their significance was concealed by the apparently decisive triumph of the French in Europe. Between 1805 and 1807 Napoleon's armies defeated those of Austria, Prussia and Russia, and down to 1813 the French controlled an unprecedentedly large European empire of which only Great Britain, Russia and the Ottoman Empire were really independent. The central question of international politics during this second stage was whether the virtual division of Europe between France and Russia, to which, in the aftermath of defeat, the Russian emperor Alexander I had agreed at Tilsit in 1807, would become permanent, and whether it would be extended into a parallel division of Asia with the Ottoman Empire and India as the principal spoils. By 1813 it was clear that neither would be the case. The British gradually got the upper hand in the economic and military warfare which they constantly waged against Napoleon's European empire. Napoleon and Alexander I were increasingly at odds over European issues, and their negotiations for mutual expansion in Asia remained deadlocked. The armies of France and Russia were instead preparing for war against one another.

In these years of uncertainty about the political structure of Europe, the British and the Russians continued to consolidate their recent gains in Asia. The British faced no serious challenge within India itself to the position won under Wellesley. Lord Minto, governor-general from 1807 to 1813, concentrated mainly on counter-measures to any invasion project which might result from the Franco-Russian alliance of 1807. Even before Tilsit, conditions had favoured a revival of Napoleon's ambitions in Asia. The sultan and his ministers were impressed by the French victory over the Ottoman Empire's traditional enemies, Austria and Russia, in 1805, and steadily moved towards cooperation with Napoleon. They responded to his suggestion that they should seize the opportunity to reverse the verdict of their recent wars against the Russians. They went to war with Russia in December 1806, and broke with the British in early 1807. The Persians, too, saw a French alliance as the best means of recovering the lands they had lost to the Russians south of the Caucasus. The British had neglected the Persians after signing a mutual defence treaty with them in 1801. By May 1807, when they had awoken to the alarming implications for themselves as well as for Russia of a Franco-Turkish-Persian alliance and decided to send a mission to Tehran, Napoleon had already succeeded in negotiating the treaty of Finkenstein with representatives of the shah. A French military mission was sent to Tehran to train the Persian army, and the leader of the mission, General Gardane, was to draw up plans for an invasion of India. He recommended that a French army should march from Persian bases to the Indus via Herat, and that a French naval expedition from Mauritius should land near Bombay. Whatever its military feasibility, the plan depended in the first place on the co-operation of the shah. This would be forthcoming only if the French got the Russians out of Georgia either by armed assistance or, after Tilsit, by diplomacy. When it became clear that Napoleon neither could nor would take steps to end the war – which had been going on with Russia since 1804 – in Persia's favour, the shah abandoned his pro-French policy.

But the very possibility of the French and the Russians coming to terms with the Ottoman Empire and Persia and forming an anti-British coalition in western Asia was enough to cause alarm. Gardane's mission to Tehran was followed by Franco-Persian overtures to the rulers of Sind, who controlled the lower Indus valley through which many former invaders of India had passed. Minto launched a diplomatic offensive to win over the rulers whose territories lay in the probable path of an invading army. Secret missions were sent to the capitals of Sind, the Panjāb, Afghanistan and Persia itself. By the time the treaties had been secured in 1809, the grand design had lost its urgency, but Minto further reinforced the outlying defences of British India in 1809–10 by expeditions to capture the French islands of Réunion and Mauritius. These had long been bases for successful commerce raiding, and had figured prominently in Napoleon's dreams of restoring French power in India. Minto also took the opportunity to dispossess the

Dutch, Napoleon's allies, of the Moluccas (1810) and Java (1811), both considered as valuable additions to Great Britain's Asian empire.

While the British were taking elaborate precautions against a remotely possible attack, the Russians were having to fight hard for their position across the Caucasus mountains against the Turks and the Persians. The Russian forces were hampered by revolt, which their harsh rule had provoked among the mountain peoples living along the Russian supply route to the south. They suffered, too, from local inferiority of numbers, which could not be remedied because of the uncertain situation in Europe. Although most of the principalities of western Georgia voluntarily became Russian protectorates in the years following the annexation of eastern Georgia in 1801, one of them, Imeret'i, was the scene of bitter resistance as its king, Solomon, exploited Russia's difficulties in the hope of regaining the independence of which the Russians had deprived him in 1804. But in the long run the Russian armies had the better of the fighting on all fronts. The Turks were glad to settle for the compromise which the tsar found convenient on the eve of Napoleon's invasion in 1812; in Europe they lost Bessarabia, and in Transcaucasia the status quo was restored. The Persians suffered heavier defeats and came to terms when Napoleon was in retreat; they had to cede several provinces and abandon their claim to Georgia. The process of gradually wearing down the Ottoman Empire had been carried a stage further, and a similar process had begun with regard to Persia. Russian power in western Asia had been significantly enhanced.

The breakup of the Franco-Russian alliance and the failure of Napoleon to reduce Russia to satellite status in the war of 1812 inaugurated the third phase. As Napoleon's power dwindled during 1813–14, the Russians and the British created an alliance of European states determined not to allow the French to come so near again to the mastery of the European continent. In the post-war balance Austria and Prussia were restored to independence and France remained a major state, but, although the diplomatic activities of Metternich and Talleyrand wrung as much advantage as possible out of the situation, the outstanding fact was that Great Britain and Russia had become the leading powers of Europe. Those sources of strength which had largely accounted for their success against Napoleon were consolidated. The British were able to extend the great network of overseas bases for their navy, which had prevented invasion, protected their commerce, countered the continental blockade, and made possible the penetration of French-controlled Europe by their army. The Russians had acquired a broad tongue of Polish territory protruding into central Europe, which made greater than ever the problem of penetrating and mastering Russia's vast spaces, and made even a threat to do so riskier because the new territory put her armies in easy striking distance of both Berlin and Vienna. Moreover, in numerical terms the British navy and the Russian army enjoyed overwhelming superiority over all possible rivals. The British had 214 ships of the line, while the only other European fleets of any significance were the French with about 50 ships of the line, and the Russians with 40. The Russian army was far and away the largest in Europe, with not far short of a million men. Numerical superiority could be very misleading and subsequent events showed that the British navy and the Russian army were less impressive than the figures suggested, but for the moment interpretation at face value was the only safe course for other governments because British and Russian capacity to win a major war had just been convincingly demonstrated.

In retrospect, it is apparent that Russia and Great Britain were by then the leading powers of Asia as well as of Europe. The British went one stage nearer to proving it as far as they were concerned by putting their domination of India beyond doubt between 1813 and 1818. The principalities of central India, from which the Company's forces had withdrawn after the recall of Wellesley, were helpless victims of the Pindaris, armed bands which plundered their territories at will. The Maratha chiefs, apart from the Company the only powers of any substance south of the Sutlej river, were either complaisant or in league with the Pindaris. The Pindaris presented to the British a short-term and a long-term threat. From their strongholds in central India they could launch raids on Company territory which had to be repelled. In the longer term, they offered an ominous reminder to the British that the Mughal Empire's decline had been promoted by the failure of its rulers to suppress the spread of similar freebooting activities by the Marathas. A new governor-general, the Marquess of Hastings, decided on the destruction of the Pindaris, and gave the Marathas the alternative of cooperating in this venture or of sharing the same fate. One of the Maratha chiefs, the Peshwa, whose forebears had traditionally led the Maratha confederacy in its heyday, was sufficiently encouraged by current British setbacks at the hands of the Gurkhas of Nepal to resist, and bid for a Maratha revival. The overwhelming superiority of the power which the British had built in India was revealed when the Marathas and the Pindaris were disposed of in a series of at times almost lighthearted skirmishes. By 1818 the British had systematically eliminated all opposition. The king of Delhi still theoretically enjoyed the suzerainty over India inherited from the Mughal emperors, and the princes

The rise of Russian and British power in Eurasia 17

who had submitted were largely free to govern as they wished within their borders, but all of them acknowledged the effective British domination of the whole of India as far north as the Sutlej.

The transformation of the political map of Eurasia during the first two decades of the nineteenth century had left Russia and Great Britain looking the strongest and most secure of the world's states. Their prestige in Europe as states difficult to defeat remained high throughout the century despite growing evidence of basic flaws. A coalition was assumed to be necessary before war could be contemplated with either. As well as enjoying this formidable status in Europe, they controlled vast territorial empires in Asia, separated from one another only by an assortment of unimpressive political units: nomadic tribes, weak and unstable principalities, large but shaky empires. All were potential victims of the Russians or the British should they choose to expand their imperial boundaries. And, if they did try to improve upon these positions of acknowledged strength, they might appear, especially to one another, to be bidding for that predominance in Eurasia which had eluded Napoleon.

2
British leaders take alarm, 1828–33

The rise of Russia and Great Britain to predominance in Eurasia in no way made conflict between them inevitable. The hypotheses about international affairs which guided the behaviour of both British and Russian leaders in the decade after Waterloo assumed no basic antagonism between them. Castlereagh and Canning, who controlled the making of British foreign policy in the periods 1812–22 and 1822–7 respectively, thought of events in a global context appropriate to a country with a world-wide commercial and territorial empire. The record of the past hundred years led them to see France as still the most probable future threat to that empire; a new European war could enable the French to extend their power once again over the coasts and resources of the Low Countries and the Iberian peninsula. They disagreed as to the means of ensuring enough British control over European relationships to avert such a war. Castlereagh pinned his faith on the personal influence he could exert on Alexander I and Metternich in regular diplomatic encounters, and in promoting the rather novel preferences of these European statesmen for stable frontiers and the peaceful resolution of disputes. Canning relied more on pointed reminders of the power at his command to make European governments fear British hostility or hope for British backing. But both men envisaged the world and the hazards it was likely to offer British interests in much the same way. France was still the most dangerous potential enemy, and a stabilized and habitually peaceful Europe the best safeguard for British commerce and empire. Russia fitted into this picture as the state with apparently the most power and hence, perhaps, the most temptation to disturb the existing balance with incalculable effects, but neither Castlereagh nor Canning saw Russia as a direct threat in the foreseeable future.

Russia's rulers were less globally minded. Whereas British governments were traditionally reluctant to get involved in European politics, for the emperors Alexander I and Nicholas I Europe was of central concern, and Russia's Asian and American interests peripheral. But they, too, pictured France as the most serious potential enemy, since France was the only state which had recently proved its capacity to challenge Russian predominance in eastern Europe and western Asia, and to invade the Russian homeland itself, and they saw European stability as offering the greatest reassurance for the future. They had a further and equally important reason for regarding France with caution. The French had offered an alternative idea of political life, whose widespread adoption would transform the habitual behaviour of a Russian emperor's subjects, gentry and peasant alike. The brief French control of so much of Europe had ensured the circulation of French political attitudes to a dangerous degree even in Russia; Nicholas I had to fight off a bid by gentry rebels inspired by French revolutionary concepts at the time of his succession to the throne in 1825. Russian emperors could experience no real sense of control over their world as long as there was the prospect of a new liberal or democratic revolutionary movement on a European scale. Paris remained the most likely source. Russia's rulers put as much emphasis on stable political systems as on stable frontiers, but their assumptions about Europe's place in international politics were not incompatible with those of Castlereagh and Canning. Great Britain fitted into the picture as a formidable power whose influence on the course of European politics had to be carefully watched, but which represented no immediate threat to Russia.

In the aftermath of the Napoleonic wars, therefore, the governments of Great Britain and Russia had not marked one another out as a particular source of future danger. They were, of course, as likely to quarrel with one another as with any other European power over a crisis whose outcome might affect the balance of power in Europe. Consensus among the five powers which had made the Vienna settlement of 1815 was always fragile. During the Congress of Vienna itself Austria, Great Britain and France came near to a breach with Russia and Prussia over the distribution of Polish and Saxon territory. Great Britain made an isolated stand in 1821-3 against the decision of its European allies to suppress rebellion in Spain. Austria opposed the decision of the Russians, the British and the French in 1826-7 to prevent the suppression of rebellion in the Ottoman Empire. But there was no special pattern of alignment in these crises. Russia and Great Britain might well be at odds with one another in one crisis, as in the case of Spain, and in harmony with one another – and, indeed, with France – over the next. Even when they were at odds they, like the other powers, had no inclination to risk the kind of upheaval from which they had all just emerged. The urge to settle disputes by diplomacy rather than by war remained strong until the middle of the century.

Interpreted within this sort of framework, events in Asia would have had to be very startling indeed to distract policy-makers in either capital from their preoccupation with the European balance and with the slightest hint of any political development capable of disturbing it. The close link between Asian and European politics, so apparent at the turn of the century, was discounted now that Napoleon's ambitions had been finally thwarted. The existing empires of Russia and Great Britain seemed secure, and Asia appeared quite big enough to allow future expansion by both powers without risk of collision. Asia assumed a low priority in the thoughts of Russian emperors and British foreign secretaries alike.

A conspicuous example of this was the attitude of George Canning to the renewal of war between Russia and Persia in 1826. Canning had to decide whether the British government was under an obligation to go to Persia's aid. British interest in a treaty relationship with Persia dated from 1799, when it was hoped that the Persians might divert an impending invasion of India by the shah's traditional enemies, the Afghans. The Afghan threat quickly passed, but the course of the war in Europe suggested that Persia might be the route for an attack on India by the French and, perhaps, the Russians. Treaties with the shah in 1801, 1809, 1812 and 1814 had, therefore, a common theme: British aid to Persian armies resisting a European invader. By 1814 official anxiety about Persia had subsided in both London and Calcutta, and the main purpose of the treaty negotiated in that year was to limit British commitments, and to stress that British help would not be forthcoming if the Persians were the aggressors. It was this revised treaty with its escape clause which was at issue in 1826. War had long been expected between Persia and Russia, neither of which accepted as final the frontier fixed at the end of their previous war of 1804–13. When it came in 1826, the characteristic conditions of a disputed frontier meant that responsibility for hostilities was debatable, but there was no doubt that Persia was technically the aggressor. The British government was, therefore, entitled to leave the Persians to their fate. The question remained whether it was in their interest to stick to the letter of the treaty, or whether the fears which had led the British to seek a Persian alliance still lingered. Could they allow Russia to defeat Persia? Canning had no doubts about the matter. He enthusiastically welcomed the escape clause.

When Williams Wynn, president of the board of control in the cabinet, argued that Russian provocation on the frontier had been such that the Persians had no alternative but to fight, Canning replied, 'I am sorry – (or rather I am happy) – to say that I cannot agree with you in thinking that the Casus foederis has occurred, under the last of the incredibly foolish Treaties of which I enclose copies.' His view was that the shah had considered Russian involvement in the Greek crisis was a convenient moment to recover his lost provinces, and that by the time he realized his mistake Persian opinion had been roused to such a pitch of fanaticism that it was too dangerous for him to draw back. 'The Priests had gotten ahead, and his forty shillingers were incurably warlike.' Not only would the Persians be refused aid on this occasion, but Canning was bent on loosening British ties with Tehran. Colonel MacDonald, the new British representative, was to be disabused of the mistaken impression that he was being sent to the court of the shah 'for the express purpose of stimulating the Schah to jealousy and resistance against Russia, and of representing to the Persian Govt. the "common Interest" which Great Britain feels with Persia in the repressing of Russian encroachments'.[1]

Canning's assessment of the Russo-Persian war as being of no concern to the British government was consistent with his general picture of world politics. Frontier warfare in Transcaucasia would not normally have been a signal alerting him to a sense of danger. In the circumstances of 1826, when he was in the middle of a delicate negotiation with the Russian government designed to keep the Greek crisis under control, it was understandable that his breezy indifference to Persia's plight should be mixed with irritation. Turkish failure to suppress the Greek rebellion, which had broken out in 1821, and the Greeks' failure to establish their independence of the Turks beyond question, had meant persistent instability and conflict in an area of land and sea important to British commerce. Possible unilateral intervention by the Russian emperor on behalf of the Greeks might make Russia a power in the Mediterranean, an area in which British predominance was traditionally thought to be vital. The popularity of the Greek cause among the British meant that Canning could not side with the Turks. Canning saw his plan of joint action with Nicholas I as the best hope of controlling

[1] Canning to Wynn, 9 Oct. 1826, priv. and conf. (copy); mem. by Canning, 24 Oct. 1826, encl. in Canning to Wynn, 24 Oct. 1826, priv. and conf. (copy), F[oreign] O[ffice] 60/29.

developments. At the same time, Canning faced a crisis over the succession to the throne of Portugal, another area which British governments were accustomed to believe should be controlled by rulers friendly to them, and by the end of the year he was despatching British troops to Lisbon. To someone who did not regard Russian encroachments on Persian territory as part of a pattern of Russian expansion leading to confrontation with British India, the events in Transcaucasia were a tiresome diversion.

Canning died in August 1827. His successors revised some of his policies, because they no longer found adequate the assumptions which had been the key to them and to the policies of his predecessor, Castlereagh. A succession of dramatic events shook the faith in established ideas about international politics of British policy-makers, especially those newly in office. A rival hypothesis about Russia was already to hand, which seemed to make more sense of the present and to offer a better chance of controlling the future.

Between 1827 and 1833 a remarkable series of predictable but unexpectedly sudden developments left the Persian and the Ottoman empires at the mercy of the Russian emperor. First, the risks inherent in Canning's cooperation with Russia (and France) to put pressure on the sultan and so prevent the destruction of the Greek rebel forces were clearly demonstrated when, on 20 October 1827, naval units of the three powers clashed with and destroyed the Turkish and Egyptia fleets, which they were blockading at the bay of Navarino. Navarino was not a decisive event. It helped the Greeks, but did not win their war for them. It infuriated the sultan, but not sufficiently to unsettle his reason and make him regard himself as at war with all three of the interventionist governments. What it did was to make the sultan less instead of more willing to negotiate, so that the three powers were faced with the choice of tamely terminating their efforts, or of intervening still more forcibly and with ever-growing risks of general upheaval in south-eastern Europe. The British hesitated; the Russians and the French were set on further and decisive intervention.

While the shock, variously pleasant or disagreeable, of the battle of Navarino was being absorbed by the parties to the conflict, news of another major international development was received. The Persians, whose war with Russia had won such scant sympathy from Canning, gave up the struggle in November 1827 and sued for peace. Initially, they had taken the Russians by surprise and enjoyed a brief moment of spectacular success. Nicholas I's energies were fully engaged with the Greek affair, and he had been confident of settling the frontier disputes with Persia by diplomacy. The Russian commanders were unprepared for the sudden Persian attack, and had diverted troops to work on their newly acquired estates. A panicky withdrawal ensued, as they scrambled to save their personal possessions, but the Persian forces were incapable of exploiting the situation and the superior quality of Russian manpower and weapons soon made themselves felt. In October 1827, a Russian offensive led to the capture of Erivan and Tabrīz, major fortresses on the road to Tehran, and to the Persian overtures for peace. When the shah, pressed by the Turks to sustain his useful diversion of Russian energy, thought better of giving up the fight just when approaching winter promised relief, the Russian commander, Paskevich, used snowploughs to resume his advance on the Persian capital. Lacking further means of effective resistance, the shah came to terms, and it was fortunate for him that Nicholas I was more concerned with the coming war against the Turks than with exploiting to the full the victory his troops had won in Persia.

The treaty of Turkomānchāy, signed in February 1828, exacted an indemnity of twenty million roubles to pay for the war, confirmed Russia's naval monopoly of the Caspian Sea, and transferred the provinces of Nakhchivān and Erivan to the Russian Empire. A commercial treaty, signed the same day, tried to create a favourable framework within which Russians could trade in Persia, including the kind of capitulatory system by which European governments had traditionally protected their nationals from subjection to Muslim law. The Russians had won a clearly defined and stable frontier on the Aras, their military superiority, so long a subject for scepticism on the part of the Persians, was established beyond doubt, and close commercial relations with a demonstrably weaker state would offer the chance of comparably close political relations. Additional advantages stemmed from possession of Erivan. This military base stood on the flank of any Turkish advance from Kars into Georgia, and also facilitated a Russian advance into Asia Minor and the heart of the Ottoman Empire.

This dramatic strengthening of Russia's position in western Asia came on the eve of a third major upheaval, Nicholas I's long-awaited war against the Turks. Agreeably surprised by the battle of Navarino, Nicholas I had waited for the response to it which the sultan's prestige demanded and which, however subdued, would serve as the pretext for a full-scale war. Not that Nicholas had any sympathy for the Greeks as rebels, and the coming war was only incidentally on their behalf. Like Canning, he simply claimed the right to stabilize an area where conflict was damaging the commercial and other interests of his countrymen, and, even more than Canning, he was precluded from doing so by helping Muslim Turks to crush Orthodox Christians. The Greek rebellion had, in any case, broken out during a series of long-drawn-out disputes between the Turks and the Russians arising from the hastily concluded peace of 1812. Nicholas intended to put an end to these disputes and reorder the Levant in such a way as to give the Russian government ultimate control over events there by the time-honoured method of a decisive war. He did not have long to wait. The sultan's response was mild, considering the outrage perpetrated against his subjects by governments with whom he was at peace. He repudiated the recently negotiated convention of Akkerman, which had settled some of the points in dispute with Russia, declared foreign intervention contrary to Muslim law, and vaguely prophesied a coming war for Islam. This was used to complete the Russian case for war against the Ottoman Empire. After some delay, while the Persian negotiations were being concluded, Nicholas I's armies set out in April 1828 to chastise Persia's more formidable neighbours.

As in the war with Persia, the Russians had little to show for their efforts during the first year's campaign, but made up for it the following year by a spectacular approach to the enemy capital. In the spring and summer of 1828, Russia's forces made heavy weather simply of establishing themselves south of the Danube and capturing the key port of Varna on the western coast of the Black Sea, despite the inadequate preparations of the Turks and the many mistakes of their generals. The Balkan range, the main natural barrier to an advance on Constantinople, had still to be crossed. Russia's communications and military organization were inadequate for the task of maintaining in the Balkans more than a small proportion of the vast army at Nicholas I's disposal. The emperor's presence at the front inhibited his generals, and made for clumsy and ill-judged use of what forces were available. Nicholas had the sense to realize this in time for the 1829 campaign. His general, Diebitsch, then struck boldly across the Balkan mountains with only twenty thousand troops, captured Adrianople and was within striking distance of Constantinople itself. Meanwhile, an even smaller army under Paskevich had turned from their war against Persia to attack the Ottoman Empire from the east. Kars and other frontier fortresses in Asia Minor were quickly taken in the summer of 1828, the important base at Erzurum was captured the following year, and Paskevich prepared to move against the Black Sea ports of Trebizond and Batum. The Ottoman Empire seemed on the verge of complete disaster.

But at this point Nicholas and his advisers decided that the military and political risks of trying to take Constantinople were too great. While less than three thousand Russian soldiers had been killed in battle, something like a hundred thousand had died of disease. Diebitsch could do no more without substantial reinforcement; his swift advance had left large Turkish forces in the rear, and while the Russians were preparing a new major offensive the other powers, at first reassured by the slow Russian progress and then startled by their rapid advance might intervene. Nor did Nicholas wish to destroy the Ottoman empire. As in the case of Persia, he had been using his armies to ensure a compliant attitude on the part of a neighbouring state. The war was halted, and the treaty of Adrianople substantially strengthened Russia's position with regard to the Turks.

Russian annexations were modest. They took the Danube delta, the remaining Turkish footholds on the Black Sea coast behind the Russian frontier in Transcaucasia, and a frontier province which had once formed part of the old kingdom of Georgia. Other conquered territories were returned to the sultan. More important provisions related to trade and to Christian peoples within the Ottoman Empire. The long military and diplomatic struggle which the Serbs had waged since the early years of the century, with spasmodic Russian support, was rewarded by autonomy. Russian influence was expected to flourish there. For Moldavia and Wallachia Russian influence was written into the treaty. These frontier provinces, the future Rumania, were to be ruled according to a constitution drawn up by Nicholas's advisers; its working was to be supervised by Russian consuls; elected leaders could not be dismissed by the sultan without Russian consent; and Russian troops were to occupy the area until a war indemnity had been fully paid. Although Moldavia and Wallachia remained technically part of the Ottoman Empire, something close to a condominium had been established and, since the sultan agreed not to build any defences there, a Russian government could easily intervene to enforce its rights. Nicholas I had thus greatly extended Russian influence over the thinking and behaviour of the Balkan peoples, and thus his prospects of controlling events in the area. The commercial clauses, removing restrictions on the freedom of Russian merchants to trade in the Ottoman Empire and to use the waters of the Danube, the Black Sea and the Straits, could also be expected, as in the case of the recent treaty with Persia, to bring indirect political dividends.

The significance attached to these developments varied, of course, according to the interpretative framework into which they were fitted. There is no reason to believe that Canning would have experienced any difficulty in fitting them into his accustomed view of international politics. It would have been characteristic of him to react to Navarino by further pressure on the sultan, if necessary by sending a British fleet to the Straits as a timely reminder to the Turks and the Russians alike. The Russians might not have gone to war; had they done so, their peace terms might have been still more moderate. Such a course of action would have been consistent with the policies he had been pursuing. His death ushered in a period of divided counsels in British policy-making, which did not end until Palmerston had established his authority in the field of foreign affairs in the early 1830s.

Three men shaped the British response to Russia's triumphs: Wellington, Ellenborough and Palmerston. After Goderich's brief ministry in the closing months of 1827 immediately following Canning's death, Wellington became prime minister. His government lasted nearly three years from January 1828 until November 1830. He appointed Dudley as his foreign secretary, and after him Aberdeen, but the Duke could, of course, speak with greater authority on international politics than either of them. As president of the board of control Wellington appointed Lord Ellenborough, a man of strong personality, whose views the prime minister respected and who was allowed a relatively free hand in determining Indian policy. Despite his deep involvement in Canning's diplomacy, Wellington had all along been uneasy about its possible effects, while Ellenborough had been a persistent critic of government policies abroad since 1815. Both men were, therefore, susceptible to ideas of changing British policy in face of the dramatic turn of events. So was Palmerston. His consuming interest in foreign affairs had begun only in 1827–8, when he first held cabinet rank, and although a Canningite he could bring a fairly open mind to bear on what appeared to be a fundamentally changed situation. When Grey succeeded Wellington as prime minister in November 1830, he made Palmerston foreign secretary and, in contrast to Wellington, largely delegated the conduct of foreign policy to him. Between 1827 and 1833 Wellington, Ellenborough and Palmerston fumbled in their reaction to events in the Balkans and western Asia, as they adjusted themselves to a revised view of international politics which seemed to all three of them vindicated by recent Russian actions.

This revised view did not discard the containment of French power as a vital British interest, nor the maintenance of European peace and stability as the most likely means of ensuring this, but it involved another major assumption which was accorded an importance just as great. The assumption was that the Russians had already embarked upon a systematic expansion of their power in Asia and the Balkans to the future detriment of British security in India and of British commercial expansion in the rest of the continent. Those who made this assumption might differ as to how systematic was the expansion, how great the impending threat and how distant its implementation, but they all set Russian moves in Eurasia within a similar historical framework, and interpreted them as ultimately dangerous to Great Britain's commercial and territorial empire.

The idea that Russia could become a major threat to the British empire in Asia dated back to the turn of the century. As early as 1791 Henry Dundas, president of the board of control in Pitt's government, had commented in a very general way on the possible danger to India should the Russians ever supplant the Turks in the Levant, but there is no evidence that he or his colleagues took such a possibility very seriously. It did not contribute to Pitt's decision in the same year to try and prevent the Black Sea port of Ochakov going to Russia as part of a peace settlement with the Ottoman Empire. This was a move in a piece of purely European diplomacy, and the hostile reception at home which led to its abandonment suggested that politically conscious sections in Great Britain still viewed Russia in terms that were either vaguely favourable or merely indifferent. But when Napoleon's attack on Egypt in 1798 made the invasion of India by a European power seem practical politics, Russia's geographical position and its growing reputation for territorial aggrandisement at the expense of the Poles and the Turks made the tsar an obvious candidate for the role of invader along with Napoleon. Apart from some journalistic speculation in Great Britain itself, the idea won early support among governing circles in India. Sir John Malcolm, Wellesley's emissary to Persia in 1800–1, was impressed by the shah's fear of Russian ambitions, and communicated his own alarm at the long-term consequences for India if Persia collapsed before a Russian attack. Shortly before his murder in March 1801, the emperor Paul was preparing moves against the British in India. His successor, Alexander I, abandoned the expedition, but by 1808 British opinion in India had come to regard Russia as a more probable future threat than France. Admittedly, the Perso-British treaty of 1814 and the consolidation of power in India under Hastings encouraged the belief that Persia was safe, and that any advancing Russian army could be checked effectively at the Sutlej. At home, public enthusiasm for the Russians as victorious partners in the triumph over Napoleon diverted attention from hypothetical threats in Asia, and the nation's leaders were still sceptical of danger.

But, although without wide acceptance, the belief in an emerging Russian threat to India remained in circulation and was developed. Just after the war, Mountstuart Elphinstone and Henry Pottinger described their wartime missions to Kābul and Baluchistan in books which excited interest in the virtually unknown regions beyond India, and occasioned discussion of what Russia might do there. So did Malcolm's *History of Persia*, which likewise provided hard information on a still mysterious country. There was enough interest in the alarmist pamphlet, 'A Sketch of the Military and Political Power of Russia in the Year 1817', by Sir Robert Wilson, a notable soldier and military writer, for it to run through five editions in just over a year and to provoke extensive newspaper debate. Malcolm's continued advocacy was important because of his friendship with Wellington, and he privately pressed his views both on the Duke and on Canning. Two particularly lucid statements by Lieut.-Colonel George de Lacy Evans coincided with the defeats of Persia and Turkey in 1828–9. By then the theme of the Russian threat had become familiar to British observers of international politics, despite the scepticism with which almost all of them still greeted it. A new working hypothesis was available.

The form which it was to take throughout the nineteenth century was already clearly outlined in these early statements by Wilson, Malcolm and Evans, and the subsequent flood of books and pamphlets provided detailed support and advice within the same basic framework. These writers varied in their presentation of material, but they all subscribed to six closely linked propositions. First, all 'civilized' states tend to expand into the territory of weaker 'barbaric' peoples. Evans put it crudely: 'no military nation has ever yet VOLUNTARILY abstained from conquest, while there was anything yet within its grasp to conquer'.[1] Malcolm was more sympathetic to what he saw as a dilemma comparable to that of the British in India; the more deeply the Russians became involved in countries like Persia, the more often would they feel the need to demonstrate their supremacy in the area, and each demonstration would bring a further extension of power which the Russian government could honestly claim had been unsought. Like Peel, Gorchakov and many other later observers, he believed in 'an impelling power upon civilisation when in contact with barbarism that cannot be resisted',[2] and throughout the century there was mutual respect among the British and the

[1] George de Lacy Evans. *On the Designs of Russia* (London, 1828), 104.
[2] J. W. Kaye, *The Life and Correspondence of Major-General Sir John Malcolm*, 2 vols (London, 1856), II, 359–61; cf. mem. by Malcolm, 28 Sept. 1826 in Malcolm to Canning, 10 Nov. 1826, F.O. 60/29.

Russians for the 'civilizing missions' of their empires. Nor would many Russians have wished to dispute the second proposition, that the history of Russia since the reign of Peter the Great had been marked by an unbroken extension of wealth, armed force, influence and territory, with the implication that this growth in power was likely to continue. The third proposition would have attracted as much controversy in Russia as it did among the British. Now that most of Russia's European boundaries ran with those of Great Powers, the future victims of this urge to expand would be the declining Turkish and Persian empires, together with the nomadic peoples and weak principalities of central Asia. Evidence for the likelihood of this was seen in the increasing success with which Russia had been dismembering Turkey and Persia, and in the record of missions and expeditions to central Asia which had persisted despite early disasters. The events of the 1820s confirmed a pattern of expansion apparent since the end of the seventeenth century.

The other three propositions concerned the implications for Great Britain. First, since there was no power capable of resisting the Russian armies between their own frontiers and the borders of British India, the British would have to face up to the probable consequences of the Russian government pursuing an expansionist course. These were, in ascending order of gravity: the exclusion by means of Russian tariff barriers of British merchandise from vast areas of Asia with which trade had been steadily growing; the undermining of British power and prestige in India at the approach of a rival Great Power whom the conquered princes of India could see as a liberator; and the possible collapse of British control over India should the Russians attempt an invasion, or simply create a military diversion large enough to overstrain British resources. Secondly, control of India bestowed immense benefits on Great Britain in terms of commerce, power and prestige, which would be growingly at risk unless some clearly defined limit was set to Russian expansion in Asia. Thirdly, this could be achieved by the growth of British influence over the intervening empires and principalities, and their reinforcement to constitute a barrier to further Russian advance. Malcolm was concerned primarily with propping up the Persian Empire, Evans with asserting British influence in central Asia and eventually China. These six propositions remained the essence of the case for making precautions against Russian aggrandisement a vital British interest during the rest of the nineteenth century.

The events of 1827–9 induced members of a British government to take the new hypothesis seriously for the first time. Not that many members of the cabinet had much time during these years to speculate on the world's future as they busied themselves with urgent problems within the British Isles, and the future status of Greece was the only international problem which aroused any general interest in government circles. The foreign secretary, Aberdeen, did reflect gloomily and at length on what he believed to be the certain and imminent disintegration of the Ottoman Empire, but he was largely absorbed in negotiating the details of a Greek settlement. Only Wellington and Ellenborough found that the idea of a growing Russian menace in Asia made the international situation more comprehensible, but they were important converts and they took prompt and appropriate measures. Both had long been anti-Russian in outlook and predisposed to suspect the tsar's intentions, but hitherto they had feared a general Russian threat to the European balance of power rather than any specific threat to the British Empire. Ellenborough began to picture events differently soon after he became president of the board of control in September 1828, Wellington apparently after reading Evan's second book in the autumn of 1829.

Ellenborough was an able and energetic man, whose administrative and oratorical talents were admired by Wellington and Peel. Since his abrasive personality made him many enemies, he never achieved his ambition to be foreign secretary, but as president of the board of control he found scope for his passionate interest in military and diplomatic affairs. His imagination was easily aroused by bold conceptions of world politics, and he readily responded to the arguments of men like Malcolm, whose 1826 memorandum to Canning on Russian expansion was part of the wide reading on Asian affairs which he undertook on entering office. He was soon attacking the custom of treating European and Asian problems as if they were quite separate, and he was for reversing Canning's policy towards Persia. He unsuccessfully argued the case for risking war and sending the British fleet to the Straits as Russian forces approached Constantinople in the summer of 1829. As early as September 1828 he had recorded in his diary the view that 'now our policy in Europe and in Asia ought to be the same – to bring down the Russian power', and within a year of going to the board of control he was interpreting international developments according to their possible effect on British interests in Asia. He had the predictable yearning for a sense of control over the area of the globe for which he felt responsible. 'Every success of theirs in that quarter makes my heart bleed', he wrote, when Russian troops captured the Turkish stronghold of Erzurum in Asia Minor. 'I consider it a victory gained over me, as Asia is *mine*.' With the

British leaders take alarm, 1828–33

ending of the Russo-Turkish war he grew convinced that he was witnessing the beginnings of a great historical process in which he could play a major part. He wrote to Wellington:

> I feel very anxious on the subject of the progress of the Russians in that quarter. I feel a presentiment that, step by step as the Persian monarchy is broken up, they will extend their influence and advance their troops, more especially under such a man as Paskewitch, till, without quarrelling with us, they have crept on to Cabul, where they may at their leisure prepare a force for the invasion of India.[1]

It was in this frame of mind that Ellenborough read Evans's book *On the Practicability of an Invasion of British India*. Besides presenting the usual case as to why the Russians should want to move on India and arguing that the intervening principalities would offer no greater obstacle than had the Indian princes to the British, Evans provided a military analysis of how Russian troops could cope with such difficult terrain. Not that Evans saw any reason for pessimism if the British took certain obvious precautions. An intelligence outpost at Bukhārā, accurate information about the Hindu Kush and its passes, and the presence of British agents at Kābul and Peshawar were essential first steps and the British should not hesitate to use a display of power to persuade Afghan and other rulers of the region to reorganize their political systems to make them more useful components of a British defence structure.

When Ellenborough read Evans's book on 29 October 1829, he was already convinced of the reality of the threat and was as optimistic as Evans as to the British ability to counteract it. What Evans did was to communicate a sense of urgency. Ellenborough had pictured the political future of the whole of Eurasia in clear and vivid terms, but his timescale was less dramatic. He had assumed that the Russian advance would be slow and gradual. A few days before, he had written to Wellington, 'That Russia will attempt, by conquest or by influence, to secure Persia as a road to the Indus, I have the utmost conviction.' But he added: 'It is evident that the latter and surer mode, that of influence, is the one she now selects.' This was in keeping with his remarks on 22 August about the Russians creeping on to Kābul step by step. Now he became convinced that the Russians could be ready to strike within the next two or three years. From the material in Evans's

---

[1] Lord Ellenborough, *A Political Diary, 1828–1830*, ed. Lord Colchester, 2 vols (London, 1881), 26 Sept. 1828, I, 227; 22 Aug. 1829, II, 88. To Wellington, 22 Aug. 1829, in *Despatches, Correspondence and Memoranda of Field Marshal, Arthur, Duke of Wellington, K.G., January 1819–December 1832*, ed. 2nd Duke of Wellington, 8 vols (London, 1867–80), VI, 100.

book he concluded that invasion was not merely practicable but easy unless the British government stirred itself to act like an Asian power. If it did, the difficulties which the ill-equipped Russian armies would suffer in an enterprise of this kind could be exploited. He was for occupying Lahore and Kābul as soon as Russian troops moved against Khīva. He would then be confident of defeating them before they ever reached the Indus. But his European-minded colleagues were without a forward policy and without the information on which it could be based. 'We know nothing of those passes, nothing of the country beyond them, nothing of the course of the Indus...' Ellenborough now busied himself with plans for remedying these defects as a matter of urgency. The Indus was to be explored, British trade with central Asia promoted, and British agents were to keep an eye on Russian activities.

He discovered that the prime minister agreed with him.

> The Duke then said we must look not to India only, but to all Asia, and asked me if I had read Evans's book. I told him I had; that forty-eight hours after I read it I had sent a copy to Macdonald and another to Malcolm. I told him all the views I had with regard to the navigation of the Indus and the opening of a trade with Cabul and Bokhara. He said our minds appeared to have been travelling the same way.[1]

As in the case of the Russian advance towards Constantinople, Wellington was much gloomier than Ellenborough as to the likely effect of any positive action to check the expansionist tendencies of the government in St Petersburg. He did not endorse Ellenborough's idea of an automatic military advance if the Russians moved, but he supported a programme of intelligence reports and the extension of British influence by money and by trade. So did the chairman and deputy-chairman of the East India Company, whom Ellenborough tackled two days after his conversation with Wellington; they welcomed especially 'the project of repelling the Russian commerce from Cabul and Bokhara, by carrying our goods directly up the Indus'. The Indus and its tributary streams were to be surveyed under cover of a ceremonial visit to Ranjit Singh of the Panjāb, who was to be presented with five dray horses in return for his coronation gift to William IV. If the Indus could be opened to British commerce, it was hoped to undersell the Russians in central Asia and to see political influence spreading, as usual, in the wake of trade. The governor-general, Lord William Bentinck, and most of his

[1] Wellington, *Despatches etc.*, VI, 238–9; Ellenborough, *Political Diary*, 30 Oct. 1829, 16 Dec. 1829, II, 122–5, 149–50.

advisers gave strong approval. Ellenborough believed he had initiated measures of incalculable value.

Ellenborough's measures did, at least, mark the beginning of an important new trend in British international policy. But they might well not have done so. Within a year Wellington's government was out of office, and there was no good reason to expect that the cabinet formed by Grey in November 1830 would find the new analysis equally persuasive. Whig repugnance for Russian methods in suppressing rebellion in Poland was strong, but none of the new cabinet was noticeably alarmed by the growth of Russian power in Asia, and there was as yet little alarm expressed in parliament and the press. Works like those of Evans were recognized by newspapers and periodicals to be worthy of careful discussion, but the tone of the debate was moderate and the verdict mildly sceptical. The danger, if it existed, was felt to be remote. Had the Russian government played an undramatic role in Asia over the next few years, Grey and Palmerston might have continued to picture the world beyond Great Britain in much the same way as Castlereagh and Canning. The alarm of Wellington and Ellenborough would then have looked merely eccentric, and later governments would perhaps have taken as calm a view of Russia's piecemeal empire-building as had Canning in 1826.

The events of 1830–1 with which Palmerston had to deal on entering office certainly had a familiar enough ring to a man whose formative years had coincided with the revolutionary and Napoleonic wars. Revolution had just broken out again in France and a few weeks later the Belgians had made a bid for independence from Holland. The new regime of Louis Philippe in Paris hoped to exploit the Belgian revolution. A Belgian nation-state under French influence would weaken part of the barrier built against France at the Congress of Vienna. French intervention in the Italian peninsula in support of revolutions seemed on the cards. At the same time Austria and Prussia were combining to supply money, arms and diplomatic support to the absolutist cause in the Portuguese civil war, while Palmerston backed a constitutionalist solution as more favourable to Great Britain's traditional interests there. As it happened, the new French monarchy was in the last resort too anxious for British goodwill in face of possible hostility from the three absolutist powers to oppose British policy over Belgium, but this opening bout of strenuous and complicated diplomatic action over the Low Countries and the Iberian peninsula would scarcely have encouraged Palmerston to believe that putative Russian designs in Asia could assume an importance comparable to the preservation of the European balance of power in a form favourable to Great Britain. And in 1830–1 Nicholas I was fully stretched coping with disaster within his own empire. The Polish revolution took nearly a year to suppress, and central Asia's current significance for Russia was as the source of the great cholera epidemic introduced by merchants from Bukhārā. The old working hypothesis served Palmerston admirably as a guide to events during his hectic initiation to world politics.

In 1832–3 a series of dramatic developments jolted Palmerston into rethinking the status of Asia in the international system. In November 1831 the Ottoman Empire, still recovering from the recent conflict with Russia, was once more plunged into war. The sultan's powerful vassal, Muḥammad ʿAlī of Egypt, made a bid to wrest control of Syria from his suzerain, and he was hoping in the process to overthrow Maḥmūd and become ruler of the whole Ottoman Empire. In 1832 he came near to success. His forces advanced into Asia Minor and, in December 1832, inflicted a heavy defeat on the sultan's army at Konya. The Egyptians were in striking distance of Constantinople itself, where Maḥmūd had reason to believe that there were plots to topple him in favour of Muḥammad ʿAlī. The sultan had made repeated appeals for British aid during the summer and autumn of 1832 as fortress after fortress fell to the enemy, but he received only vague assurances of goodwill. In desperation he turned to the Empire's ancient enemy, and in February 1833 Russian ships and troops were sent to defend Constantinople. Muḥammad ʿAlī contented himself with the rich enough prizes of Syria and Adana. The Russian reward was a defensive alliance with the Porte, the conditions of which appeared to make the Ottoman Empire a virtual satellite of Russia. As in 1828–9, a British government watched a major redistribution of power take place in south-eastern Europe and western Asia, and took no effective action.

There is no need to puzzle overmuch about Palmerston's passivity in this crisis during 1832. Intervention to save the Ottoman Empire was not an obvious course except to those who thought in the new way. It was generally agreed that the survival of the Empire was desirable for the sake of the balance of power, but that its collapse was inevitable. Wellington and Aberdeen had assumed its dissolution to be imminent in 1829; Grey and Palmerston took the same view in 1831–2. Intervention to ensure that British interests did not suffer during the process of dissolution was obvious enough in principle, but, as in 1829, it was anything but obvious what form intervention should take. British naval forces were fully stretched in support of diplomatic action over the Belgian and Portuguese crises, and there were no ships to spare in defence of Constantinople or as a threat to the Egyptians. There would be cabinet and parliamentary opposition of the strongest kind to increased naval estimates. And even if sufficient naval power could have been mobilized it was by no means clear how to use it. Unilateral action against Muḥammad ʿAlī might prove unfortunate if the sultan's power collapsed in spite of it and Muḥummad ʿAlī became the strongest ruler in western Asia; on the other hand, Palmerston was not attracted by the idea of backing Muḥammad ʿAlī in the hope of his future alliance because, in contrast to the Ottoman dynasty, his empire was liable to die with him. But above all Palmerston had to think quite differently before he could convincingly urge the cabinet to act. When the crisis began he still saw the apparently impending collapse of the Ottoman Empire in almost entirely European terms, as a rather regrettable jolt to the balance of power but one which could be settled within the European concert like the much more important Belgian crisis. To see the Empire's collapse in Eurasian terms as bringing nearer the day when the Russians would mount a threat to British India would take time; indeed, it was far from certain at the beginning of 1832 that Palmerston would come to see it that way at all. Unlike Wellington and Ellenborough, Palmerston had been anxious for good relations with Russia, and he had no special interest in India. The question is not why he did nothing but how he eventually came to believe that action was essential.

The changes in Palmerston's thinking cannot be traced as easily as with Ellenborough, who conveniently charted them in his political diary, but there is enough evidence for a rough chronological picture. There appear to have been two stages to the transformation. First, in the spring and summer of 1832, when Palmerston was receiving alarming reports from British consular officials in Egypt and Syria as to the military capacity and ambitions of Muḥammad ʿAlī, he was also reading a number of memoranda from men who were, or had been, on the spot in western Asia. These memoranda had been commissioned by the president of the board of control, Charles Grant, because the board was worried about the decline of British influence in regions adjoining India. They variously recommended the shoring up of Persia, Afghanistan, or the Ottoman Empire in Asia, but they were all agreed as to the danger to India inherent in every forward move made by the Russians. Sir Henry Willcock, formerly at Tehran, explicitly linked British inertia in western and in central Asia as facilitating the general Russian advance. The British government did not consider itself justified in intervening to save the Ottoman Empire and Persia; the same would happen, he prophesied, with regard to the smaller Asian states between the Oxus

(Amu Darya) and the Indus. The Russians would gradually advance 'to our very frontier in India without affording the slightest tangible ground for the expression of umbrage on our part'.[1] Palmerston took these memoranda, which were circulated to the cabinet, seriously and began to express concern as to possible Russian moves in central Asia. Russian possession of Khīva, he noted, would place them 'nearly in command of the navigation of rivers which lead down to the very frontier of our Indian Empire'.[2] This was written on 31 August 1832. A fortnight later he spoke with Stratford Canning on his return from Constantinople, and on 18 September expressed the opinion that it was in Great Britain's interest to maintain the Ottoman Empire. By this time, then, Palmerston had been sufficiently impressed by the remarkable consensus among diplomats and consuls with expert knowledge of western Asia to give broad credence to a general Russian threat.

In the closing months of 1832, Palmerston was interpreting the Turco-Egyptian crisis as much within the context of India's strategic needs as that of the balance of power in Europe. He assumed that the Russians, 'the most active intriguers and the most universal meddlers in the world', would seek to profit from the sultan's discomfiture by lopping off a province in north-eastern Anatolia, and that they would form an alliance with the victorious Egyptians to the detriment of British security in India.[3] Support for this interpretation of the crisis came from Stratford Canning, who, in a famous memorandum of 19 December 1832, summarized the case he had been advancing throughout the year for Great Britain's interest in maintaining the Ottoman Empire against Russia and Egypt, and especially from Henry Ellis, formerly at Tehran and now a member of the India board, who argued forcefully that a triumph for Muḥammad ʿAlī might be followed by a Russo-Egyptian partition of Persia. Palmerston also received Captain Chesney's report on the political value of promoting a new route to India via the Euphrates valley, where British influence was needed to bolster the defences of an area currently offering 'an easy and irresistible inlet to a northern enemy'.[4] Palmerston's correspondence suggests that these documents strongly influenced his thinking. But although he believed that Nicholas I would exploit the defeat of the Turks for territorial gain, and although he acknowledged the potential danger of a subse-

---

[1] Willcock to Backhouse, 6 Mar. 1832, F.O. 60/29.
[2] Quoted by M. Vereté, 'Palmerston and the Levant crisis, 1832', *Journal of Modern History*, vol. 24 (1952), 148 n. 1.
[3] *Ibid.*, 148–9.
[4] Quoted by J. B. Kelly, *Britain and the Persian Gulf, 1795–1880* (London, 1968), 267.

quent Russo-Egyptian alliance, he does not seem to have been very alarmed at the end of 1832. There is nothing to suggest that he then saw the situation in the dramatic terms he used in retrospect to condemn his cabinet colleagues for their failure to act, or that his advice that help should be given the sultan was offered to the cabinet with any particular vehemence.

His composure is understandable if he expected the powers to cooperate sufficiently to prevent the crisis getting out of hand. His experience with the Belgian crisis was reassuring. Despite quarrels and formal breaches among the powers as the crisis dragged on, there was always enough agreement to keep events under control and to preserve Palmerston's faith in collective action. None of the major governments at that time seemed anxious to allow a complete breakdown of international order. Too much at odds over Belgium for formal conferences to continue, the powers were quietly engaged in formal but effective diplomacy in late 1832 and the early months of 1833, at the very time when events in the Ottoman Empire were reaching a climax. Palmerston approved of this negotiation behind the scenes of outward antagonism, which were necessary to preserve an appearance of consistency and strength. 'But though there is no Conference,' he wrote, 'there can be no reason why Gentlemen should not meet together and talk these matters over, and, if the Gentlemen, who do so, happen to be the Plenipotentiaries of the Great Powers of Europe, why, all one can say is, that some public good might arise out of their private conversations.'[1] He may well have assumed that the governments of the powers would no more in the last resort allow Muḥammad ʿAlī to dictate events in the Ottoman Empire than they had allowed the king of Holland his way over Belgium. There were good grounds for such an assumption. The French and the Austrian governments were anxious to work with the British in imposing a settlement, and in December 1832 Nicholas I himself had invited the British to give naval support to the sultan. It is not surprising, therefore, that his solution was the Canningite one of working with the Russians in order to exercise some measure of control over them and to limit their gains from any intervention. The fortunes of war inevitably meant a redistribution of power in the area by which Russian capacity for long-term expansion would be enhanced, but the changes could be regulated by European diplomatic action. It was not that Palmerston underestimated the dangerous possibilities inherent in the Turco-Egyptian crisis, but his experience in

[1] Quoted by Sir Charles Webster. *The Foreign Policy of Palmerston, 1830-1841*, 2 vols (London, 1951), I, 175.

handling the Belgian problem may have led him to exaggerate the degree of restraint and patience that the tsar would be willing to exercise while the leisurely processes of diplomacy got under way. He does not appear to have expected Nicholas I to save the Turks by unilateral military action.

The second stage in Palmerston's conversion did not come until the summer of 1833. Even when Maḥmūd, rebuffed a second time by the British cabinet, accepted an offer of Russian support in February 1833, and when Russian troops and ships arrived to defend Constantinople, Palmerston had not panicked. Suspicion of Russia had already become the rule. 'In the absence of grounds for judgment,' he wrote to Ponsonby, newly appointed ambassador at Constantinople, 'one must go by the general rules and believe that where Russian agents are employed there must be intrigue on foot.'[1] He distrusted Metternich, too. But he continued to work throughout the first half of 1833 for a formula to which the Russians, the Austrians and the French could equally subscribe. At least Russian intervention had ended the immediate danger of Ottoman collapse, and they could scarcely remain to consolidate their hold in face of European displeasure any more than could the French in Belgium. It was only when the Russian government established a special treaty relationship with the Porte at Hünkâr Iskelesi, and when it became clear that Metternich had been persuaded at Münchengrätz to support the arrangement, that Palmerston's worst suspicions were confirmed and he abandoned any hope of a generally agreed European settlement. From then on Palmerston was convinced not merely of a general Russian threat but that the threat had urgently to be countered by whatever measures of intrigue and intervention were necessary to assert British influence in countries between the British and Russian empires. His acceptance of the new hypothesis was now complete, and he saw the Russian government, despite its denials, as 'intently engaged in the prosecution of those schemes of aggrandizement towards the South, which ever since the reign of Catherine have formed a prominent feature of Russian policy'.[2]

For the rest of the century most British cabinets were to interpret Russian moves in Europe and Asia as part of a grand design patiently pursued whenever a favourable opening occurred. Why Wellington, Ellenborough and Palmerston found the suggestion of a grand design convincing in the crucial years of its adoption at government level

---

[1] Quoted by H. C. F. Bell, *Lord Palmerston*, 2 vols (London, 1936), I, 181.
[2] R. L. Baker, 'Palmerston and the treaty of Unkiar Skelessi', *English Historical Review*, vol. 43 (1928), 86.

British leaders take alarm, 1828–33 39

between 1827 and 1833 is clear. But were they right? Did the new interpretation of Russian policy correspond more closely with reality than the assumptions of Castlereagh and Canning? Had Canning been right in his assessment of the Russo-Persian war in 1826? If so, would his view have been still appropriate by 1833? Was there a threat to British India implicit in Russian military and diplomatic activity between 1826 and 1833?

Strictly speaking, the question need not be asked. In attempting to explain the behaviour at international level of men like Canning and Palmerston, it is important to establish how and why they thought the way they did about world politics. To decide whether they were right or wrong in their assumptions contributes nothing by way of explanation. It would settle the controversies of their day, but one hundred and fifty years too late to alter the course of events which was the purpose of the original controversies. Refighting old battles with the advantage of hindsight is an enjoyable pastime, but a futile one if the only point is to justify or condemn the use governments made of the power and influence at their disposal. But an answer might also contribute to a controversy which is only too much alive: how often does international conflict arise from illusion and misunderstanding as to an opponent's intentions?

In one sense, the answer is straightforward. Russian policy had not changed. Nicholas I looked at the world beyond Russia in much the same way as had Alexander I in the years since 1815. The stabilization of Europe was still the highest priority of the government in St Petersburg. Asian affairs were a side issue. In the wars against Persia and the Ottoman Empire, Nicholas had used force to resolve quarrels with two troublesome neighbours but his aims were limited to stabilizing the situation in Russia's favour. There is nothing to suggest that he or his ministers saw the Russian decision to fight as part of a grand design in Asia, or that the successful outcome of the wars tempted them to pursue such a design. The suspicions of Ellenborough, Wellington and Palmerston as to Nicholas's intentions during these years were quite unfounded. In one of its functions, that of interpreting the current behaviour of other governments, the new working hypothesis had failed. The assumptions of Canning would have been as correct in 1833 as they had been in 1826. But such hypotheses have a second function, that of imaginative anticipation of danger and opportunity without which no international statesman is likely to feel in control of his world. It is not possible to discuss which attitude more accurately anticipated events, because the attempt to provide against events predicted is itself one of the most crucial factors determining the course of events, and the predominance of a different interpretation would have brought different consequences. It is possible to discuss whether it was sensible in 1828–33 to imagine and prepare for threats from Russia which had as yet no place in Russian official thinking. Here, the answer is less straightforward.

A strong case can be made in retrospect for attributing the changed attitudes of 1828–33 to unnecessary panic. For the indefinite future any Russian emperor was likely to be sufficiently obsessed by the prospect of revolution in Europe to keep much the same priorities in foreign policy, and to continue to regard territorial expansion in Asia as of minor importance. The upheavals of 1830–1, including as they did part of the Russian Empire, served to enhance the probability of this. The British could, it would be reasonable to argue, rest secure in Asia, and look on Russian bids for improved frontiers and extended influence there as being, like their own moves, consolidatory in character. British interests in the Ottoman Empire could be defended through the European diplomatic network. There was nothing unlikely about a view of international politics which discounted any serious danger from the Russians in Asia in the foreseeable future. The difficulty is that there was also nothing unlikely about the view which had displaced it. However mistaken its protagonists may have been about Nicholas I's policy around 1830, at least two of their reasons for apprehension about the future look sound enough, again in retrospect. First, Russian power and influence in western Asia *had* increased considerably with the recent victories over the Turks and the Persians, and so, accordingly, had the Russian government's capacity for expansion towards India. Since there was every reason to expect further crises from which the Russians could profit, the steady growth of Russian power was a process likely to continue even without any grand design. It could thereby gradually reach proportions which would become very dangerous indeed to the British should a future Russian government adopt the sort of policy already attributed to them by leading British politicians. The second reason was that such fundamental switches of policy were a risk that every government had to allow for in its dealings with Russia. The making of foreign policy was the personal prerogative of the Russian emperor. Foreign governments had to take into account the possibilities that his behaviour might prove capricious or that he might be overthrown. Men of Palmerston's generation could have justifiably recalled that the Emperor Paul had begun his reign by abandoning a war against Persia to concentrate on the cause of conservatism in Europe, but that, once he believed conservatism to have been saved by the advent of Napoleon, he had promptly turned to plans for the invasion of India. It would have been rash to have assumed around 1830 that Paul's son, Nicholas I, would turn out to be so remarkably single-minded and consistent, or to have assumed that he would remain emperor for so long. His grandfather and his father had been assassinated, and Nicholas himself had been the target of conspirators at the very start of his reign. A vision of the future in which a Russian emperor exploited an increasingly favourable position in Asia to threaten British India was just as likely as one in which even the same emperor refused to be distracted from his chosen role as the guardian of the monarchical order in Europe. Either interpretation may be said, therefore, to have offered equally reasonable guesswork about the future.

On the face of it, those who saw little sign of danger have the greater claim to realism. Their assessment of existing Russian policy has been vindicated, and their prediction of its future course was rationally enough based. Their cool and sceptical tone has greater appeal to later and uninvolved generations than the Russophobia which triumphed in the 1830s. In their anxiety about the future, the Russophobes fell an easy prey to delusions about the present. It is always a short step from fear of what a powerful neighbour might do to the belief that he is already in the process of doing it, from horrified realization as to the possible effect of a neighbour's increased power to the conviction that the increase in power was planned with such an effect in mind. Between 1828 and 1833 Ellenborough, Wellington and Palmerston took that step, and in the years that followed David Urquhart and other writers persuaded most British observers of international politics to follow them. Yet it is at least arguable that pessimism about the future, even if it bred delusions about the present, was the better basis for policy-making by the time of Hünkâr Iskelesi. In any situation involving potential conflict it is normal for the scale of the precautions to be in proportion to what is at stake. When this rule is observed, the prospects of maintaining the state's integrity are greatly enhanced because its leaders are more alert to sense impending danger and to counter it quickly and decisively. The higher the stakes, the greater is the risk in assuming that even a remote threat will not materialize. In this case, the stakes were very high indeed, and the threat very far from remote. Should tsarist ambitions with regard to India be revived, those British politicians who had thought the change to have already taken place might well be better equipped to meet a crisis than those who had been prepared to wait and see. In this sense, the new interpretation was probably the more appropriate guide to action in 1833. It remained to be seen whether the action taken by way of precaution would be dramatic enough to stimulate the Russians into a comparably sweeping reappraisal of world politics.

3

Palmerston's counter-offensive, 1833–41

By the middle 1830s it was widely believed among the British that their empire would be endangered without a vigorous assertion of British power and influence in Asia. There was no grand design, but with politicians in London and agents in Asia tending to interpret events within the same broad speculative framework, it was only to be expected that the more dynamic would tackle the problems confronting them in appropriately aggressive style. By 1860 the British had fought and defeated the Russians, the Chinese, the Egyptians, the Persians, the Afghans, the Burmese, the Balūchīs of Sind, and the Sikhs. They had annexed Sind, the Panjāb, Lower Burma, Aden and Hong Kong. They had suppressed a major revolt against their rule in India. They had forced on Russia and China, the only other great powers in Asia, treaties which limited their rulers' freedom of action in humiliating fashion. In terms of power politics it was an impressive record. All the wars by which this new position of power was achieved have since been regarded as discreditable by the British, who have been ashamed of the impression left of imperialist bullying, or of some gross bungling on the road to victory, or of both. But the upshot from the point of view of the defeated was an extraordinary assertion of British power in relation to every state on the Asian mainland.

Palmerston began his campaign against the Russian 'threat' by energetically contesting Russian influence throughout western and central Asia and in the capitals of Europe. Central to this diplomatic battle, waged with gusto by ambassadors, consuls and other agents, was Constantinople. It was there that Russia's representatives had gained an apparently spectacular triumph on 8 July with the signing of the treaty of Hünkâr Iskelesi. Initial British and French fears that Russia had acquired the right to send warships through the Straits into the Mediterranean proved to be without substance. The treaty simply provided that the Russian government should supply military and naval assistance to the Turks if the Ottoman Empire were attacked, but that by way of reciprocity the Turkish government needed only to ensure that the Dardanelles were sealed to foreign warships when Russia was at war. This was in keeping with existing international law concerning the Straits. Strictly speaking it was a straightforward defensive alliance between two sovereign states to which other governments had no right to object. But it was correctly sensed abroad that Nicholas I and his ministers intended the treaty to be the first step to a very different relationship. The help already given in 1833 and promised for the future at Hünkâr Iskelesi would begin the process of accustoming the Turkish government to the idea of Russia as their only reliable and fully committed ally. The Ottoman Empire, still weak and vulnerable to Egyptian attack, was certain to appeal again for aid until, as Palmerston put it, 'the Russian Ambassador becomes chief Cabinet Minister of the Sultan'.[1] 'There is no doubt', wrote Orlov, the Russian negotiator of the treaty, 'but that in a year or two at the most, we shall be summoned back, but we shall have the great advantage of coming back, thanks to our antecedents, without arousing suspicion and of coming back in such a way as never to leave again, if need be.'[2] Nicholas I's policy was to preserve and control the Ottoman Empire as a defensive barrier for Russia against the powerful maritime states, France and Great Britain. But this could not be achieved overnight. Hünkâr Iskelesi was only a promising start. Palmerston's aim was to render abortive the embryonic vassalage which it symbolized.

Disrupting Russian plans for an exclusive alliance with the Turks did not prove difficult. The British ambassador at Constantinople between 1833 and 1841 was Lord Ponsonby, who quickly mastered the arts of palace intrigue required in the battle for influence with his Russian counterpart, Butenev. The Russian government was always much more generous than the British in supplying money for bribes, but Ponsonby had other and decisive advantages. Sultan Maḥmūd had turned to Russia for aid only when the alternative seemed to be imminent defeat and overthrow, and had met their conditions for a firm alliance only because no other system of security was available. His distrust of the Russians had not been removed, and he would welcome

---

[1] Quoted by Webster, *Foreign Policy of Palmerston*, I, 305.
[2] Quoted by P. E. Mosely, *Russian Diplomacy and the Opening of the Eastern Question in 1838 and 1839* (Cambridge, Mass., 1934), 21.

the freedom of manœuvre which a real change in British policy would bring him. But he had to be sure. Ponsonby had a forceful personality which carried conviction. Although he had to avoid promises which might have encouraged the sultan to attack Muḥammad ʿAlī, his hints, backed by British naval reinforcements and manœuvres, persuaded Maḥmūd that the prospects of escaping from exclusive dependence on Russia were good. Ponsonby's extravagant behaviour won him many enemies among his fellow diplomats at Constantinople and at home, but Palmerston firmly supported him, and he won sufficient influence with the sultan to neutralize Russian hopes that Maḥmūd would look only to them in future. On the other hand, Palmerston's hopes of using British influence to promote reform of the Ottoman Empire's army, finances and administration to the point that it would be strong enough to resist both Russian and Egyptian threats, and hence become, in effect, a defensive barrier for the British against Russia, were unfulfilled. He underrated the problems of instituting rapid and effective change, and both the advice and the advisers he sent to Constantinople accomplished little. Nor could the British exclude Russian influence altogether. Maḥmūd's interest was to keep both powers in play until one of them offered direct help in driving Muḥammad ʿAlī out of Syria, a price neither the British nor the Russians were prepared to pay. But Palmerston and Ponsonby had prevented a Russian monopoly of influence at Constantinople developing out of the position won in 1833. Hünkâr Iskelesi had proved an abortive triumph.

British success was signalized in the commercial convention signed in August 1838. Pressure on the Turks to conclude such a convention was part of a general government drive at this time, in face of growing protectionism in Europe, to improve conditions under which British merchants could trade abroad. Since Russia was one of the chief offenders from the British point of view, the extension of Russian frontiers in Asia would make less attractive what were believed to be markets of great potential value. This gave added point to the policy of checking Russian advances, especially as trade routes important to the British ran close to the Russian frontiers in western Asia. It gave added point, too, to the policy of preventing the Ottoman Empire – widely publicized by David Urquhart and others as a country whose trade links with Great Britain offered immense scope for development – from coming under Russian domination. But although the essential aim of the convention was to meet grievances of British merchants about impediments to trade, its signing was evidence that by the summer of 1838 the sultan had come to believe that Great Britain was the power more likely to help him overthrow Muḥammad ʿAlī.

In the Ottoman Empire local conditions favoured British diplomacy. Elsewhere in Asia the odds were stacked against the British diplomatic offensive, and the political and commercial gains which were its objective suffered initial frustration. In Persia, for example, a situation closely comparable in many respects to that presented by the Ottoman Empire redounded to the Russian government's advantage. Like the Ottoman sultans, the shahs ruled over what had once been a great empire and a major centre of civilization. From the fifteenth to the eighteenth centuries Turks and Persians shared control of western Asia because neither was capable of toppling the other in their recurrent wars. Persia had now sunk into an even deeper decline than the Ottoman Empire, and was even less able to resist the new giants of Asia, Russia and Great Britain. Recent defeat had left Turkish and Persian rulers alike frightened of the Russians and sceptical of the British as willing and effective allies. With no prospect of regaining territories taken by Russia, both the Turks and the Persians concentrated in the 1830s on other areas which had slipped from their grasp: the sultan on the provinces of his overmighty subject, Muḥammad ʿAlī; the shah on the Afghan lands which, a century before, had formed part of the vast empire of Nādir Shāh. Shah and sultan alike would unhesitatingly throw in their lot with whatever power would help them in their ambitions. But there the comparison ended. Despite their antagonism, it was common policy in London and St Petersburg to try to restrain Maḥmūd from attacking Muḥammad ʿAlī for fear of a train of consequences beyond the control of either government. But whereas the British felt the same way about the expansionist aims of the shah of Persia, the Russians gave him every encouragement. Their influence waxed accordingly.

In face of this, British diplomatic efforts were naturally unavailing. Palmerston had since 1833 been trying to repair the damage done by Canning's indifference in 1826 and by the subsequent decision to end, in return for a single cash payment, the obligation to subsidize the Persians if they were attacked. A revised treaty was being discussed with Fatḥ ʿAlī Shāh at the time of his death in November 1834. Palmerston had also secured Russian agreement on support for the heir apparent in the event of a disputed succession. During the brief Tory ministry of November 1834 to April 1835 it was decided to raise the status of British representation at Tehran. In 1823 control of the British mission there had been transferred to the East India Company, Persian affairs being regarded as of importance only to India and as irrelevant to Great Power relationships. Control now reverted to the Crown. Palmerston confirmed the change when he returned to office, and took measures to ensure close working between the foreign office and the board of control. The first representatives under the new arrangement were Henry Ellis and John McNeill, both firm believers in the Russian menace and with long experience of the country. McNeill wrote one of the most famous Russophobe pamphlets shortly before taking up his post in 1836. They were both able and energetic men, but they had no chance of restoring the close links with Persia which British policy now required. The new ruler, Muḥammad Shāh, wanted the one thing it was their duty to oppose at all costs – Herat.

Herat, revered by Persians as an ancient centre of their culture, had been under Afghan control since 1747, and many attempts had been made to regain it. It was a valuable military base. It lay in a fertile valley where troops could mass for an advance to Qandahār and the Indus, bypassing the formidable mountain barrier of the Hindu Kush. Its position made Herat the key to India, a favourite route for conquerors in the past. The Persians themselves had three times in the course of their history used Herat as a base from which to conquer northern India. The British were understandably alarmed at the prospect of Herat's absorption by a state which seemed on the way to becoming a Russian satellite. Simonich, the Russian ambassador to Persia, was apparently urging the shah to take Herat as the beginning of a drive to the east. The Russian government denied his involvement. To Palmerston and his colleagues, however, Simonich's activities fitted a pattern of events for which they were well prepared. Under the Persians, they believed, Herat would become a Russian advance post against British India.

Nor could the Persian conquest of Herat be an isolated incident in the politics of Asia. The political units occupying the lands between Persia and India were highly unstable. A successful Persian thrust would bring a still greater degree of uncertainty. Herat was one of several principalities into which the short-lived Afghan empire had disintegrated in the early nineteenth century. The two principal centres of Afghan power were Qandahār, farther along the route to India from Herat, and Kābul, astride another vital road south to the Khyber Pass and India, and north to the passes of the Hindu Kush and central Asia. Between the Afghans and British India were Sind and the Panjāb, along the course of the Indus, the river which Ellenborough hoped would carry British commerce and political influence into the heart of Asia. The Afghan principalities were in conflict with one another and with the Panjāb, and the Persians were their traditional enemies; the Panjāb was at odds with Sind. All took the British into account as potential allies or enemies of great importance in the power struggles of the region. But a Persian capture of Herat would bring dramatic proof of the value of Russian support. Russian power would become as crucial a factor as that of the British in the calculations of the rival princes on the frontiers of India. The Russian government could establish a consulate at Herat once it was part of Persia. If its agents could outbid the British, their influence might extend to the Sutlej, and soon spill over to encourage disaffection within India itself.

The projected Persian attack on Herat threatened the concept of a security system for India. Ideally, the British aspired to predominant influence throughout the region which separated their empire from that of Russia: in Persia, Afghanistan, Sind, and the Panjāb, as well as among the more remote principalities and tribes of central Asia. It was hoped that growing dependence on British commerce, confidently expected to have a decisive edge over that of Russia or any other exporting country, would unite the quarrelling rulers under British influence, expressed by a network of commercial and political treaties. But this would take time. Russian backing for an attack on Herat suggested that the necessary time was unlikely to be available. To counter the move and its probable consequences, the British were forced to try short-term diplomatic expedients of the kind Russia had practised with regard to Persia, especially the promise of aid in war. Here they were at a disadvantage. Given existing political conditions, they could aid one ruler only at cost of alienating the neighbour he wished to attack. For example, the Afghan princes between them controlled the main invasion routes to India. Alliance with them was essential to any security system. But the price demanded by Dost Muḥammad Khān of Kābul was, as in the case of Persia, the very one the British could not afford to pay. Dost Muḥammad's ambition was to establish his supremacy over the other Afghan principalities of Qandahār and Herat, and, more urgently, to recover Peshawar, wrested from Afghan control in 1834 by Ranjit Singh of the Panjāb. Ranjit Singh commanded a strong and efficient army, and Dost Muḥammad appreciated the value of a powerful ally. The British would unquestionably be the most effective ally against the Panjāb in terms both of strength and proximity. The British were well aware of how valuable to their defences would be a united and friendly Afghanistan across the Russian route to India. But the price was the ending of their alliance with Ranjit Singh, which dated from 1809 and was the only surviving remnant of the defence structure built up by the diplomatic offensive beyond India's frontiers during the Napoleonic Wars. They respected Ranjit Singh as their strongest and most reliable neighbour. They could strengthen their defences at one point only by undermining them elsewhere. Yet the only alternative sources of aid for Dost Muḥammad were the Persians and the Russians.

To the men in London and Calcutta who firmly believed that the Russian emperor would exploit this dilemma in order to extend his influence towards the frontiers of India, the situation seemed explosive. A sequence of dramatic events like the fall of Herat to Russia's Persian protégés could swiftly transform the outlook not only of princes beyond the frontier but of those within India itself. Russia would seem the power of the future, to whom it would be expedient and profitable to pay court. But although there was general agreement as to just how great the potential danger was, Palmerston and his colleagues had difficulty in deciding which of the various measures urged upon them were most appropriate.

Four contrasting programmes of action were canvassed in the mid-1830s. Sir Charles Metcalfe, one of the most experienced of the British administrators in India, believed that security lay in staying put on the Sutlej frontier and building on the alliance with the Panjāb, which he himself had negotiated in 1809. The Sikhs under Ranjit Singh should be allowed to expand as they wished in the direction of Sind and Afghanistan, and the British would need to look no further for a powerful buffer state to stand between them and the advancing Russians. Of the other three programmes, the boldest was that put forward by Alexander Burnes, whom Sir John Malcolm had in 1830 entrusted with the Indus expedition to Ranjit Singh. Burnes had won great fame by his subsequent journey to Bukhārā in 1832, which he described in a popular contribution to the growing literature on central Asia. Although Burnes stressed the difficulties of Ellenborough's project of pushing British influence into the heart of Asia by making the Indus a great commercial highway, he confirmed the view that British exporters could drive their Russian counterparts out of the central Asian market by the cheapness of their products, and he also confirmed the gloomy forecasts of how easily the Russians could despatch troops as well as goods to the region if they were not so excluded. On his way to Bukhārā Burnes had visited Kābul, where Dost Muhammad impressed him as the man of destiny in that part of Asia. The programme he pressed on his superiors was that of a great Afghan buffer state developed by British aid and serving the function which Metcalfe envisaged for the Panjāb. From Tehran the British representative McNeill urged a still wider though more flexible programme. Since he believed the fate of Herat to be the key to the future, he wanted direct British intervention against Persia to save it. As a long-term solution he argued for the inclusion of Herat in a unified Afghan state under any prince capable of holding the tribes' allegiance and willing to follow a course in foreign affairs favourable to the British. Unlike Burnes, he held no special brief for Dost Muḥammad. All three programmes shared a common vision of a friendly and powerful Asian state interposed as a barrier between the British and Russian empires.

It was a fourth and less dramatic programme which was initially adopted by Palmerston and by Lord Auckland, who had been appointed governor-general in 1835. This attempted to preserve a balance of power in the region on the grounds that it was too dangerous to rely on the uncertain friendship of either a Sikh or an Afghan empire. Ellenborough had advocated this in March 1835 during his return to the board of control in the short-lived Tory administration of that year. Each prince in the region should be made to feel that his security depended on British support, so that the British could rely on close and friendly ties with the Panjāb, Sind and an eventually united Afghanistan. Given the mutual antagonism of the rulers involved, the programme presented obvious difficulties, but Auckland took as his starting-point the superior strength of Ranjit Singh's Panjāb. The amirs of Sind and the Afghan princes alike had cause to fear Ranjit Singh's territorial ambitions at their expense. This provided Auckland with a bargaining counter, because Ranjit Singh was convinced of the value of his old treaty relationship with the British and would be reluctant to jeopardize it by moves to which they were strongly opposed. Although Auckland had to be careful not to strain this relationship too far by asking Ranjit Singh to abandon what he saw as the defence of his vital interests – for example, Peshawar – the governor-general could offer to restrain Ranjit Singh from attacking the rulers of Sind and Afghanistan provided the latter bound themselves to observe British interests in their conduct of foreign affairs.

The policy met with partial success. It worked in the case of Sind. The threat of leaving them to the mercies of Ranjit Singh had been used against the amirs in 1832 when Henry Pottinger negotiated commercial treaties with them to open the Indus to merchants from India. In 1835–6 Ranjit Singh underlined the reality of the threat by making war against Sind, one of whose dependent peoples had been raiding the Panjāb. The British, of course, had no intention of allowing Ranjit Singh to seize control of Sind and the mouth of the Indus, but Pottinger successfully persuaded the amirs that his government would intervene to save them from disaster only on rigorous terms. These included a British agent permanently resident at the capital, Haydarābād, and British control of all future relations with the Panjāb. With the acceptance of a treaty on these lines in April 1838, Sind was well on the way to protectorate status. Ranjit Singh scaled down his demands in face of British representations. The British had enhanced their capacity to control events immediately beyond their frontier.

At the very time when Pottinger was concluding the treaty with Sind, Alexander Burnes was leaving Kābul, having failed to win Dost Muḥammad's compliance with much more modest terms. Burnes was empowered to offer the same bait – the restraint of Ranjit Singh – and was to demand in return only that Dost Muḥammad should spurn the overtures of the Persians and the Russians, and demonstrate his willingness for a reconciliation with Ranjit Singh. But Dost Muḥammad was not sufficiently afraid of either Ranjit Singh or the British to be impressed. He wanted to win Peshawar and his co-religionists there back from Sikh rule, and a British alliance would have point only if it contributed to this. Nor could he lose face by humbling himself before Ranjit Singh. Burnes, unable to promote his own scheme of encouraging the ruler of Kābul to hope for British support in his expansionist ambitions, gave up after six months of bargaining in April 1838. He left the field open to a Russian agent, Vitkevich, who had arrived the previous December. British manipulation of the balance of power along the Indus remained incomplete.

By 1838 the diplomatic offensive which Palmerston, Auckland and their subordinates had launched after the treaty of Hünkâr Iskelesi had enjoyed some measure of success in the Ottoman Empire and on the Indian frontier. But it had failed in Persia and Afghanistan. After a number of false starts, the shah of Persia's forces had begun the siege of Herat at the end of 1837. The Afghan princes of Qandahār were ready for a deal with Persia, and at Kābul Dost Muhammad himself was negotiating with a Russian agent. Reports were current of forthcoming Russian expeditions to the central Asian principalities of Khīva and Bukhārā. Within the Ottoman Empire, moreover, Muḥammad ʿAlī was said to be planning a declaration of independence, which would certainly mean renewed war with the sultan and probable intervention by Russia. The prospect loomed of an alliance between Russia, Persia and the Afghan princes being formed just when the Russians were poised to strike at Constantinople and the heart of Asia. At the same time, the British faced possible war with the Burmese and with the Gurkhas of

Nepal. From London and from Calcutta it looked as if events could go spinning out of control if decisive action were not taken.

Nor was there much consolation to be derived from Palmerston's diplomacy within Europe. He had tried to fortify British plans for a European guarantee of Turkish security in place of Russia's exclusive alliance by moves to cooperate with the French and to isolate Russia from the Austrians. But his proposed expedients met with opposition from some of his colleagues as well as from Metternich, and they came to nothing. He even tried to counter traditional Russian influence among the south Slavs of the Balkans by sending Colonel Hodges on a mission to Prince Miloš of Serbia, but the Russian connection was too strongly established for quick results, and the Austrians preferred even Russian influence on their frontiers to the virus of British liberalism. The British government's morale was nevertheless high. Events seemed to them to have confirmed the working hypothesis which had guided their policies. The anticipated confrontation with Russia was probably near. They had the intoxicating sensation of having been proved right; there were none of the doubts and misgivings which had greeted the crises of 1829 and 1833. What the failures with the Persians and the Afghans suggested to them was the need for stronger measures in pursuit of the same policies, not the scrapping of those policies or the way of thinking which inspired them. The diplomatic offensive of 1833–8 was followed, therefore, by greater readiness to use war and the threat of it to ensure success. Between 1838 and 1860 the British were normally engaged in warfare beyond their frontiers somewhere or other in Asia.

There were two main clusters of violent conflict, the first lasting from 1838 to 1842, and the second from 1854 to 1860. In the first of these Palmerston and his colleagues, convinced of the reality of the Russian threat, believed it would grow or diminish according to their ability to control the behaviour of three men: the rulers of Egypt, Persia and Kābul. Muhammad ʿAlī of Egypt could create sufficient havoc in the Ottoman Empire to encourage the Russians to seize Constantinople before any other power did. Muḥammad Shāh of Persia and Dost Muhammad of Kābul could, by enlisting Russian aid in pursuit of their territorial ambitions, provide the Russians with valuable bases from which to promote their influence or to wage war in the direction of India. On the other hand, the successful intimidation of all three would disrupt any plans Nicholas I might have for exploiting their ambitions. The use of British power against Egypt, Persia and Afghanistan between 1838 and 1842 constituted, therefore, three aspects of a single crisis from the point of view of the British government. A second crisis in these years, Britain's military involvement in China, had separate origins, but its consequences were related to the overall problem of how power and influence were to be distributed in future on the Eurasian continent, and it will be treated alongside the first.

The quickest and easiest results were obtained in tackling the Persian side of the problem. The Afghans in Herat had held out against the shah's forces. The British and Russian ambassadors set up camp with the besieging forces. McNeill advised a negotiated settlement and demanded the redress of various local grievances held by British representatives in Persia. He was rebuffed, and signalled his displeasure by leaving the shah's camp at the beginning of June 1838. The shah instead accepted Simonich's advice to make an all-out assault on Herat with the help of Russian officers, which was realized at the end of June. The assault failed, and as Eldred Pottinger, a British officer, contributed to its defeat, British prestige soared and that of Russia plummeted. The shah soon heard that five hundred sepoys from the Bombay garrison had been sent by Auckland to the Persian Gulf, and that they had occupied the island of Kharg. In August, Captain Stoddart delivered him an ultimatum from Palmerston to abandon the siege of Herat or face retaliation. The nature of the retaliation was not mentioned, and Palmerston had, in fact, ruled out an attack on the Persian mainland lest it lead to a direct confrontation with Russian troops, but, in the circumstances, the small force at Kharg looked like the spearhead of an invading army. The shah, frustrated and alarmed, abandoned the siege in September 1838, and agreed to the demands made earlier by McNeill. The British remained on Kharg while the terms were being implemented. The occupation was prolonged, because the shah evaded implementation as long as possible, and in the meantime the British accumulated further grievances requiring redress. It was not until 1841 that the shah evacuated a fortress about forty miles from Herat, signed a commercial treaty, and made the necessary gestures of apology. Kharg was evacuated in March 1842. But the essential demand, withdrawal from Herat, had been speedily obtained.

The ease with which the shah of Persia had been intimidated was gratifying, but it was taken for granted that he would renew his bid for Herat as soon as more favourable circumstances occurred. The long-term solution to India's defence problems was still believed to be firm alliance with India's neighbours. The British could not take the measures required to convert Persia into such an ally without directly clashing with the Russians, because it would involve intervention to replace the existing shah. On the other hand, intervention of this kind was possible in Afghanistan, with which the Russians had no common border and where they could thus do little to counter British moves. By the summer of 1838 Palmerston and Auckland had independently come to the same conclusion; that only the installation of a pro-British ruler in Kābul would guarantee the balance of power which diplomacy alone had failed to secure on India's frontiers. Dost Muḥammad was to be overthrown by giving military aid to one of his many rivals. A suitable rival was readily available. Shāh Shujāʿ had ruled Afghanistan between 1803 and 1809. After his overthrow he had gone into exile, and had eventually in 1816 become a pensioner of the British government in India. He had made an unsuccessful bid to regain his throne in 1834 in collaboration with Ranjit Singh and with the tacit connivance of Lord William Bentinck, then governor-general. Dost Muḥammad had defeated the attempt, but it was during this affair that Ranjit Singh had won Peshawar from the Afghans. Now the British were to give Shāh Shujāʿ the full backing of their armed forces for his restoration. A treaty of alliance was made between Auckland, Ranjit Singh and Shāh Shujāʿ which was intended to be the foundation of a new security system in the region.

In 1839 the plan was carried into effect. The Army of the Indus moved into Sind on the first stage of its expedition to Kābul. The amirs of Sind were forced to accept terms even more severe than those recently mposed on them as the price of their continued 'independence' during the operations in Afghanistan. The British forces, together with those they had enabled Shāh Shujāʿ to raise, occupied Qandahār in April 1839, the chiefs fleeing at their approach. In July the fortress of Ghazna was stormed during a surprise attack. Dost Muḥammad fled from Kābul, which was entered in August. Shāh Shujāʿ was made ruler of Qandahār and Kābul, and part of the British contingent remained to see him firmly established. The rest of the Army of the Indus returned to India in November 1839, less than a year after it had set out.

For two years it looked as though the British bid to reconstruct in their interest the politics of this part of Asia had triumphed. Dost Muḥammad made an unsuccessful attempt to recover his position in 1840. He then surrendered to Sir William Macnaghten, Auckland's envoy with Shāh Shujāʿ, and was despatched to captivity in India. Macnaghten continued to send optimistic reports from Kābul during 1840 and 1841. Moreover, the Russians failed in a comparable expedition to replace the khan of Khīva in 1839-40, the effect of which would have been to reduce Khīva to the dependent status of a Russian outpost.

Palmerston had dexterously robbed the Russians of their main pretext for action against Khīva. In 1839 he sent an agent, Captain James Abbott, to persuade the khan to negotiate with the tsar and release Russian subjects held in slavery. Abbott succeeded, and later another British officer, Richmond Shakespear, brought the slaves out of Khīva. It was poor operational planning that made the Russians call off the expedition, not Abbott's diplomacy, but the upshot was that the British had displayed on all fronts superior military and diplomatic prowess in central Asia.

In fact, the British achievement was a good deal less solid than it looked, and in 1841 it crumbled. Ranjit Singh had died in June 1839, and the predictable period of instability after the great man's death had been alarmingly prolonged. Under his weak successor the Panjāb had ceased to be the stable and reliable frontier state on which all calculations about the balance of power had been based. Instead of being the powerful ally which could be used to frighten British India's other neighbours into compliance with British wishes, the Panjāb was beginning to look as much a candidate for subjection as Sind. The assumption that Herat was too dependent on British aid for its survival to risk defiance was also undermined in 1841. Successive British agents in Herat had found it very difficult to cultivate good relations with its rulers. In February 1841, Major D'Arcy Todd broke off relations on his own initiative after a quarrel over intrigues with the Persians. He was promptly disowned by his superiors, but the rulers of Herat indicated the fragility of British precautions over the 'key to India' by threatening to submit to Persia. When Palmerston proposed the extension of British operations to occupy Herat, Auckland made it clear that the expense would be ruinous; the Afghan commitment was already costing a million pounds a year and producing a deficit in the Indian government's finances. Nor was there yet any sign that the outpouring of money to make sure of Afghanistan was coming to an end. Although Auckland's advisers had been unanimous that Shujā' would be welcomed by the Afghans, many of the tribal chiefs, without whose support no ruler in Kābul could survive, were in growing opposition to him. The early withdrawal planned by the British would clearly mean his collapse. The easy triumph at Kābul had by no means removed British anxieties at a stroke as had been hoped. British relations with the Panjāb, Herat and Kābul were shaky and uncertain.

The Tories had all along been sceptical of the policy of using British arms to overthrow one regime and set up another. They still shared the belief in the Russian threat, but favoured subtler counter-measures.

When the Whigs fell from power in the summer of 1841, Sir Robert Peel's Tory government replaced Auckland as governor-general by Ellenborough, who went out determined to conduct a staged withdrawal from Afghanistan. The timing was, however, determined by the Afghans themselves. Chiefs hostile to Shāh Shujāʿ organized a rising in Kābul against the British presence in November 1841. After General Elphinstone proved unable to mobilize his forces effectively against the tribesmen Macnaghten negotiated terms for a withdrawal of British troops from Afghanistan. With the unquenchable optimism which had misled him as to the seriousness of the opposition, Macnaghten hoped there would be characteristic divisions among the chiefs who could then be played off one against the other. He easily fell into a trap set by Muḥammad Akbar Khān, a son of Dost Muḥammad, who offered him a separate and more favourable treaty to prove Macnaghten's bad faith to the other chiefs. Macnaghten was killed at a meeting with Akbar Khān, and his mutilated remains were exhibited. The Kābul garrison and its women and children were evacuated in January 1842 under Akbar Khān's promise of safe conduct, but few survived the journey through hostile territory. The planned withdrawal was postponed until the humiliation could be redeemed. General Pollock's reoccupation of Kābul in September 1842 and the ritual of destruction and killing which accompanied it gratified the British desire for revenge. It did not restore faith in the policy which had ended in such disaster. By December 1842 the British army was back behind the Sutlej, and Ellenborough did not intend it to take the road to Kābul again.

The programme of a balance of power in the lands between the Hindu Kush and British India was in ruins. Ranjit Singh was dead, and the Sikhs were uncertain allies. The amirs of Sind had become increasingly restive and recalcitrant as the British tried to tighten their grip on the country and its communications during their occupation of Afghanistan. Shāh Shujāʿ was assassinated in 1842, and in 1843 Dost Muḥammad returned to Kābul to resume his rule, in no mood to participate in British alliance schemes. The British had learned the hard way how difficult it was to control a country far from base without conquering it. Temporary occupation made excessive demands on the talents of their agents. On the other hand, Palmerston and his colleagues had some grounds for their unrepentant attitude. Miscalculations by men on the spot had led to unnecessary bloodshed and humiliation; different agents reacting differently might have carried it off. Shāh Shujāʿ might not have long survived the British withdrawal, but his successors would have been wary of provoking fresh British intervention. Even with the

Kābul fiasco, the expeditions of 1839 and 1842 had shown the Afghans how vulnerable they were to British hostility. Dost Muḥammad took care, one brief episode apart, not to incur it again. The British had demonstrated their striking capacity to the ruler of Kābul as convincingly as they had to the shah of Persia.

The third ruler whose policies the British saw as crucial to the security of their empire was Muḥammad ʿAlī. The pasha of Egypt's own empire-building threatened British imperial interests in two directions. The control of Syria, which he had won in 1833, was a constant source of antagonism between him and the sultan, and renewed war might occasion Russian intervention and seizure of the Straits. Secondly, his plans for further territorial expansion were thought to include the pashalik of Baghdād and the Arabian coast of the Persian Gulf. This would bring him to the approaches to India. Controversy about future communications with India had already given Palmerston the opportunity to publicize British interest in Baghdād and the Persian Gulf. The traditional route around the Cape of Good Hope was politically trouble-free, but there was an obvious need for speedier delivery of political, commercial and personal correspondence than it could provide. The coming of steam navigation itself had offered no immediate solution, because the early steam vessels were not up to long oceanic voyages. They could, however, give fast service in the Mediterranean, the Red Sea, the Persian Gulf and the Arabian Sea. This encouraged experiments with routes across Egypt and western Asia. The most obvious of these involved a short land journey at Suez to link steamships in the Mediterranean and the Red Sea. In the 1830s there was also great interest in the Euphrates route. After crossing the Syrian desert, passengers and cargo would be conveyed by steamboat down the Euphrates to the Persian Gulf. Muḥammad ʿAlī did all he could to encourage the Egypt–Red Sea route, hoping to profit from transit dues. Should he declare his independence and extend his power to the Euphrates and the Persian Gulf, he would, no doubt, be equally cooperative. But British governments disliked the idea of both the short steam routes being dependent on the goodwill of the same ruler, whose closest ally was France and whose successors might well look to Russia. Thus, although its feasibility was still untested, the Euphrates route attracted enthusiastic support on political grounds. It was still largely under the sultan's control. It included a region at which the Russians might strike in the future, perhaps as a possible route for invading India, and it was useful to establish a vital interest there which a British government could easily justify defending. Both Muḥammad ʿAlī and Nicholas I, therefore, were to be warned off the pashalik of Baghdād, through which the Euphrates ran, by an exploratory expedition under the command of the route's chief advocate, Captain Francis Chesney. The expedition began work in 1835. It suffered many mishaps, including sabotage by Muḥammad ʿAlī's officials in Syria, and it was clear by 1837 that the Euphrates was not a suitable route. But the survey was continued until 1842, its armed steamboats being a convenient means of showing the flag and of relaying intelligence in western Asia at a time of crisis.

An Egyptian threat in the Persian Gulf was the first to reach crisis proportions. Muḥammad ʿAlī had first extended his power to Arabia at the invitation of the sultan himself. In the late eighteenth century, the Wahhābi sect had waged war there to restore primitive simplicity to the Muslim world. They came to dominate Arabia, including the holy cities of Mecca and Medina. In 1811, the sultan had deputed Muḥammad ʿAlī to destroy their power. By 1818 the pasha's troops had driven the Wahhābi from Mecca and Medina, but they continued to control eastern Arabia, and when Muḥammad ʿAlī resumed operations against them in 1837 his aim was probably to probe the southern approaches of the Baghdād pashalik under cover of pursuing the sultan's business in Arabia. His forces overthrew the current Wahhābi leader, and one of Muḥammad ʿAlī's prisoners from the earlier campaign was installed as a puppet ruler. During 1838 the pasha extended his power to practically the whole of Arabia. His forces garrisoned the principal ports along the eastern coast of the Persian Gulf, and in March 1839 the important island shaikhdom of Baḥrayn submitted. It was widely believed that all this was preliminary to a bid for the pashalik of Baghdād, badly governed and only too vulnerable to attack.

Palmerston and Hobhouse, Grant's successor at the board of control, reacted strongly to the alarming reports sent by their agents in the Persian Gulf and Baghdād, and were sceptical of Muḥammad ʿAlī's reassurances. Palmerston told Muḥammad ʿAlī he would not be allowed to establish himself on the Persian Gulf or at Aden. Hobhouse instructed Auckland in June 1838 to take Aden, and, if Muḥammad ʿAlī declared his independence, as he was currently threatening to do, to occupy the island of Kharg in the Gulf as a base which the British could use in countering an Egyptian attack on Baghdād. The British had had their eye on Aden for some time as the best naval and coaling station on the steamship route between Bombay and Suez. As the full extent of Egyptian operations in Arabia became known, the authorities in India hastened to anticipate its absorption by Muḥammad ʿAlī. In January 1838 Captain Stafford Haines came near to purchasing Aden from its sultan, inclined to regard the British as a lesser evil to the approaching Egyptians, but his chiefs finally dissuaded him. An expedition from Bombay was sent to bombard and occupy it in January 1839. Kharg had, of course, already been occupied as a result of Auckland's precautionary show of strength against Persia in the Gulf. But Captain Samuel Hennell British Resident at Bushire, and other agents in the Gulf area did not believe these measures would be enough to meet the situation. Since 1819–20, when an expedition to the Trucial Coast had attacked the bases from which tribes preyed on British shipping, the British presence in the Gulf had remained strong enough to act as a deterrent to piracy. A tenuous treaty relationship with the maritime tribes was maintained by the personal influence of men like Hennell backed by a small cruiser squadron. These men on the spot sensed the crumbling of their prestige as the Egyptians were allowed to dominate the mainland with no more than token opposition from the British. Auckland, his resources stretched by the Persian and Afghan crises and the impending one with China, shrank from commitments such as offering protection to friendly tribes, which his agents believed was the only alternative to the collapse of British influence in the Gulf. From London, Palmerston and Hobhouse were clear that British influence had to be preserved, but were less clear as to the means.

Palmerston's militant approach to Muḥammad ʿAlī's activities was heightened in April 1839, when Maḥmūd at last made his expected bid to recover Syria. The sultan calculated that whatever the military outcome the Russians and the British would be forced to take his side. His death prevented him from learning both that the military outcome had been the total defeat of his forces by Ibrāhīm at the battle of Nezib in June 1839, and that his political calculation had proved correct. Palmerston was more convinced than ever that only the expulsion of Muḥammad ʿAlī from Syria, and the restoration of a clear desert frontier between Egypt and the rest of the Ottoman Empire, would stabilize that part of Asia. He now wanted general European agreement to force this through. Initially, he encouraged the desire of Metternich and Louis-Philippe to take the lead in ensuring that the European powers controlled the crisis, because he expected to need their support in preventing unilateral Russian intervention by the treaty of Hünkâr Iskelesi. But the French had no intention of coercing the ruler who had so long been their protégé and who might provide the means of establishing French ascendancy in the Levant. Louis-Philippe wished to play a major role in the crisis, but by evolving a compromise favourable to Muḥammad ʿAlī. It quickly became apparent to Palmerston that the kind of cooperation with the French which had been useful in recent crises involving Belgium, Spain and Portugal would not be possible on this occasion. If he wanted to coerce Muḥammad ʿAlī in Syria as well as in the Persian Gulf, he would have to reckon with the prospect of conflict with the French.

What looked like becoming a dangerous situation, with the British simultaneously at odds with the French and the Russians, was simplified by a Russian initiative. Nicholas I was more than ever determined to keep events in western Asia under control at a time when his forces were heavily engaged in trying to crush renewed resistance to Russian rule in the Caucasus. David Urquhart and his associates had already in 1836 deliberately engineered a minor crisis by running a British ship, the *Vixen*, through the blockade imposed by the Russians as part of their operations against the Circassians on the east coast of the Black Sea. The tsar decided on a direct deal with the British to safeguard his interests, and in the hope that France would in the process be isolated. Since the treaty of Hünkâr Iskelesi had not reduced the Ottoman Empire to satellite status, Nicholas proposed to secure his Black Sea coasts against attack by means of a general European agreement to closure of the Straits to warships of all powers, including Russia. He was prepared to endorse Palmerston's proposals to deprive Muḥammad ʿAlī of Syria by force. To Palmerston this general programme was immediately acceptable, and by December 1839 a detailed agreement had been worked out which had Austrian backing. The French remained unalterably opposed to any coercion, and were convinced that the other governments could not act without their consent. It took Palmerston until July 1840 to win a cabinet majority in face of arguments that the risk of war with France was far too high a price to pay for intimidating Muḥammad ʿAlī. Palmerston was sure that the French would not fight. He attributed the cooperative attitude of Nicholas I to the tough policies the British had been pursuing in Asia, and he was convinced that the French, too, would back down to a determined coalition of the three eastern powers. The British cabinet, at any rate, backed down to Palmerston's threat of resignation and to his vision of an Ottoman Empire divided between Russia and France as the only alternative to a deal with Nicholas I, a deal which seemed to many of them totally inconsistent with the hostility to Russia they had understood to be the keynote of British policy. By a convention signed in July 1840, Muḥammad ʿAlī's army was to be driven out of Syria by forces acting on behalf of all the European powers except France.

In February 1840 Palmerston had recommended measures by

Auckland to force Egyptian withdrawal from the coast of the Persian Gulf. Ports controlled by Muḥammad ʿAlī should be blockaded, supplies sent by sea from Egypt should be cut off, and Baḥrayn should be occupied if its submission to Muḥammad ʿAlī turned out to be anything more than nominal. These measures proved unnecessary, which was just as well since naval reinforcements destined for the Gulf had been diverted to fighting the Chinese. By June 1840 the Egyptian army was pulling out of Arabia. It had met with increasing local hostility and communications problems, and the troops were now needed to defend Syria and perhaps Egypt itself against European intervention. The peremptory terms offered by the convention of July 1840 justified the precaution. If he surrendered at once, Muḥammad ʿAlī could retain Egypt on a hereditary basis, and govern Acre for the rest of his life. If he did not surrender within ten days, the offer of Acre would be withdrawn, and ten days after that he could not be guaranteed Egypt itself. Although the ultimatum was backed by the governments of Great Britain, Russia, Austria and Prussia, the job of enforcement would, in practice, be left to the Turkish army, the British navy and Lebanese rebels. In the circumstances, the contribution of the British navy would have to be decisive.

The British applied themselves with energy to their role. Swift action was necessary to demoralize both the Egyptians and the French, because the whole plan was something of a gamble. The French enjoyed slight naval superiority in the Mediterranean, and Minto at the Admiralty, heavily committed in Asian and American waters, could not guarantee adequate reinforcements in time. Nor was it at all certain that coastal operations by the Royal Navy would be enough to turn the scales against Ibrāhīm's forces in Syria. At Constantinople, Ponsonby helped to organize a new Turkish offensive, and sent money and arms to Syrian dissidents. Richard Wood, the British agent in Syria, worked to revive Syrian resistance after an insurrection earlier in the year had failed for lack of Turkish support. Napier's naval squadron blockaded Syrian ports, and during September 1840 Beirut, Tyre and Sidon were captured. By early October Ibrāhīm's army had been driven from the coast, and the Lebanon was in revolt. The British admiral, Stopford, acutely aware of the French threat, hesitated to press home the advantage gained, but Palmerston's confidence in French neutrality was unshaken, and his forceful instructions overcame Stopford's doubts. In November 1840 Acre's reputation as a great defensive bastion quickly crumbled before the guns of the British fleet. With the fall of Acre, Muḥammad ʿAlī abandoned the struggle. The French, as Palmerston had calculated, did not take up the challenge. Thiers, his bluff called, was replaced by the more conciliatory Guizot and, in July 1841, France joined the other powers in a general treaty closing the Straits to warships while the Ottoman Empire was at peace.

At the same time as British forces were in action against the Egyptians, the Afghans and the Persians, they were engaged in a comparable exercise in intimidation against the Chinese. While the other three operations were facets of a single crisis, the war with China had quite separate origins. But the timing was not altogether a coincidence. The more aggressive politicians, traders and officials were united in thinking of the promotion of British trade as a national interest justifying the use of force against governments which put obstacles in the way of the free flow of commerce, or at least against governments vulnerable to the kind of power at Great Britain's disposal. The imagined expansion over most of Asia of Russia, a protectionist power not vulnerable to diplomatic or other pressure, had in the 1830s lent a general sense of urgency to the activities of politicians, who saw trade with a continent containing about half the world's population as vital to British prosperity as well as by far the most effective means of curbing Russian influence there. Businessmen were quick to utilize the prevailing mood, which was likely to be as impatient of the Chinese reluctance to adapt themselves to British needs as it had been with the Afghans and the Egyptians. Thus, although China was not as yet a subject of contention between the British and Russian governments, the Chinese unwittingly added to the general sense of frustration the British were experiencing through their difficulty in protecting their vital interests in Asia against Russia, and they incidentally exposed themselves to the sort of aggressive treatment which currently seemed to Palmerston the obvious remedy in such cases.

Thus, when the Manchu rulers of China, in accordance with the traditional Chinese interpretation of world politics, refused to negotiate on equal terms with British officials about the regulation of the booming Sino-British commerce, and when they tried to halt the importation of opium which had become a cardinal element in the trade, Palmerston was easily persuaded that vital British interests were at stake which only a show of force could secure. These arguments were put to him by the British agent at Canton, Captain Charles Elliot, and by leading British merchants in the China trade like William Jardine. From India, Auckland accordingly sent twenty ships and four thousand troops to intimidate the rulers of the Chinese Empire. Again, this was something of a gamble. If the Manchus had not soon come to terms, the British might have been drawn into a war of attrition of immense cost and uncertain outcome. In fact, a small expedition was quite sufficient. In two short campaigns during 1840–2 the British showed that their forces could attack China's coasts at will and advance inland without meeting effective resistance. The Manchu rulers, perhaps alarmed at the effect on their discontented subjects of prolonging this display of their military weakness, yielded to the demands presented by the British negotiator, Sir Henry Pottinger. By the treaty of Nanking of August 1842 they were committed to pay for the cost of the war to the British, to cede the island of Hong Kong, to fix low tariffs and to allow trading at five ports instead of only Canton. Palmerston's policy of intimidation had obtained in full the trading conditions long sought by British businessmen.

In their simultaneous intimidation of the Chinese, the Afghans, the Persians and the Egyptians around 1840, British political leaders had demonstrated their capacity for determined and aggressive action to correct what seemed to them a potentially dangerous situation. Their policy, moreover, had all the appearance of success. The symptoms of danger vanished, at least for the time being. The four rulers against whom force had been used hesitated to provoke its repetition. The Russian government, too, had recalled its agents from Tehran and Kābul in response to British protests, and had abandoned the treaty of Hünkâr Iskelesi. But it would be wrong to conclude from this that intimidation had worked in the case of the Russian government as well. Despite appearances, Nicholas I had not backed down before a display of British pugnacity.

The events of 1838–42 left Nicholas I's view of world politics unshaken. The conservative cause in Europe and sealing the Black Sea against foreign warships remained his highest priorities; France with her suspect political tradition still seemed his most probable enemy; and Asian politics continued to be a side issue. Developments which looked dramatic enough from the standpoint of London and other capitals could be fitted by the emperor and his ministers into the familiar framework of interpretation. Any threatened change within the Ottoman Empire was examined for its possible weakening of Russian capacity to exclude hostile warships from the Straits. When Muḥammad 'Alī looked like declaring his independence in 1838, a step which might have led to complete disintegration of the Ottoman Empire and uncertainty as to who in future would control the Straits, Nicholas made careful preparations based on his experience of earlier crises of authority for the sultan. His ships and troops were ready to seize the Straits. He visited various German rulers to check on their ability to hold back any Franco-British offensive against Russia in Europe. He countered Palmerston's moves to summon a European conference on the impending crisis at which Russia might be isolated. He was confident that his forces would win if it came to war. At the same time, he continued to believe that drastic changes within the Ottoman Empire would be more likely to work in Russia's favour if he cooperated with at least one of the other interested governments. Between 1833 and 1839 he regarded Metternich as his associate in the event of Ottoman disintegration. Münchengrätz had been the necessary complement to Hünkâr Iskelesi. Disillusioned by Metternich's behaviour when the crisis was renewed in 1839, he looked elsewhere for collaboration. He reverted to the course which had proved successful at the beginning of his reign: a direct deal with the British government. It advanced two of Nicholas's principal aims. It gave him a greater sense of security in the Black Sea than Hünkâr Iskelesi could any longer do, and it isolated France. Nicholas was so gratified with the feeling of control over the affairs of Europe which he could derive from the handling of this crisis that he suggested to Palmerston a permanent Four Power alliance against France, which was tactfully declined. Throughout the crisis Nicholas moved confidently and coolly. Although the deal with Palmerston came at a time when the British were adopting aggressive policies in Asia, Nicholas's initiative can be explained without reference to this. It was a skilful move to secure his traditional objectives, not a gesture of conciliation.

Nicholas and his advisers had, indeed, a much better understanding of British policy in Asia than did the British of Russian policy there. Their reaction to the British demonstrations of their striking power was cool and calculated, and meant no shift of priorities in their overall foreign policy. Russian official attitudes to Asia were unchanged. Nicholas had no grand design for expansion in Asia, and certainly no intention of trying to invade or even threaten India. But this did not mean that he was hostile to the idea of expansion in Asia. Russia had a long tradition of expanding its frontier to control neighbouring nomadic tribes and weak states whenever circumstances – ambitious men on the spot, border fighting etc. – stimulated it. Expansion in Asia had since the sixteenth century been unsystematic and spasmodic, but it had always been taken for granted that it would continue and that Asia, as far as the settled frontiers of solidly based states, was destined for Russia. There was never any sense of hurry because there were never any serious competitors, with the possible exception of the Chinese.

Palmerston's counter-offensive, 1833–41

Nicholas accepted this tradition. Although his attention was concentrated on Europe and on the Ottoman Empire, he was prepared as a matter of course to look favourably on the arguments of frontier officials for extending Russian control in particular cases provided the move did not conflict with overall Russian policy. Similarly, he assumed predominant Russian influence in Tehran to be as obvious a need as predominant Russian influence in Constantinople. If the British were alarmed at improvements in the Russian ability to strike at India they must be reassured as to Russian intentions, but the reassurance would not take the form of renouncing Russia's manifest destiny in Asia.

In 1838–9 Nicholas and his advisers worked out a measured response to British hostility in Asia. Nesselrode understood the fear aroused in London and Calcutta by Russian behaviour in Tehran and Kābul. Simonich was recalled and the methods by which he had asserted Russian influence at Tehran were disowned, but not the policy itself. His successor, Duhamel, was instructed to withdraw Vitkevich from Kābul and to distract the shah from his obsession with Herat. Less ostentatious and provocative ways had to be found of asserting Russian influence in Persia. Nesselrode believed that the British government's fear of Russia would not be carried to the point of war, and that Palmerston and his colleagues would rely instead on a propaganda campaign to foster distrust of Russia in other capitals. Nicholas agreed. Recalling Simonich cost Russia nothing – especially as the failure at Herat had discredited him with the Persians – and was good counter-propaganda. Similarly, when the British expedition to Afghanistan was launched, Nesselrode was able to convince Nicholas that Dost Muḥammad and the Qandahār chiefs had been encouraging Russian overtures in pursuit of schemes which offered no advantages to Russia. Vitkevich's mission to Kābul had poisoned relations with Great Britain without any corresponding gain. The Afghan chiefs had brought British hostility on themselves by their intrigues. The British expedition was justifiable and presented no threat to Russia. On the other hand, at British triumph in Afghanistan following on the Persian failure at Herat, with which Simonich had incautiously associated Russia, would have to be offset by some dramatic counter-measure. Hence the Khīva expedition.

General Perovsky, the governor of Orenburg, was currently engaged in a struggle with the nomadic Kazakhs. The khan of Khīva was giving support to the Kazakhs, and Perovsky wanted an expedition to bring Khīva under Russian control. His case was not accepted by Chernyshev, the minister of war, but Nicholas saw it in March 1839 as a means of restoring Russian prestige in Asia at a time when the British would have no legitimate grounds for complaint. The effect created by the Herat affair was soon to be neutralized by the British failure in Afghanistan, which was just as well for Russia in view of the fate of the Khīva expedition. But the decision to conquer Khīva – long anticipated by British writers and politicians as the prelude to an invasion of India and bound to be publicized as such – does not suggest that Nicholas felt the need to retreat before an assertion of British power in Asia.

British moves in Asia between 1838 and 1842 did not have the effect on Nicholas I and his ministers that Russian moves in 1828–33 had on British political leaders. There were, it is true, already those in Russian official circles who offered an alternative view of events, and believed that only vigorous action could turn back a British programme of expansion which would eventually absorb central Asia. Men on the spot like Simonich, Vitkevich and Duhamel thought in these terms, and so did the veteran diplomat, Pozzo di Borgo, then ambassador in London. Nicholas I was less scornful of these ideas than his foreign minister, Nesselrode, and intended to be on guard against an outbreak of 'English madness', but his notion of what was probable in the conduct of any British government remained the same. Had the British been more successful his viewpoint might have been shaken. Had Afghanistan become a British satellite; had Macnaghten pushed the British presence beyond the Hindu Kush; had the British agents, Charles Stoddart and Arthur Conolly, flourished at the court of Bukhārā instead of dying there unavenged in 1842; had the grand design been realized in these years and even supplemented, which was by no means impossible, the arguments of Pozzo and others might have looked more realistic to Nicholas. As it was, he found no cause for alarm. On the contrary, he was more impressed by the isolation of France and with the Straits Convention of 1841, and, after the crisis was over, he continued to look to the British as much as to the Austrians to keep France in check, and to prepare against the day of the Ottoman Empire's collapse. Given his persistent preoccupation with these issues, the mixed fortunes of the British and the Russians in their relationships with the governments of Asia and the prospect of future quarrels with one another there were trivial compared to their proven capacity to work together in Europe.

Thus, only one of the factors which had transformed British thinking about international politics in the years 1828–33 was present to influence Russian policy-makers around 1840 – the availability of a new working hypothesis. There was no new man at the head of affairs, and the emperor and his closest advisers were not confused and uncertain as to how to interpret and react to the dramatic events confronting them. Nicholas I's deep-rooted convictions about the nature of the world he was trying to control were undisturbed by the violent British reaction to the growth of his power.

4

The British and the Russians lose control, 1841–53

For the next ten years there was a lull in Russo-British hostility. There was even a prospect during the 1840s that belief in a Russian threat to India might once and for all be classified as alarmism, and that developments in Asia might again become of subsidiary importance in the making of British foreign policy. For Peel's government between 1841 and 1846 the French threat eclipsed that of Russia, and beyond Europe quarrels with the American government surpassed in gravity any in Asia.

Peel's foreign secretary, Aberdeen, reacted against Palmerston's style in dealing with crises. Once the government had wound up the Afghan and Chinese affairs, he concentrated on trying to reduce the number of Great Britain's enemies through conciliation and compromise. In particular he strove to restore amicable relations with the French. In opposition he and his colleagues had argued that the French had been unnecessarily humiliated by Palmerston during the Egyptian crisis, and that the entente of the early 1830s should be revived. There was, however, no corresponding inclination in Paris, and French empire-building proceeded in north Africa and the Pacific with no more regard for British susceptibilities than Palmerston had shown for those of France. Nor was Aberdeen much more successful in promoting a spirit of compromise in British relations with the American government. Rebellion against the British in Canada had coincided with the intensification of old boundary disputes left unsettled after the war of 1812–14. Palmerston, preoccupied with the complex of crises in Asia, was less belligerent than Russell and others, who resented American sympathy and support for the rebels and expected war in the near future, but in 1841, with events in Asia apparently going well, he had privately threatened the American government with war. The crisis over the Canadian rebellion and the Maine boundary dispute with which it was associated died down, partly as a result of Aberdeen's willingness to make concessions, but American aspirations to territory claimed by Canada and Mexico brought further and growing tension until it looked as though the British would be fighting simultaneous wars with both the French and the Americans. The expected wars did not materialize, but the same antagonism persisted, especially with regard to the French.

For Palmerston, too, they were the main problems when a change of government brought him back to the foreign office in 1846. As the advent of steam brought the prospects of a French invasion of the British Isles closer, Palmerston concentrated his energies on trying to curtail French bids to expand their influence in western Europe. He intrigued against them with varying effect in Spain and Italy, and helped to ensure that the 1848 revolutions on the continent were not accompanied by any revolution in the distribution of power there. He accepted American predominance on the north American continent as an accomplished fact, confirmed his predecessor's agreement on the forty-ninth parallel as Canada's boundary, and confined himself to attempts at discreet containment of American influence in the Caribbean and in Latin America. Had chance or anger produced a more violent sequence of events in this decade, America might have displaced Russia for politically minded British as the principal threat to their empire, with France consolidating its role as the only direct threat to their homeland. But the high drama was missing, or at least no writer or orator emerged persuasive enough to portray the events as such, and the struggle to preserve a balance of power in north America failed to catch the imagination of either the public or of enough influential political leaders.

Nor was there in Asia during these years the kind of drama to encourage in either Great Britain or Russia the idea that any grand design was about to be realized. Nicholas I, on the contrary, saw no reason to be diverted from his goal of a deal with the British and Austrian governments in anticipation of that final collapse of the Ottoman Empire which he was sure its next internal upheaval would bring about. His proposals for distributing the spoils varied so much on different occasions as to make it clear that any terms providing Russia with a bare minimum of security requirements would serve. Any prior arrangement would be preferable to a hectic scramble in crisis conditions, just so long as neither the British nor the French got Constantinople and thereby access to the Black Sea and Russia's southern coast. In 1833 he had suggested to the Austrian ambassador that a new Greek empire might replace the Ottoman if Muḥammad ʿAlī overthrew the sultan. In the 1840s his solution was that the Habsburg Empire should have Constantinople. Informal proposals to this effect were made in September 1843, March 1844 and December 1845. The British could take Egypt and share the Aegean islands with France. Metternich was unresponsive. In a memorandum he drafted in December 1852, Nicholas was less self-denying and more radical still. He now thought of Russia's share as being Moldavia and Wallachia, and part of Bulgaria, but his restraint as to Constantinople still held. Since Metternich had expressed no interest in adding it to the Habsburg Empire, it could be a free city, with a Russian garrison at the Bosphorus and an Austrian garrison at the Dardanelles. The Austrians could also take the Dalmatian coast, the French Crete, the British Egypt and perhaps Cyprus and Rhodes. Serbia and Bulgaria were to be independent. Nicholas was striving to understand and acknowledge what other governments saw as their vital interests in the hope that they would in turn appreciate the Russian government's need to close the Black Sea to potential invaders. His projection of Great Power aspirations in the event of collapse was realistic enough to judge from their later behaviour. He had come up with a grand design, but one aimed at preserving the balance of power, not at throwing the British out of Asia.

Nicholas, indeed, went out of his way to reassure the British government in the 1840s about his objectives in Asia and at the Straits, and to try and create a lasting atmosphere of trust between leaders in both countries. He believed he had succeeded. The crisis of 1839–40 had proved it was possible for the Russians and the British to cooperate over the Ottoman Empire to the exclusion of the French. As with the Greek crisis at the beginning of Nicholas's reign, it showed that a politician of the calibre of Canning or Palmerston could carry the cabinet with him on a deal with the Russian emperor. Nicholas had, therefore, grounds for believing that he could do business on the basis of mutual regard for British and Russian interests with a government in which Palmerston was foreign secretary. After his visit to London in the first week of June 1844, Nicholas believed he could make a deal with the Conservatives as well, should circumstances make it necessary. Peel and Aberdeen, faced with possible war against the French and the Americans, were only too willing to be reassured by the Russian emperor in person of his policy of restraint in areas of vital concern to them. They agreed with him that the Ottoman Empire's continued existence was in the interests of British and Russian governments alike. They accepted that if it was seen to be finally disintegrating, talks between the British and the Russians, as the governments whose combined power on land and sea was sufficient to enforce a settlement, would be necessary to secure their own interests and to uphold the balance of power. They noted his assurance that the Habsburg government would support such an arrangement, and they had no reason to object to Nicholas's desire to exclude France from such preliminary talks. They acknowledged the correctness of the memorandum setting down the substance of the conversations, which was drawn up by Nicholas's foreign minister, Nesselrode, when he too visited London later in the year. Both sides were pleased with the upshot of the conversations. Nicholas and his ministers were relieved to have evidence that Peel and Aberdeen would be as ready as Palmerston to negotiate directly with the Russian government should Ottoman collapse appear imminent. Peel and Aberdeen, after their disillusioning experiences with the French and the Americans, were relieved to have evidence that Nicholas would not try to seize the Straits in a crisis, and to hear both the emperor and Nesselrode insist that they would avoid action leading to a clash of interests in Persia and central Asia.

The 1844 conversations signified the new mood of mutual trust between the Russian and British governments. There was just about as much and as little justification for it as there had been for the mutual hostility of the 1830s. On the British side there was an element of wishful thinking as strong as the alarmism which had preceded it. After all the criticism he had received, Palmerston was naturally anxious to believe that his policies had succeeded and that Russian ambitons had been checked. After the failure of their policy of conciliation in respect of France and America, Peel and Aberdeen were only too willing to believe it had succeeded with Nicholas I. Yet all that had really changed was the thinking of British political leaders about the same kind of situation. The future of the Ottoman Empire, Persia and Afghanistan was as uncertain as it had been a decade before. Russian long-term aims in Asia were precisely the same, though some of the means used in the 1830s to secure them had been dropped as ineffective, like Hünkâr Iskelesi, or counter-productive, like the mission to Kābul. Russia's capacity to threaten India was, if anything, greater than it had been. At the time the conversations were taking place, Russian forces were engaged in successful operations against the Kazakhs, and they were about to establish a new line of forts on the steppe lands eastwards from the Caspian Sea, from which they would be better placed than in 1839 to strike at Khīva and the other central Asian khanates. In 1842, the khan of Khīva had been persuaded to sign a treaty with the Russians, by which he was to keep the peace and facilitate Russian commerce. Although it remained a dead letter, such a treaty, whose predictable violation could supply pretexts for punitive expeditions, was, like the new line of forts, the sort of sign which a year or so earlier would have meant impending danger to observers in London. Now it was interpreted more calmly. The evidence for a Russian threat to India was as great – or as small – as in 1833, and British leaders, as Nicholas was soon to discover, still believed in it. But their belief that it was imminent and that urgent action was required to counter it had been weakened now that the great crisis had come and gone with India looking no less secure than before. Russian moves in the future would have to constitute a much more clearly defined threat before provoking a violent British reaction.

On the Russian side, Nicholas I remained unperturbed by evidence that British power in Asia was growing on a scale which could well have been seen as lending support to the theory of a British threat to Russia. Abandonment of the projected alliance system with Afghanistan, Sind and the Panjāb had not meant the end of the urge to reconstruct the political geography of the north-west frontier in a manner reassuring to the British. The lesson of Kābul had been learned, and Afghanistan was left alone. Grandiose designs were looked upon with suspicion. Over-elaborate means had been employed for the relatively modest end of securing a network of dependable allies beyond the frontier. During the next few years a much more drastic solution was achieved by simple and haphazard opportunism. Sind and the Panjāb were conquered and brought within the frontiers of British India. It was a dramatic extension of British power, the sort of move to confirm the suspicions of those in Russia who expected a systematic British advance towards the heart of central Asia.

It is true that neither the British government of the day nor the East India Company and its governor-general, Lord Ellenborough, favoured the annexation of Sind. When Peel came to defend the step he had strongly opposed, he addressed the House of Commons in language strikingly similar to that which Malcolm had used twenty years earlier and which Gorchakov, in a memorandum already quoted, was to use twenty years later. 'Whatever may be the principle which may regulate the conduct of civilized nations when coming into contact with each other,' he said during the debate about Sind on 8 February 1844, 'when civilization and barbarism come into contact there is some uncontrollable principle of a very different description, which demands a different course of conduct to be pursued.' He feared that because there was 'some great principle at work' it was impossible 'to apply the rules observed among more advanced nations'.[1] To the opposition a simpler explanation seemed sufficient. What had proved uncontrollable was not the working out of some great principle, but the behaviour of the British commander in Sind, Sir Charles Napier.

Napier was sixty when he arrived in Sind in 1842, still searching for a role in keeping with his grandiose ambitions. His diary suggests that he saw the appointment as his last chance, and that from the start he thought in terms of adding Sind to the British Empire as his claim to fame. The new governor-general, Lord Ellenborough, was in tune with the personality of Napier, a man as spirited and turbulent as himself. He preferred Napier's judgment of the situation in Sind to that of the political agents, on whose advice his predecessors had tended to rely when formulating policy. The Sind–Baluchistan political department was closed down, and Napier was for all practical purposes given a free hand. He took full advantage of it. The confused and conspiratorial politics of Sind could always be relied upon to throw up suspicious circumstances, which Napier could be relied upon to interpret as evidence of duplicity on the part of the amirs. In fact, the amirs had behaved all along with remarkable restraint in face of severe provocation. It was Napier who was guilty of deception by misleading Ellenborough as to the state of affairs there. When the amirs assembled pathetically inadequate forces to defend themselves against Napier's ostentatious displays of force, the latter welcomed the pretext he had been looking for. The main Sindhi forces were crushed in February 1843, and the rest at another battle the following month. Ellenborough accepted Napier's claim that the conquest had been necessary; so, outwardly, did the government in London. The East India Company did not, and had Ellenborough recalled. The property rights of the amirs were taken up, in the end successfully, by some scandalized public figures in Great Britain. 'Peccavi', the famous pun attributed to Napier, was endorsed by them without laughter. But Napier became a national hero, and the British government kept the direct control he had won over the lower Indus.

During the debate on Sind in which an embarrassed Peel had taken refuge in the 'uncontrollable principle', the radical member Roebuck had prophesied the principle's next manifestation. '... I am a prophet! I say you will possess the Punjab in less than two years in spite of yourselves. (Laughter) My hon. Friend may laugh; but remember I said two years ago, you would have Scinde, and Scinde you have!'[2] Roebuck

[1] *Hansard*, 3rd ser., vol. LXXII, col. 443–4.
[2] *Ibid.*, col. 390.

was right. No one capable of uniting the Panjāb had emerged since the death of Ranjit Singh in 1839. Shortly before his death he, too, had forecast British absorption of his state. Now the tribal and religious strife which he had overcome was revived in a murderous struggle for succession. The best equipped contenders waited beyond the Sutlej to see whether the Panjāb would fall to a ruler able to make it again the stable, independent ally which the British had found so reassuring. By 1845 they had tired of waiting, and Lord Hardinge, Ellenborough's successor, prepared to intervene. Between December 1845 and February 1846 a short but fierce war was fought which destroyed the independence of the Panjāb. Annexation was as yet ruled out as being attainable only with prolonged fighting and excessive expense, but by the treaty of Lahore of March 1846 the current ruler was, as Hardinge put it, 'in fetters, and under our protection, and must do our bidding'.[1] The last battle had taken place two years almost to the day after Roebuck's Commons speech.

Annexation itself was only three years away. '... I cannot consider it politic to annex the Punjab, if it can be avoided', Hardinge wrote to Peel after the signing of the treaty of Lahore. Peel took the same view. The 'reflecting few', he told Hardinge,

> consider that the annexation of the Punjab would have been a source of weakness and not of strength; that it would have extended our frontier at the greatest distance from our resources, and at the weakest points; that it would have been a perpetual blister, from bringing us into contact with new tribes, unused to our sway, unconscious of its advantages, unable to appreciate the benefits of government on settled principles; that you would have been with reference to Afghanistan and all the bordering countries in a much worse position than you were in September last with reference of the Punjab, at a greater distance from your resources, with a hostile country and difficult rivers in your rear.[2]

Lord Dalhousie, Hardinge's successor, likewise began his term as governor-general in 1848 believing that any threat to British predominance in the Panjāb should be dealt with by a punitive expedition. But when resistance to the British presence spread during the summer of 1848 he changed his mind. By August he was advising the government in London that 'however contrary it may be to our past views and to our

---

[1] C. S. Parker, *Sir Robert Peel, From his Private Papers*, 3 vols (London, 1899), III, 311–13.
[2] *Ibid.*, III, 312, 317–18.

present views, annexation of the Punjab is the most advantageous policy for us to pursue'.[1] Another short, fierce struggle ensued, and the British army suffered a severe mauling before it finally triumphed in February 1849. Dalhousie lost no time in annexing the Panjāb to British India.

It says much for the relaxation of tension between the British and Russian governments that Nicholas I's unease at the annexation of Sind and the prospect of an occupation of the Panjāb was soothed during his visit in 1844 by sincerely expressed reassurances. For, however sincere, Peel's reassurances could have little value if he were right in arguing that relations with 'uncivilised' neighbours were not subject to normal governmental control. The mysterious forces which had made the British feel compelled to annex Sind and the Panjāb would presumably continue to operate with respect to the new frontier. Beyond it lived Bāluchī and Pathan tribes accustomed to plundering raids with which it would now be the turn of the British to deal. From Kābul Dost Muḥammad exercised a shadowy suzerainty over many of them, and was still seeking an opportunity to recover Peshawar. He had joined the Sikhs in their war against the British in 1848-9 and Peshawar was to have been his reward in the event of victory. Conditions seemed little different from those which had prompted the extension of empire between 1843 and 1849; accordingly, it would not be unreasonable to expect the same remedy to be applied in coping with them. Were those Russians who believed that there was no assignable limit to British aggrandisement in Asia and that their government would eventually have to contain it by force nearer the mark in their speculations than Nesselrode and Nicholas I?

Much the same answer may be suggested as with the alarmist version of Russian policy in the 1830s. Russian revisionists were undoubtedly wrong in ascribing an expansionist policy to British governments in the 1840s. Nicholas I and Nesselrode were right in believing Peel and Aberdeen to be sincere in their protestations. But in so far as their speculations about the workings of British policy referred to the future, the revisionists had at least as good a case as the emperor. Peel's 'uncontrollable principle' was not, after all, so very mysterious. Everyone responsible for the exercise of British power in southern Asia – the cabinet in London, the governor-general and his advisers in Calcutta, the military commanders and political agents in border areas – needed to feel that the situation immediately beyond India's frontiers was 'under control'. That is to say, any threat of force against the frontier or of

[1] J. G. A. Baird (ed.), *Private Letters of the Marquess of Dalhousie* (London, 1910), 237.

subversion of those who lived within it had to seem predictable enough to make possible preparations in anticipation and on a sufficiently small scale to ensure that the preparations would be adequate. Annexation of the territory from which the danger came was risky to attempt and expensive to implement, and most of those with whom the decision lay preferred to avoid it while any alternative method of reducing frontier threats to a tolerable level seemed likely to be effective. But alternative methods rarely were effective for any length of time, whereas annexation, for all its disadvantages, offered a practicable and clearcut solution. Hence, although policy-makers quite genuinely hoped that annexation would be avoided, it was unusual for them to exclude annexation as a possible course of action if the man on the spot deemed all other means to have failed. A sincere wish to avoid expansion was in itself of little value. Those Russians who anticipated new British inroads into Asia were at least as likely to be right as their more trusting ruler.

If anything they were more likely to be right. British, like Russian, governments were heavily dependent on the judgment of their proconsular and frontier officials. This could be attributed in part to the difficulty of keeping in touch with developments thousands of miles away, but, in the cases of Sind and the Panjāb, a constant flow of telegraphic communication would simply have enabled Napier and Dalhousie to pile up evidence in support of their conclusion. A government in London – or St Petersburg – would always be reluctant to chance the situation getting out of control through their rejecting outright the advice of the officers on the spot. It was not unreasonable for Russian observers to anticipate that men sensitive to danger and keen to eliminate it expeditiously would be prominent in the task of controlling the troubled frontiers of India. Moreover, since annexation provided another and still more distant frontier to defend, there were good grounds for expecting the British to extend their power eventually to the natural strategic frontier of the Indian subcontinent, the Hindu Kush. Yet, as the Russian example in the Caucasus had shown, the attainment of a secure mountain barrier did not obviate the temptation to go beyond it. Thoughts of penetrating the central Asian khanates had, indeed, been prevalent when the British had briefly reached the Hindu Kush in 1839–40. Such a process, as events were to show, was by no means inevitable, but it was quite possible. Either Nicholas I or the pessimists might be vindicated. But, as in the case of the British, it was arguably better to be alarmist and hence prepared to react quickly should the danger materialize, provided that the form alarmism took was not such as to provoke the very danger that was feared. Ironically, it was moves by Nicholas himself which conjured up the danger in which he did not believe.

The first occasion was in 1849. It was a year in which the British had been able to annex the Panjāb with Russian approval and the Russians had been able to intervene for the suppression of revolution in Hungary and the Principalities with British approval. Yet in the autumn a crisis in Russo-British relations arose out of a far less spectacular incident. The Russian and Austrian governments demanded the extradition of Polish and Hungarian rebels who had fled across the border into the Ottoman Empire. They severed diplomatic relations with the Porte when the demand was rejected. Although Austrian conduct was the more high-handed, it was the reappearance of a Russian threat to the Ottoman Empire which impressed British observers of international politics, especially with the Turks defending rebels with whom British opinion in general sympathized. The British and French governments supported the Turks in their stand, and British warships were ordered to Besika Bay, just outside the Dardanelles. Stratford, the British ambassador, encouraged their commander to edge them still nearer to Constantinople through a strained interpretation of the 1841 convention. The crisis was easily and quickly resolved. Nicholas I abandoned his extradition demand in response to a personal request by the sultan; Palmerston disowned Stratford's violation of the spirit of the 1841 convention, and reaffirmed British loyalty to the principle of closure of the Straits to foreign warships. To all appearances the atmosphere of mutual understanding had been severely tested and triumphantly preserved.

In fact, all the crisis had done was to reinforce the wishful thinking of both governments. Palmerston could reasonably believe that the Russian emperor had backed down before a discreet display of force. Nicholas had gracefully given way on an issue more important to the Austrians than to himself and could feel that the basic soundness of the Russian position in the area had been demonstrated. The sultan's direct appeal to him showed Turkish recognition of their special relationship with St Petersburg, while Palmerston's anxiety to reassure him about the Straits looked more significant to Nicholas than the precautionary movement of the British squadron, and helped the emperor to go on believing in a special Russo-British relationship over the Ottoman Empire. The easy resolution of the crisis obscured from Nicholas the reasons for British hostility and from Palmerston the strength of Russian determination about the Ottoman Empire.

There *was* an underlying agreement between British and Russian leaders about the Ottoman Empire, but it was narrower in scope than Nicholas believed. It had been formally agreed that the Straits should be closed to foreign warships while the Ottoman Empire was at peace. It had been less formally agreed that the preservation of the Empire was in the interests of both the British and the Russian governments, and that should the Empire nevertheless collapse any redistribution of territory must respect the European balance of power. There used to be controversy as to just how formal this second area of agreement was, and whether British violation of a binding commitment brought about the Crimean War. But the constitutional status of the 1844 agreement is a red herring as far as the origins of the Crimean War are concerned because what had been agreed in 1844 – and in 1839–41 – was still agreed in 1853–4. The Straits convention had been so easily arranged and the 1844 conversations had gone so smoothly because neither side was in fact conceding anything fundamental; they were both simply acknowledging areas where their interests were identical then, and remained identical down to the outbreak of the Crimean War. Nicholas believed this would be enough to ensure cooperation between London and St Petersburg in any foreseeable crisis over the Ottoman Empire. He believed that the British had conceded all he needed, and that he had conceded all the British needed. In this he was wrong. The real conflict of interest between Great Britain and Russia over the Ottoman Empire had never even been discussed.

It was assumed by everyone in St Petersburg concerned with foreign affairs that Russia's relationship to the Ottoman Empire was different from that of the other powers, and that the difference was so fundamental as to be obvious to all. It was no longer taken for granted that Russian armies would gradually conquer the Empire and occupy Constantinople. But although it had been thought convenient since 1829 to preserve enough of the sultan's dominions to constitute a harmless buffer state shielding Russia's Black Sea coasts from the maritime powers, the Ottoman Empire was not to be an independent, neutral buffer but one in which Russian influence had at all costs to count for most. The Russians had come to accept by 1841 that any attempt to formalize this special relationship, as in the treaty of Hünkâr Iskelesi, would be alarming to other governments and would revive old fears of Russian conquest. There had, therefore, been sincere efforts to understand and explicitly acknowledge Austrian and British interests in the area on the assumption that they were compatible with informal Russian predominance. Formalization was now reckoned to be unnecessary as well as tactless. Russian governments had made it clear enough in the past on many occasions that they would fight if their interests in the region were threatened either by the sultan or by some outside power. The close proximity of Russian ships and troops meant that informal predominance could become a formality quickly enough in case of need. But that the sultan should always in the last resort accept that he was too dependent for his survival on Russian goodwill to cross the tsar on any issue vital to Russia was a basic assumption of Nicholas I's foreign policy.

British political leaders recognized that the undoubted Russian capacity to seize Constantinople gave Nicholas I the edge over other governments in any battle for influence in the Ottoman capital. They accepted that there was in practice a special relationship between the Russian and Ottoman Empires. But none of them assumed, as Nicholas I did, that the favourable Russian position was a right comparable to the right to a secure frontier and deserving the same sort of tacit acknowledgment on the part of other Great Powers. Nor did they see Russian superiority as an unalterable feature of the international scene. To the Russians their special relationship, however vague, was a vital interest to be defended in the last resort by war; to the British it was simply a temporary diplomatic advantage to be whittled away over the years. This was the basic conflict of interest underlying events after 1833. It had been concealed during the 1840s by mutual recognition of related vital interests, and by the fact that the British had been successful enough at Constantinople to give them hope for the future but not successful enough to give the Russians any real cause for alarm. Palmerston's policy of promoting westernization under British auspices, so that the Ottoman Empire would gain the strength necessary to serve as a barrier against Russia, had been continued by Stratford, the British ambassador from 1842 to 1852, but vigorous defence of the Empire's Christians and the recommendation of alien ideas and practices made the British as many enemies as friends. Stratford's spectacular record of personal intimidation and intrigue did not mean, therefore, either effective modernization or British diplomatic ascendancy in matters crucial to the government in St Petersburg. But should the Russians ever try to formalize their special relationship in such a way that the British would feel permanently excluded from the counsels of the Turkish government, or should the Russians ever feel they were in danger of losing their position as the one power the sultan could not afford to offend, then leisurely rivalry would turn to conflict. British and Russian assumptions about the Ottoman Empire were ultimately incompatible.

This became clear when the French successfully challenged the Russian position at Constantinople in 1852. Napoleon III, for domestic political reasons, intervened in the age-old dispute between Orthodox and Catholic clergy over custody of the Holy Places, the various religious buildings in Palestine sacred to Christianity but currently within the Ottoman Empire. The Orthodox Church had long enjoyed a position of ascendancy over the Catholics in the administration of the Holy Places. Initially, the Porte tried to satisfy the French by concessions of little substance. Thereupon, Napoleon in the summer of 1852 mounted a show of force. The French warship *Charlemagne* passed the Dardanelles, technically violating the Straits Convention, and a French naval squadron was sent to Tripoli, ostensibly to force the surrender of two French deserters. The Porte, apparently impressed by these hints of coercion, and, especially, by the formidable appearance of the *Charlemagne*, resolved the Holy Places dispute in favour of the Catholics in December 1852, snubbing Nicholas I's purely diplomatic representations on behalf of the Orthodox Church.

The French naval demonstrations and ensuing diplomatic triumph signified a slump in Russian influence at Constantinople, which could only worsen if it were allowed to go unchecked. The circumstances were especially alarming to Nicholas I. Although Orthodox rights in Palestine were not in themselves vital to Russian security, the Turks were sensitive enough of Nicholas's role as defender of his co-religionists in their Empire for their yielding to France to look like a deliberate affront, or a recognition of France as a power more to be feared than Russia. Either way, what the Russians saw as their security was impaired, the more so as the beneficiary was the country Nicholas I regarded as the prime enemy of the conservative principle it was his life's work to defend. His policy of keeping Russia's strength in relation to the Ottoman Empire as unobtrusive as possible to reassure the Austrians and the British, whose cooperation in orderly partition was deemed essential to inhibit French exploitation of the Empire's expected collapse, seemed to have actually facilitated the subversive aims of Russia's most dangerous enemy.

Nicholas I, therefore, responded forcefully. It so happened that his conservative ally, the Austrian government, was also currently at odds with the Porte. The Turks were engaged in one of their periodic wars to give some substance to a shadowy suzerainty over the Montenegrins. For various reasons both the Austrians and the Russians favoured Montenegro's *de facto* independence, and the Austrian government, along whose frontier the war was being fought, took steps to intervene just at the time the Russian government was planning its move against the Porte. Diplomatic representations backed by the threat of force were prepared in Vienna and St Petersburg, and the two governments kept in close touch with each other. The Austrian mission about Montenegro came first. The Porte at first rejected Count Leiningen's demands, and an Austro-Turkish war, in which Russian forces would have taken part, seemed imminent in February 1853. At the last moment the Porte backed down, and the evacuation of Montenegro was secured. Menshikov's mission for Russia followed immediately, and took much the same form as Leiningen's – demands to be followed, if necessary, by threats and breaking off relations. On the face of it, Menshikov was demanding less of the Turks than Leiningen. The latter had demanded a humiliating withdrawal from a war the Turks had been waging successfully to regain control of part of their empire. Menshikov wanted them to change their minds about what was for the Turks a minor and uninteresting dispute between two groups of the sultan's subjects, and offered to protect them from French wrath, should any be forthcoming. But he also wanted a written guarantee that no such situation would occur again. This the Porte refused. When in May 1853 Menshikov, like Leiningen before him, broke off negotiations and boarded ship to return home, the Turks did not this time back down. A month after diplomatic relations had been broken off, Nicholas I ordered his forces to occupy the Principalities of Moldavia and Wallachia, where Ottoman sovereignty had been limited by the treaty of Adrianople, as the first stage in the process of intimidation.

It was the guarantees for the future which proved more galling to the Turks than the Austrian demands over Montenegro. A compromise over the Holy Places was worked out relatively easily with the help of Lord Stratford de Redcliffe, who had returned to Constantinople as British ambassador. The Turks had, in any case, got used to the bullying and intervention of stronger powers over specific issues. But they were not resigned to the idea of perpetual inferiority. Since 1774 they had been compelled by treaty to accept a vague Russian right to make representations on behalf of the Christian religion and churches in the Ottoman Empire. Now this right was apparently to be spelled out as applying to Orthodox churches and clergy, the leaders of some twelve million of the sultan's subjects, whose privileges were to be supervised by a foreign government with the power to give effect to its representations. The Turks would be acknowledging the tsar's right to inflict an indefinite number of humiliations on them for the indefinite future. The draft treaty which Menshikov took to Constantinople was meant to signalize the lasting subordination of the Ottoman Empire to the Russian government, to formalize the informal predominance of the last resort which the Russians had so long regarded as essential to their security. Nicholas I agreed with Menshikov that 'sans une crise de contrainte il serait difficile à la Légation Impériale de ressaisir le degré d'influence qu'elle avait exercé antérieurement sur le Divan'.[1] He was planning further measures of intimidation if the Russian occupation of the Principalities did not bring results. And he assumed that the Austrian government would be as willing to help as he had been with regard to Montenegro.

While Nicholas I clearly expected resistance from the Porte, it is equally clear that he did not think that either the Austrians or the British had any reason to be offended. His assumptions about Austria were not unreasonable, given recent Austrian words and deeds. In the case of Great Britain, he had been careful to conduct the crisis with full regard to what he conceived to be British vital interests. He was at pains to convince the British ambassador to St Petersburg, Sir Hamilton Seymour, that, in the event of the Ottoman Empire collapsing, the Russian government would cooperate with the British to ensure that the balance of power was preserved in any share-out. The secret defensive alliance which Menshikov was to offer the Porte so that the latter would have no need to fear France, had none of the references to the Straits contained in the troublesome treaty of Hünkâr Iskelesi. Neither he nor his ministers seem to have taken seriously the possibility that preventing the formal subordination of the Ottoman Empire to Russian influence through active protection of the sultan's Orthodox subjects could also be a vital British interest. Nor, apparently, did they question whether Austrian and British cautious consent to cooperation in the event of the Ottoman Empire collapsing through internal revolt would still be forthcoming if the collapse were brought about by Russian intimidation from without.

Not that British official hostility to the Menshikov proposals was by any means certain. It depended on whether the majority of the cabinet would take them at their face value as confirming traditional Russian concern for their co-religionists, or whether they would assume them to be the means of bringing the Ottoman government more firmly under Russian control. The ministers of Lord Aberdeen's coalition government most concerned with the question – Russell, Clarendon, Palmerston and Aberdeen himself – had all been involved in earlier crises affecting the Ottoman Empire, and were accustomed to viewing with varying degrees of suspicion Russian moves in that part of the world. But initially most of the cabinet, including Aberdeen and Clarendon,

[1] A. M. Zayonchkovsky, *Vostochnaya Voyna*, 4 vols (St Petersburg, 1908–13), supplement to vol. I, 399–401.

were reluctant to interpret the Menshikov mission in terms of 1833 without supporting evidence. Aberdeen was only too anxious to believe the assurances of the Russian ambassador, Brunnov, that the Porte was merely being asked to confirm past practice, and that no new Russian rights would flow from the proposed agreement. Palmerston, on the other hand, was convinced from the start that Turkish independence was at stake, and that movements to warn the tsar he must abandon his pressure on the Porte should be quickly authorized.

At the beginning of June, following Menshikov's breach with the Porte, the British fleet was sent to Besika Bay in case it should be needed, but the majority of the cabinet were as yet unconvinced by Palmerston's view that the situation called for more drastic measures. Faith in the interpretation of Russian aims which had guided British policy in the 1830s had been sufficiently weakened in their minds for them to wait for some more overt act of aggression than a form of words which might or might not in practice undermine Turkish independence. But Nicholas I's programme of graduated intimidation would provide precisely the kind of evidence to convince them that the proposals did mean more than they said. With the occupation of the Principalities it became increasingly difficult to refute explanations of Nicholas I's conduct in terms of Russian expansionist traditions, which were vehemently canvassed by journalists as well as by cabinet colleagues and in which the hesitant ministers themselves more than half believed. At the very least it seemed risky to assume that no dangerous designs were afoot. The philanthropic language of the Menshikov proposals began to seem a less reliable pointer to future Russian intentions than the aggressive behaviour used to advance their acceptance by the Turks.

None of the British cabinet thought war necessary to dispose of the dispute. Palmerston himself advocated strong measures in the belief that they would deter the tsar from carrying the crisis to the point of war. The French government could enjoy the prospect of exploiting dissension among the Vienna powers, but Napoleon III was looking for diplomatic not military triumphs. From the Austrian point of view Nicholas I had, by his occupation of the Principalities, gone far beyond the policies which had made cooperation over the Ottoman Empire normal during the past twenty years, but their attitude was merely that of a reproachful ally. Nor did Nicholas I intend to press the matter to the point of risking a European war. He and his ministers had not anticipated British and Austrian opposition to their moves against the Ottoman Empire, and less forceful means could be substituted if the risks inherent in a quick solution were too great. Conditions seemed right for a diplomatic settlement involving all the powers and allowing the Russian government to retreat with honour from an over-exposed position. During July 1853 numerous ideas for a compromise were exchanged among the capitals of Europe. A French suggestion of a conference at Vienna was eventually taken up, and a French-inspired formula was adopted by the Austrian, British, French and Prussian governments. By the terms of the Vienna Note of 31 July, the sultan was to promise to make no change in the existing privileges of the Christian communities of his Empire without having arrived at a previous understanding with both the Russian and French governments. Nicholas I accepted the Vienna Note. The sultan did not.

Posterity has been unsympathetic to the European political leaders whose countries became involved in the Crimean War. But historians have at least paid them the compliment of examining exhaustively their motivations. The sultan and his ministers have been less fortunate. They were once pictured merely as puppets of Stratford's will to war. Even Professor Temperley, who successfully absolved both them and Stratford of this charge and who appreciated their resentment of the Vienna Note, relied heavily on 'fanaticism', 'obscurantism', and the peculiarities of the 'oriental mind' in explaining the Porte's decision to defy the European powers and to make war on Russia.[1] This sort of interpretation may, of course, be correct – one cannot say one way or the other on the basis of non-Turkish sources – but there seems no need to resort to it. Ottoman policy, while irritating and inconvenient to the diplomats gathered at Vienna, was neither outlandish nor puzzling.

The Turks were being asked to agree that two European governments, frequently hostile to them in the past, should have the right to decide whether the sultan should in future be allowed to make changes affecting two religious groups among his subjects, a limitation on sovereignty which every European government would have found unacceptable except in the aftermath of a disastrous war. The Turks had made a rather vague concession of this kind to the Russians in 1774 in part settlement of one such disastrous war. They were now expected to extend and more closely define this concession not because they had suffered any defeat but because it was reckoned to be a way of restoring tranquillity to the European powers. They were to sacrifice their already much-damaged self-respect and independence to the susceptibilities and political calculations of the French and Russian

[1] H. W. V. Temperley, *England and the Near East. The Crimea* (London, 1936), 345–8, 358–61.

emperors. The emotional response to this demand was precisely what might have been expected in any part of the world. It might have been muted, and sullen compliance might have been forthcoming, had resistance to the demand seemed futile, but there was every reason for believing that conditions for resistance were particularly favourable. As in 1839, the Ottoman government could embark on war in defiance of the wishes of the major European governments with the virtual certainty that they would not be allowed to suffer catastrophic defeat. Thus, in 1839–40, had they turned the tables on Muḥammad ʿAlī. On the same kind of calculation, the Turks now had the best chance of being on the winning side against Russia since Peter the Great's reign. Stratford's manner in advising them to accept the Vienna Note might have been, as has been surmised, reassuring enough, and the threat of violent indignation within the Empire if they did not act was severe enough to bolster the inclination of Turkish political leaders to follow such a rational if risky course. But if the governments of the powers failed to understand Turkish psychology it was because they assumed Turkish psychological makeup to be fundamentally different from their own in such matters. What took them aback was that the Porte, instead of accepting a submissive role in keeping with its lowly rating as a power, behaved just like any major European government.

The desire for a peaceful solution was still strong in all capitals except Constantinople, and there was further diplomatic wrangling in search of a formula satisfactory to all parties. In retrospect, these disputes over wording, with the issue of war or peace hanging on whether one phrase or another was to be adopted, appear ridiculous. Certainly life for the sultan's Christian subjects, on whose behalf the exercise was allegedly being conducted, was likely to go on much as before whatever the outcome. But preferences in wording had great significance. The basic conflict between the Russians and the British – and between the Russians and the Austrians – could remain latent as long as both sides left their relationship with the Ottoman Empire vague and ill-defined. The crisis over the Holy Places had provoked an attempt by the Russian government to define its relationship more precisely and so ensure that Turkish policies would henceforth be reassuringly predictable. In an atmosphere of mutual mistrust the various governments looked for signals by which they might divine one another's intentions, and insistence on, or rejection of, forms of words in proposed written agreements has always been deemed in diplomatic circles to be fraught with meaning.

The wording of the various Russian proposals contributed as much as Menshikov's truculence and the occupation of the Principalities to winning over the doubters in the divided British cabinet to the belief that the Holy Places dispute was being used to make the Ottoman Empire a virtual Russian protectorate. Suspicion had grown to the point that, when Nicholas I accepted the Vienna Note, Clarendon, the British foreign secretary, seems to have felt there was a catch somewhere. When the Russian government on 7 September 1853 rejected Turkish amendments to the Vienna Note, Clarendon, whom the combined arguments of Palmerston and the press had gradually moved from his earlier non-committal position, saw it as a clear sign that the Russians did have designs against the Ottoman Empire which acceptance of the amended note would make it difficult for them to vindicate. Nesselrode's subsequent interpretation of the Vienna Note as meaning that the Porte must 'take account of Russia's active solicitude for her co-religionists in Turkey' was characterized by Clarendon as 'violent'. Lord John Russell, although mistrustful of Nicholas I from the start, had believed the Turks should accept the Vienna Note as it stood, but when he heard of the Russian rejection of the Turkish amendments he took it as conclusive proof of Russian plans to subjugate the Ottoman Empire. 'If that is the case,' he wrote to Aberdeen, 'the question must be decided by war, and if we do not stop the Russians on the Danube, we shall have to stop them on the Indus.'[1]

As disputes within the British cabinet were settled in the long run in favour of its more belligerent members, and as the latter were forcefully and emotionally supported by the majority of journalists, it is tempting to assume that the government bowed submissively to 'public opinion' in eventually opting for war. But there is a simpler and more probable explanation. Both politicians and journalists were divided as to the significance of Russian moves against the Ottoman Empire. *The Times* threw its considerable influence on the side of the caution which Aberdeen and Clarendon urged within the cabinet. How the debate would go depended on which interpretation seemed belied by events. As each prospect of a peaceful solution was dashed, the alarmists sounded more and more convincing, until, as in the 1830s, the most trivial sign of Russian aggression looked like dramatic confirmation of their view. The advocates of caution had from the start been afflicted by doubts which never troubled their opponents. As usual in international politics, the consequences of failing to identify a danger eventually seemed more awesome than the consequences of preparing for war. By September 1853 the alarmists had reinforced the doubts of their opponents that

[1] Quoted by J. B. Conacher, *The Aberdeen Coalition, 1852–1855. A Study in Mid-Nineteenth-Century Party Politics* (Cambridge, 1968), 182.

Nicholas I was not to be trusted. His willingness, after a conference at Olmütz that month with Austrian leaders, to deny unequivocally that he had any intention of securing new rights in relation to the Ottoman Empire or of interfering in its internal affairs, carried no conviction in London. The alarmists had by now won the day as to the reality of a Russian threat. It is possible that some ministers were intimidated by the fierce emotions which the newspaper campaign had released. It is more likely that they had run out of arguments to account for the pattern of Russian behaviour. The balance of probability lay with the alarmist version of events. Consideration for public opinion, such as Clarendon expressed, could conveniently sanctify the change of mind which politicians always find so embarrassing.

The British cabinet's divisions and uncertainties down to September 1853 may have looked undignified in retrospect, but they were appropriate enough at a time when Russian intentions were probably unclear to the Russian government itself. Unfortunately, they reached agreement on the reality of a Russian threat just when the Russians were genuinely trying to get back to a pre-Menshikov position and to restore Russo-Turkish relations to sufficient vagueness to satisfy all parties. This confused state of affairs might have been sorted out but for the Turkish declaration of war on Russia on 4 October 1853. Although this was a logical enough development in the crisis, it created for the British government a fundamentally different problem from the one they had been wrestling with since Menshikov's mission. There was no reason to believe that the Turks would fare any better than usual in a war against Russia, and there was every reason to believe that Nicholas I, frustrated and exasperated by his failure to control the sultan's behaviour, would this time exploit his victory to the full. Hitherto, the British cabinet had been concerned to forestall a Russian diplomatic victory conferring subtle advantages in the long term. Now they faced the imminent prospect of the Ottoman Empire being defeated and dismembered by the Russians with incalculable repercussions throughout eastern Europe and western and central Asia. To prevent the situation sliding out of control they had either to ensure that the state of war remained a bloodless affair of gestures, or to intervene in sufficient force to prevent a Turkish collapse. The Russian government made clear its wish for peace talks and its intention of remaining on the defensive. The British tried to persuade the Turks not to initiate hostilities, and made their support conditional on the Porte accepting the Vienna Note in revised form and accompanied by guarantees. The Turks obviously thought the British were bluffing, and they had in any case already begun the war in earnest by attacking Russian forces across the Danube and in the Caucasus.

Since the Russians could hardly be expected to exercise restraint indefinitely, the British government had to be prepared for intervention. Its members would have preferred to aid the Turks in some way which would not involve the British themselves in war with Russia. This would be difficult, but not, perhaps, impossible if the aid were confined to money, arms and advisers. It was made near to impossible by the British assumption that intervention must include the familiar recourse to naval action as swift, economical and effective. Already in late September, during the disturbances in Constantinople which had been the prelude to the Turkish declaration of war, it had been decided to bring the British and French squadrons through the Dardanelles to the Ottoman capital. At a crucial cabinet meeting on 8 October 1853 it was agreed that the warships might enter the Black Sea if such a move were needed in defence of Turkish territory. Aberdeen and the more pacific of his colleagues deluded themselves into believing that because they thought of any such move as defensive it was reasonable to expect the Russians to categorize it as such. The whole point of Russian policy in the region was to keep British or French warships a safe distance from Russian territory. No Russian ruler could possibly accept their domination of the Black Sea while his forces were engaged in war with the Turks. Nicholas I was certain to interpret their presence there as an act of war. The British would find themselves on a collision course with the Russians should the Russo-Turkish war take a dramatic enough turn for the cabinet to set in motion their policy of limited intervention.

This was the significance of the Turkish naval disaster at Sinop. Nicholas I's circular expressing willingness to remain on the defensive despite the Turkish declaration of war had been issued before it became clear that the Turks were bent on actual hostilities. His policy held for the Balkans out of respect for Austrian susceptibilities, and Russian forces did not react strongly to Turkish skirmishing across the Danube. He saw no such reason for restraint on his Asian frontiers with the Ottoman Empire, where Turkish victories would encourage the flourishing resistance to Russian rule in the Caucasus. At the end of November 1853 Russian forces inflicted a heavy defeat on a Turkish army moving against Georgia. This coincided with the Russian Black Sea fleet's victory over a Turkish naval squadron which had recently sailed from Constantinople three hundred and fifty miles along the coast of Asia Minor to Sinop, and had been surprised in port. It was the battle of

The British and the Russians lose control, 1841–53

Sinop which provided the dramatic turn of events sufficient to swing even moderate opinion in Great Britain in favour of war. The ease of the Russian victory underlined Turkish helplessness, the likelihood of rapid collapse, and British failure to anticipate such events despite having the means at hand. *The Times* saw Sinop as ending the case for moderation, which it had hitherto preached, and the passionate outcry among journalists registered general dismay at this demonstration of Russian naval power. The mood of virtuous indignation was misplaced, but the sense of alarm was well founded. Hysterical language was clothing a rational enough assumption. The longer the British government hesitated to act in the hope of avoiding general war, the more likely were disasters like Sinop, whose cumulative effect might be too catastrophic to undo.

By December 1853 the British cabinet could be divided into two broad categories: those, like Palmerston, Russell, and Clarendon, who expected and even preferred war as an outcome to the crisis, and those, like Aberdeen, Wood, and Graham, who were more or less resigned to war but still hoped somehow to avoid it. Sinop provided the pretext the former group needed to convince their colleagues that the moment had arrived for naval action of the kind envisaged in the October cabinet meetings. They met no resistance. 'Some rather strong measures', Aberdeen told the queen, 'were adopted in consequence of the catastrophe at Sinope, by directing the presence of the English and French fleets in the Black Sea; but no violent or very hostile decision was taken.'[1] Nor did the more pacific members of the cabinet resist the decidedly violent and very hostile proposal of the French government that, once in the Black Sea, the British and French fleets should intercept all Russian warships and force them to return to base. They accepted that Sinop had made measures to save the Ottoman Empire so urgent as to justify increasing the risk of war. Offensive action in the Black Sea was, in any case, thought of in London and Paris as simply raising the diplomatic stakes. It seems to have been quite genuinely believed that, although there was a strong risk of war implicit in the decision, Nicholas I might behave 'reasonably' and back down to a display of superior force. Palmerston thought war likely in the long run, but not as a result of this particular action. He did not expect Nicholas I to declare war 'for so polite an attention as a request that he will not expose his Black Sea fleet to the various dangers, which might beset their ships if they left their good anchorage at Sebastopol', and he believed that the tsar

[1] Quoted by J. B. Conacher, *The Aberdeen Coalition, 1852–1855. A Study in Mid-Nineteenth-Century Party Politics* (Cambridge, 1968,) 238–9.

would 'become reasonable in proportion as he finds that his difficulties and dangers will increase by his remaining unreasonable'.[1]

Nicholas I did not declare war. It was in his interest to postpone any extension of hostilities as long as possible while his war preparations were still under way. But Palmerston was wrong in thinking that Nicholas could stomach the Franco-British presence in the Black Sea unless it could really have been construed as a diplomatic gesture aimed at controlling the Turks as much as influencing the Russians. When it became clear that their intention was simply to interfere with Russian military operations and facilitate those of the Turks, Nicholas recalled his ambassadors in February 1854. The French and British ambassadors were handed their passports. Their governments declared war at the end of March after their ultimata demanding evacuation of the Principalities had expired.

The lull in Russo-British rivalry had ended in a war which has generally been regarded as occurring almost accidentally. Certainly, there was reluctance on the part of both the Russian and the British governments to fight, and the British cabinet gave the appearance of 'drifting' towards war without clear purpose or direction. But the war was no chance mishap. Belief in a fundamental Russian threat to British imperial interests had been weakened during the 1840s, but it had by no means been dispelled and certain dramatic events like a Russo-Persian or a Russo-Turkish war could be expected to revive it in full. Admittedly the crisis of 1853 was dramatized by journalists to an exceptional degree. The odium which the tsar had incurred yet again during 1849 as 'an aggressive tyrant' and 'an enemy of the liberty of nations' was still fresh when Russia appeared once more in a bullying role which also recalled old fears for British interests at Constantinople. But, although bombarded with alarmist interpretations of Russian policy, most members of the British cabinet avoided any violent reaction, and those whose reaction was violent needed no press campaign to induce it. Public opinion did not 'drive' the British government into war.

The Crimean War was brought about by the Turks. Without their decision to wage war on the Russians, the crisis would almost certainly have been resolved peacefully. However much the crisis had revived the British view that Russian policies in Asia constituted a threat, war as a means of coping with the threat would be reserved for extreme circumstances. The Turks created those extreme circumstances. Once a Russo-Turkish war was in progress, the British could retain a sense of controlling the Russian threat in one of two ways. They could mobilize

[1] Quoted by Temperley, *The Crimea*, 382.

the rest of Europe in a show of unity and strength which the Russians could not ignore, or they could help the Turkish armed forces to win. Since they did not trust the Austrians and were unsure of Napoleon III, they resorted to the second alternative. There was initially hope of saving the Turks by aid short of military participation, but after Sinop this hope faded, and it was decided that only direct use of naval force in the Black Sea would serve. The predictable outcome was war, an outcome which the Russians and the British alike would have much preferred to avoid. They had brought it upon themselves. Scorning to treat the Turks as equals, they had both underrated what the Turks could still accomplish by independent action. The Turks could and did create a situation which gave the leaders in London and St Petersburg little freedom of action, because their ingrained habits of thought left them psychologically equipped to respond to it in a very limited number of ways. Whether by calculation or otherwise, the Turkish leaders tempted the Russians to achieve what the British had for twenty years regarded as intolerable. They had thereby regained a little of the sense of control over their own affairs of which the other powers had largely deprived them. The war which they had set in motion was a desperate expedient, but it was no accident.

5

Russian leaders take alarm, 1853–60

The military achievements of the Crimean War can be simply stated. The Russians captured Kars, their enemies captured Sevastopol. As a war it was unspectacular, though spectacular changes in Europe – the rise of Piedmont and Prussia, the destruction of a viable European states system – have been attributed in part to it. It undoubtedly had considerable importance for the development of Russo-British rivalry, in which, as far as the British government was concerned, it had its origins. Its importance in an Asian as well as a European context was enhanced by its being one of a series of events in Eurasia during the 1850s which altered the dimensions of the Great Game.

The character of the war helps to explain its importance in the history of the Great Game. It was very difficult for either side to strike at the enemy decisively enough to make for a spectacular outcome. The French and the British could attack Russia directly and to some purpose only through the Baltic and the Black Sea. They placed their hopes of a decisive blow in each area on the destruction of bases essential to Russian coastal defences and to Russian control of each of the seas. This simple strategic objective was by no means easy to realize. In the Baltic, British and French naval power could blockade the Gulf of Finland, prevent some thirty Russian ships of the line from commerce raiding in the North Sea, and, by merely offering a threat so near to the Russian capital, divert large numbers of troops from active service elsewhere. The fortress of Bomarsund in the Åland Islands was bombarded by a combined force of British and French ships in August 1854, briefly occupied, and its defence works destroyed. A year later, Sveaborg, in the Gulf of Finland, was bombarded. But both Napier (of Acre fame), who commanded the British squadron in 1854, and Dundas, who replaced him for the 1855 expedition, were agreed that the destruction of Sveaborg, Revel, and the island fortress of Kronstadt covering St Petersburg, could not be accomplished with the forces at their disposal. The possibility of mounting in 1856 operations on the massive scale required was still under consideration when the war ended. Had the British and the French tried to invade Russia's Baltic provinces and struck at St Petersburg itself, even with the growing prospect of Swedish participation against Russia, they would presumably have faced the same sort of frustrating struggle already experienced in the Crimea.

There, it had taken a year to capture Sevastopol, the principal Russian base on the Black Sea. As in the Baltic, the Russian fleet acknowledged its hopeless inferiority by remaining in port and leaving the British and the French unchallenged command of the Black Sea. An allied army landed without opposition on the Crimean coast in September 1854, and defeated a smaller Russian army standing between it and Sevastopol at the battle of the Alma. In Sevastopol itself formidable defences were hastily prepared under the direction of Colonel Totleben, and the invading forces resigned themselves to a winter siege. Diversionary attacks by the main Russian army in the Crimea were defeated at the battles of Balaklava and Inkerman in October–November 1854 and at the battle of the Chornaya in August 1855. Sevastopol was not finally abandoned by the Russians until September 1855. The British and French forces had achieved the temporary crippling of Russian power in the Black Sea which had been their objective, but the capture of Sevastopol would hardly have been chosen as the means had such a protracted and bloody campaign been anticipated.

The Russians were far worse placed, and had little hope of bidding for a decisive victory. They could not strike at the homelands of either the British or the French. Their continuing warfare in central Asia had been producing results too slowly and gradually to make the British fear the sort of breakthrough which would bring an imminent threat to India. The Russians could not even think in terms of diverting resources to mount such a threat because of their fear for Russia's own frontiers in Europe. Despite its vast size, the Russian army faced so many immediate and potential enemies in 1853–6 that its strength could never be concentrated in the Crimea where it was so urgently needed. The Franco-British threat in the Baltic, and the fear that the Austrians might enter the war with even graver effects than the invasion of the Crimea, condemned too much of the Russian army to a non-combatant role for it to achieve numerical superiority in the main fighting area, and perhaps save Sevastopol. With more troops, General N. N. Muravyov, the cautious viceroy of the Caucasus, might have been encouraged to strike earlier at the key Turkish frontier fortress of Kars, and set in motion a really dangerous offensive in Anatolia. As it was, Kars was not taken until the end of November 1855, in time to constitute one of the few Russian bargaining counters at the conference table, but too late to affect the course of the war. And the Russians, like the British and the French, failed to find generals with the genius that would have been necessary to create spectacular victories out of such an unpromising situation.

When the Great Game was being pursued in earnest by the British during the 1830s, Palmerston and his colleagues had been sustained by their optimism as to the result of war with Russia, should it come. Nicholas I had seen Russia as a fortress proof against any outbreak of British 'madness'. War had come, and the optimism of both governments had been confounded. This was partly due to awkward if not immutable geographical facts, partly to remediable enough military and naval weaknesses, but partly also to an inhibiting dependence on the reactions to their conflict of other European governments, a dependence which the geographical facts and the military weaknesses combined to make unavoidable.

The Austrians had pointedly demonstrated the vulnerability of Russia's military route to Constantinople; in the summer of 1854 the Russians felt obliged to accept an ultimatum from the Austrians demanding withdrawal from the Principalities. With the sultan's concurrence, the Austrian army occupied the area themselves, placing a neutral land barrier between the combatants, and ensuring that the war would be conducted well away from Austria's frontiers and from the easily inflamed Balkan populations who were Austria's neighbours. The effect on the course of the war of Austria's possible participation in it has already been remarked. In January 1856, it was above all the immediate threat of Austrian entry into the war, and possibly that of Prussia and Sweden as well, which convinced the Russian emperor and his advisers that, although they might shrug off the loss of Sevastopol and continued war with the British and the French, a war with practically the whole of Europe could not be profitable in the long run. The British, too, found their freedom to wage war restricted. Austrian diplomatic activity to restore peace had persisted throughout, and the French were anxious for a quick end to the war once Sevastopol had fallen. The British found themselves unable to contemplate a further year's warfare with only the Turks for allies, and they had to abandon hope of substantial Russian cessions in the Caucasus, such as Circassia and Georgia, and even of the Crimea itself. The other European states had shown they could exercise a decisive influence on the outcome of a Russo-British war. Admittedly, this particular war was over the Ottoman Empire, which was a general European interest, but even a conflict between the Russians and the British over territories deep in Asia would almost certainly involve Europe because the British could best bring their naval superiority to bear on Russia by penetrating the Black Sea and the Baltic, and the Russians could best keep them out by alliances with other powers. The Crimean War showed that the Great Game for ascendancy in Asia might be resolved in favour of whichever government mobilized most support in Europe.

In addition, the war revived and extended the Great Game. It had been a somewhat one-sided affair, even in the 1830s, and during the following decade the concept had lost much of its power to shape British foreign policy as Russian expansion came to be seen as a long-term trend without immediate menace. But the Crimean War had been none the less a product of the Game in that the British government would scarcely have seen the 1853 crisis as warranting war had not the need to defend the Ottoman Empire against Russian domination been a cardinal assumption of British policy-makers; and it was in the 1830s that it became an assumption so strong as to remain unquestioned in the years when a sense of danger about India itself was waning. There was now no prospect of the Great Game fading out of international politics altogether. It was given new vitality by the climate of frustration and belligerence which permeated political life in both Great Britain and Russia in the years 1853-6. Moreover, it ceased to be essentially a British preoccupation. The Russian government now embarked on a programme of vigorous expansion in Asia, apparently vindicating the direst prophecies of the British alarmists.

Nicholas I had died in March 1855, and it was left to his son, Alexander II, to make peace and decide how the Russian government should now view the world. After the failure of the Turks, the Austrians and the British to behave in the way he had predicted, even Nicholas I would presumably have been responsive to some sort of reinterpretation of international politics. The sequence of events had been far more dramatic than that in the years 1838-42, which had done nothing to shake his sense of understanding and control. The Crimean War shattered three of his basic assumptions: first, that common allegiance to the conservative principle and mutual expressions of respect for one another's interests in the Balkans would be sufficient to sustain an alliance with Austria; secondly, that a deal had been struck with the British firm enough to survive any crisis; thirdly, that Russia had been kept in a condition to fight and finance a protracted war. Having lost the war, Alexander II had to sign a treaty which deprived the Russians of two conditions thought essential to their security: a fleet and bases in the Black Sea, which now was to be neutralized; and a special relationship with the Ottoman Empire, which was to be admitted to the concert of Europe, and whose independence and integrity were formally guaranteed by all the powers equally. And the sequence of alarming events was not yet over. Russia's most intransigent enemies during the Crimean War had been the British. As if to clinch the claim of Russian alarmists that British activities formed a pattern of aggression and imperial expansion, Palmerston's government promptly went on to fight two further wars in Asia against neighbours of Russia.

The British decisions to go to war with the Persians and the Chinese a few months after the ending of the Crimean War were not, in fact, directly linked, and they did not exemplify systematic aggression to extend British imperial power. But it was no coincidence that war should have been chosen as an instrument of policy three times in as many years, any more than simultaneous wars against the Egyptians, the Afghans and the Chinese had been a coincidence around 1840. The mood induced by war against the Russians had simply made it seem more obvious to try and settle quickly by war disputes which might otherwise have been left to gradual smothering by normal diplomatic processes. And the war with Persia signified more than a mood of impatience and belligerency. It betokened the return of the 'threat to India' theme in British policy-making.

The Perso-British conflict centred on a renewed bid by the shah for Herat. Although British governments were now less prone to panic at recurring threats by the shah to Herat, they still intended to counter any Persian attack on it by repeating the expedition to the Persian Gulf, which, they believed, had contributed to its relief in 1838. The right enjoyed by the Russian government to station consuls anywhere in the shah's dominions meant that Herat's incorporation in Persia could turn it into a Russian outpost for intrigue against the British in India and ultimately, perhaps, a base for invasion. In the Crimean War, the shah tried unsuccessfully to sell his support to the highest bidder. When the British simply urged his neutrality, and warned him of the consequences of joining the Russians or of moving on Herat, the shah tried to alarm them by courting the French and by offering the Americans, once more at odds with the British, a favourable commercial convention if they would protect Persia's coasts. As the Crimean War drew to a close without the shah having achieved anything except British resentment at his tactics, the incorporation of Herat became again his principal goal. A sense of urgency was imparted by the news that Dost Muḥammad of Kābul was preparing to bring both Qandahār and Herat under his rule. In December 1855, Dost Muḥammad took the first step with the occupation of Qandahār. A recent coup had put a former pensioner of the shah in control at Herat, and the shah received a convenient request for Persian aid. In February 1856, Persian forces took the road to Herat.

The British had already broken off relations with Persia the previous November. The shah had quarrelled with the British ambassador, the Hon. Charles Murray, over one of the Persians employed by the embassy, and had had his wife kidnapped. Murray withdrew his embassy from Tehran. The British government approved, and were in no hurry, at first, to settle the dispute. Antagonized by the shah's behaviour during the Crimean War, Clarendon thought it good tactics to keep the shah in suspense for a time. But by May 1856 news about the Persian advance on Herat was arriving. The ruler who had summoned the Persians had been overthrown, and, with the Persians openly approaching in the role of conquerors rather than allies, an appeal for help had gone out to the British. At the same time, Dost Muḥammad had sought British approval for his own designs on Herat. Opinion in London and Calcutta had for some time been hardening in favour of Herat's inclusion in a united Afghan state as the best solution from the point of view of British interests in India. 'Affghanistan', declared Palmerston in June 1856, echoing the old idea of Alexander Burnes, 'is now the true Bulwark of British India.' He believed Persia had become 'the advanced guard of Russia', and it was essential to prevent the shah from annexing Herat.[1] A cabinet meeting on 5 July 1856 decided to demand immediate Persian withdrawal from Herat, and to support Dost Muḥammad's aspirations to it. In September 1856, when it became clear that the shah did not intend to comply, an expedition prepared by the Indian authorities was ordered to sail for the Persian Gulf. Lord Canning, the governor-general, son of the British foreign secretary who in 1826 had stood out against British involvement in Persia, proclaimed a state of war in November 1856.

The war was a short one. For compelling military and political reasons peace was restored in March 1857. Militarily, it was an absurdly unequal contest. Although the British commanders had good cause for

[1] Quoted by J. B. Kelly, *Britain and the Persian Gulf, 1795–1880* (London, 1968), 464.

apprehension about the terrain over which they would have to fight, the Persian army itself was a negligible obstacle. The expedition occupied the island of Kharg without resistance in December 1856, and then successfully attacked Bushire. In January 1857, Sir James Outram arrived to take command and with powers to negotiate. The following month he easily defeated a Persian force in a feint attack, before directing the main British thrust along the Kārūn River with five armed steamers and nearly five thousand men. In March, thirteen thousand Persians abandoned Muhammarah after the armed steamers had overcome the defending artillery. For the loss of five killed the British had won control of an important stronghold on the way to Iṣfahān.

The two armies fought the engagement without knowing that their governments had already ended the war. While Outram's troops had been providing the shah with sufficient military reasons for coming to terms, loud opposition in parliament was making it politically advisable for Palmerston and his colleagues to settle the affair quickly. Rather than risk probable defeat over the issue, Palmerston and Clarendon contented themselves with a peace treaty which gave them all the points deemed vital, and they did not persist in claims likely to prolong negotiations. The shah could not exploit this, because the war was even more unpopular in Persia itself and caused widespread disorders. He agreed to withdraw from Herat, which his forces had captured the previous autumn, and to abandon claims to suzerainty over Afghan lands; the British ambassador was restored to Tehran, and the dispute which had caused his breach with the shah was honourably resolved; and the British were granted most favoured nation treatment in commercial relations and the stationing of consuls.

Palmerston and Clarendon were gratified to find that the Russian government was needled by the prospect of a British consular presence as diffused as their own in Persia. For them the war was a necessary and successful stroke of policy. They discounted the condemnations of those who feared it might be, as Clarendon remarked, 'the beginning of that fight with Russia for India which must some day come, but which the people of England are very desirous to see postponed'.[1]

Within a few weeks of the British government's decision to send an expeditionary force to the Persian Gulf, British ships were firing the first shots in a war against China. The British government had not directly authorized this particular use of coercion, but it was in any case currently negotiating with the French for an expeditionary force to the Pei-ho river. Ever since the Treaty of Nanking had ended the first

[1] Quoted by J. B. Kelly, *Britain and the Persian Gulf, 1795-1880*, 492.

British war with the Chinese in 1842, its operation had disappointed British merchants and officials. British merchants had continued to blame Chinese government restrictions for the failure of trade to expand in the way they had expected. British officials in Hong Kong and the five treaty ports had continued to complain of the Chinese government's failure to treat the British government as an equal and to treat its representatives accordingly. Palmerston, frustrated in his attempts to deal directly with the government in Peking, had said in September 1850 that 'the Time is fast coming when we shall be obliged to strike another Blow in China'. 'These half civilized Governments,' he added, 'such as those of China Portugal Spanish America require a Dressing every eight or Ten years to keep them in order.'[1] He seemed to be on the point of using force at the time he had to resign from the government in December 1851. His successors at the foreign office during 1852, Granville and Malmesbury, had neither a belligerent temperament nor much interest in China, and as the Taiping rebellion spread there was some reluctance to risk the worsening of trade conditions by the even greater disruption which coercion might bring. The Crimean War soon postponed any precipitate action. But, once it ended, Palmerston and Clarendon were, as in the case of Persia, in just the mood to match the impatience long felt by the men on the spot. Hence Clarendon's negotiations with the French.

The men on the spot were Harry Parkes, the British consul at Canton, and Sir John Bowring, governor of Hong Kong and superintendent of trade. On 8 October 1856 Parkes was presented with the problem of what to do about the Chinese boarding of a lorcha, which was flying the British flag and which they should therefore have treated as British territory. Parkes believed that without a strong reaction to the incident British shipping in general would risk similar violation. Bowring, to whom he referred the case, was a passionate Benthamite and free trader, only too anxious to press his ideas of rational behaviour on the Chinese whenever the opportunity offered. He approved of Parkes's demands for redress, although he was aware that the legal status of this particular lorcha, the *Arrow*, was debatable. When the Chinese authorities in Canton made only partial amends, Bowring authorized a show of force in the area, and decided to use the *Arrow* incident as a pretext for ending the exclusion of foreigners from the city of Canton. Hostilities against Chinese shipping and fortifications began on 23 October. They were of very limited character, because the Chinese

[1] Quoted by J. K. Fairbank, *Trade and Diplomacy on the China Coast. The Opening of the Treaty Ports, 1842–1854* (Cambridge, Mass., 1953), 380.

did not have the power to cope with the British warships whose guns controlled the waters around Canton, and the British could not attempt to capture Canton without substantial reinforcements. Hostilities having begun, it would have been difficult for the British government to disavow Bowring when news of the events finally began to reach London in December 1856. Rather than do so, Palmerston and his colleagues used the *Arrow* affair as the occasion for that enforcing of treaty revisions which they had already been preparing.

In contrast to the conflict in Persia, the war with China dragged on for four years. Not that there was much actual fighting. After the initial clashes at the end of 1856 there was a long interval because Lord Elgin, appointed to take command and negotiate a settlement, felt obliged to divert the reinforcements intended for the China war to the more urgent task of suppressing the risings in India which broke out in 1857. It was not until December 1857, over a year after the *Arrow* incident, that the British and French forces were ready to take Canton. Its capture was the first of four brief spells of military activity. The second occurred in May 1858 when Elgin and his French counterpart, Baron Gros, arrived with their forces in the Gulf of Pechihli. The forts at Taku, covering the mouth of the Pei-ho, were taken, and the invaders' gunboats sailed up the river to Tientsin. After Elgin's threat to advance on Peking, which was largely bluff, the Chinese negotiators reluctantly conceded in June 1858 the right of a British representative to reside at Peking. This was taken by both sides to be the crux of the matter, as it implied Chinese acceptance of the British government's claim to be treated as an equal by the Chinese emperor. The French – and the Russian and American representatives who were in Tientsin to take advantage of the situation – had been prepared to settle for occasional missions to Peking, and the British themselves, once the principle had been conceded, agreed to save the emperor's face by not insisting on a resident ambassador for the time being. The opening of more ports to commerce, freedom for foreigners to travel in the interior of China, legalization of the booming opium trade, and regulation of their tariff scales to suit British merchants, were among other concessions wrung from the Chinese at this time. A third outburst of hostilities came a year later in June 1859, when Chinese batteries at Taku crippled several of the gunboats attempting to escort the British and French plenipotentiaries up the Pei-ho for ratification of the treaty of Tientsin. It took over another year to reassemble sufficient allied forces in the Gulf of Pechihli to storm the Taku forts again, and fight their way to Peking. In October 1860, Elgin and Gros made a ceremonial entry into the Chinese capital, from which the emperor had withdrawn. The Chinese would henceforth have to accept the permanent presence of foreign envoys in their capital. And their rulers would have to consider whether they had lost control of their world because their interpretation of it had been faulty.

The British attacks on China and Persia provided dramatic support to those who offered Alexander II a fresh interpretation of world politics. So did the Indian Mutiny. For if the British were engaged in systematic aggression in Europe and Asia, the Indian uprisings suggested there was no longer any need to despair of checking their aggression. The vulnerability of their empire in Asia was being demonstrated at the very time they were occupied in fighting Russia's neighbours. The brutal vigour of Dalhousie's westernization programme had offended and alarmed most sections of Indian society, including one section well placed to challenge it – the Indians in the Company's Bengal army. In isolation, the celebrated grievance over cartridges greased with the fat of animals having religious significance could have been hastily rectified. Coming as it did after a series of other shocks, which had been interpreted as a campaign against Indian religious and social institutions, the cartridge episode could be taken as the final insult. In May 1857, mutineers at Meerut marched forty miles to Delhi to claim the leadership of the old man who still held court there as Mughal emperor. Risings against British rule elsewhere in northern India followed. Fighting continued until the end of 1858, but the British had gained the upper hand with the recapture of Delhi in September 1857, by which time adequate reinforcements were reaching India. Although the revolutionary outbreaks affected a relatively small area of the subcontinent, and although in retrospect the actual overthrow of British dominion looked an improbable outcome, the mere fact of the uprisings and the ferocity with which operations were conducted by both sides offered spectacular evidence to the outside world that British control of India might be becoming less, not more, secure with the passage of time. The future shape of Russian foreign policy depended partly on how Alexander II would interpret all this evidence of apparent British aggression and insecurity in Asia.

Alexander II was, predictably enough, bent on restoring Russia to a position in which he could enjoy a sense of control over his dominions and over neighbouring governments, and freedom to extend his dominions in the manner of his forebears. In contrast to Nicholas I he would have to be an initiator of change both at home and abroad, but, since he would be in no position to cope with war or revolution until the changes had brought results, risks would have to be minimized. Thus, although, like many rulers in the aftermath of humiliating defeat, he was inclined to listen to those who attributed the defeat to a whole complex of defects in society rather than to contingent errors by individuals, he was also inclined to compromise in adopting the remedies they advised. This was true of the social and administrative changes by which he hoped to make his subjects more efficient and more manageable in future wars. It was even more true of his attempts to ensure that they would fight any future war under more favourable international conditions, because renewed war was a more immediate and likely danger than revolution.

The most urgent task abroad was to undermine the Crimean coalition, but it was also the task requiring least effort on the part of the Russian government because traditional antagonisms among the partners revived once the war was over. The most difficult task was to strengthen Russia's frontiers, which would be particularly vulnerable during the period of recovery and reform. Here, four problems could be distinguished. First, there was the defenceless character of the Black Sea coast. This was, of course, the most serious of the four problems, and Alexander II accorded it the highest priority. But the treaty revision required to solve it could be secured only by a patient, waiting game, in which Russian diplomats exploited European antagonisms and helped to create a favourable climate of opinion. The second problem was how to prevent other governments exploiting Polish antagonism to Russian rule, and thus making the Russian salient in central Europe almost as vulnerable as the Black sea coast. This, too, depended on careful manipulation of diplomatic relationships in Europe. The third problem was how to cope with British intrigue in the Caucasus, another of Russia's discontented frontier areas, and the fourth was how to counter the spread of British influence among the governments bordering on Russia's unstable Asian frontiers. It was in tackling these last two closely related problems that the temptations of direct and immediate action were strongest, and the risks correspondingly high.

Alexander II received conflicting advice on this. Prince Gorchakov, who had succeeded Nesselrode as foreign minister in 1856, and General Sukhozanet, the war minister, largely discounted a British threat in Asia. They saw Russian activities in Asia as a dangerous distraction from the prime task of restoring Russian influence in Europe. Gorchakov pinned his hopes to an alliance with the French, who could be encouraged to check the British in Persia and elsewhere. On the other hand, Prince Baryatinsky, one of the new emperor's most trusted confidants, believed that the Russians would themselves have to check the British in Asia as a matter of urgency. He interpreted the Persian war of 1856–7 as another phase of the Crimean War, and regarded renewed war with Great Britain as inevitable. When war came Russia must be already in a position to pose such a threat to the British empire in Asia that the British would have to concentrate their forces in an area where the Russian army could confidently expect to have the advantage. This favourable position could be achieved only if the Russian government did something quickly to counter British commercial and political penetration of western and central Asia. As the new viceroy of the Caucasus, Baryatinsky saw this area as a centre from which Russian influence in the form of political prestige, religious ideas and trade could spread in opposition to that of Great Britain. But this form of penetration might not be enough in view of British economic superiority. 'England displays its power with gold. Russia which is poor in gold has to compete with force of arms.' Given a few strategic railways, the Caucasus could also be a powerful operational base, from which Russian forces could 'descend like an avalanche on Turkey, Persia and the road to India'.[1]

Alexander II inclined to Baryatinsky's view of the situation in Asia. He believed in a British threat. He saw British activities in Asia as calculated to do irreparable damage to Russian power and influence there. He accepted the need to counter it. He did not believe, as Gorchakov did, that the importance the British attached to India made an energetic Russian policy in Asia too dangerous to contemplate. He found the Indian Mutiny encouraging. Ignatyev, his military attaché in London, reported that the mere rumour of a Russian threat to India had stimulated Indian resistance to the British. Baryatinsky saw Russia looking the more attractive of the two imperial powers after the events of 1857. Since Alexander II feared especially the aid the British might give to the rebellious mountaineers of the Caucasus – and private British aid from David Urquhart and his associates had increased since the neutralization of the Black Sea – he was glad to know he could reply in kind. Asia did not, of course, displace Europe as the central concern of the Russian emperor. It was rather that Alexander, like Ellenborough and Palmerston a quarter of a century before, was beginning to see his problems in one broad Eurasian setting. He saw a general threat, and, in particular, a British threat to Russia's frontiers in Europe and Asia alike. But he was circumspect in his initial choice of counter-measures. Indeed, the moves he made, like the fears which had engendered them,

[1] Quoted by A. J. Rieber, *The Politics of Autocracy. Letters of Alexander II to Prince A. I. Bariatinskii, 1857–1864* (Paris and The Hague, 1966), 71–2.

bore a striking resemblance to those of Ellenborough and Palmerston in response to a putative Russian threat.

Admittedly, Alexander gave free rein to Baryatinsky's energies by appointing him viceroy of the Caucasus with a mandate to end the war there quickly. Baryatinsky had insisted this was possible. Conventional military opinion had assumed an indefinite continuation of the old struggle, which had reached major proportions since the 1830s when the mountaineers had found a great leader in Shāmil. Baryatinsky used his influence with Alexander II to get the troops and weapons he needed, and, with his chief of staff, D. A. Milyutin, systematically reorganized the military and administrative machine in the Caucasus. A vigorous Russian offensive was launched at a time when Shāmil's movement was already in decline. After Shāmil's capture in 1859, resistance disintegrated and Baryatinsky achieved the rapid victory he had promised to the emperor. The Russian grip on the Caucasus was further strengthened by the annexation of their protectorates Mingrelia, Abkhazia and Svaneti, whose ambiguous status had been exploited by the Turks during the Crimean War. The forcible exile of six hundred thousand Circassians from the Black Sea coast deprived the Turks and the British of their most valuable potential allies within the Russian Empire. The Caucasus would remain one of the most difficult parts of the empire to govern, but the forceful policies of Baryatinsky and his associates had stabilized it to an unprecedented degree. Alexander II could enjoy a reasonable sense of control over a vital frontier area, whose turbulence had for decades tempted Russia's enemies.

The new emperor likewise approved the empire-building already being pursued by the governor-general of eastern Siberia. Count Muravyov, appointed to the post by Nicholas I in 1847, had from the start urged a forward policy there to forestall British expansion. The Russian and Chinese empires did not, for the most part, have a clearly defined common frontier. Apart from a line of agreed frontier posts in Mongolia, the Russians and the Chinese faced each other across considerable stretches of territory still disputed, sometimes unexplored, and often controlled by the peoples who actually lived there, who were neither Russians nor Chinese. This sort of territory included coastal regions accessible to a British fleet. The British had, in fact, no interest as yet in this part of Asia and no thought of exploiting its uncertain status, but the 'Opium War' had given some colour to Muravyov's claim that the British might come to threaten lands which the Russians had always assumed would eventually fall to them. Nicholas I had accepted the need to assert Russia's claim to the mouth of the Amur by the establishment of military outposts like Nikolayevsk, and in 1853 he favoured negotiating a stable frontier with the Chinese government. He was clearly concerned with robbing the British of any future excuse for intervention, but he wished to do so by agreement with the Chinese, and his territorial claims were very modest. They did not constitute the sort of forward policy designed by Muravyov to make China dependent on Russia, and thus give Russia a dominating position in East Asia.

The Crimean War, which included a diversionary British attack on Kamchatka, gave Muravyov every excuse for stepping up Russian activity in the Amur region. His armed, though bloodless, colonization in these years made the Amur region effectively part of the Russian Empire by the end of 1856. Alexander II endorsed this extension of his frontiers, logically enough given his increasing disposition to think in Eurasian terms. Not only had the Great Game become a reality for most of Russia's leaders, but its operational range extended, in their eyes, to China, which the British had hitherto seen as a separate issue unconnected with Russia. Kovalevsky, head of the Asiatic department at the foreign ministry, linked the areas of rivalry when he declared in January 1857 that the British could not be allowed to take either Peking or Herat. The fall of Peking, made possible by news of Elgin's expedition, 'would paralyze all our beginnings on the shores of the Pacific and Amur, and the second [the fall of Herat] would put all Central Asia in the power of the English'.[1] Between 1857 and 1860, the diplomacy of Muravyov, Ignatyev, Putyatin and others skilfully exploited China's war with Great Britain and France to negotiate a formal disclaimer by the Chinese not only to the left bank of the Amur but also to the right bank as far as the Ussuri and the whole area between the Ussuri and the coast. Without incurring hostilities with the Chinese, nor the resentment of the British, who were only dimly aware of what was going on, Alexander II's agents had added to his empire a province of great strategic value in relation to China and the Pacific. The base Muravyov founded on the Sea of Japan in 1860 was significantly called Vladivostok, 'Ruler of the East'.

In tackling the British threat to central Asia, Alexander II initially refrained from warmaking, which had been appropriate within Russia's own boundaries in the Caucasus, and from territorial expansion, which the predicament of China in the years 1856–60 had made both urgent and free of risk. For the time being, he relied instead upon Russia's

[1] Quoted by R. K. I. Quested, *The Expansion of Russia in East Asia, 1857–1860* (Kuala Lumpur, 1968), 65.

traders and diplomats to counter the British. Like Ellenborough, he could hope that the enterprise of his merchants and manufacturers would, if the government negotiated at least some of the attractive trading conditions they frequently demanded, carry Russian influence to the threatened areas of Asia in a manner inexpensive, indeed profitable, to the state and unprovocative, if disturbing, to the British. Even if he did not conveniently set down a programme on these lines such as that devised by Ellenborough, the moves he authorized in 1857 suggest a coherent policy emerging in response to the various ideas in circulation. During 1857, Russian diplomats and other agents were sent on special missions to Khurāsān, Afghanistan, Khīva, Bukhārā and Kashgar in what amounted to a systematic quest for commercial and military intelligence, and for possible new political links with Russia's Asian neighbours.

In the autumn of 1857, Alexander II approved two expeditions to central Asia. One was to be led by N. V. Khanykov, an orientalist attached to the Asiatic department of the foreign ministry; the other by N. P. Ignatyev, recently military attaché in London and a fervent advocate of a forward policy in Asia. Khanykov's expedition was to Khurāsān and Afghanistan; Ignatyev's to Khīva and Bukhārā. Apart from collecting commercial and military intelligence, Khanykov was instructed, in the first place, to visit the Afghan centres of Kābul, Qandahār and Herat, and to convince Dost Muḥammad of the Russian emperor's desire for a strong Afghan state capable of resisting British expansion. Secondly, Khanykov was to try and bind the turbulent and rebellious tribesmen of Khurāsān and Sīstān, south-east of the Caspian, more closely to Persia. Persia's unstable eastern provinces, whose boundaries lacked definition and whose inhabitants were of uncertain loyalty, offered the British – and the Russians – ample scope for intrigue, and the Russians wanted no further weakening of Persia after the recent British invasion. Ignatyev was expected to meet up with Khanykov somewhere in central Asia, so that they could compare notes on British activity there. Ignatyev, too, was to gather commercial and military information. He was instructed to try and improve Russia's relations with the khan of Khīva and the amir of Bukhārā by mutual trading concessions, to discourage Khīvan intrigue among the tribes on Russia's borders, and to secure the release of Russian prisoners held in Bukhārā. If possible, he was to commit both rulers to written agreements, and he was authorized to offer some degree of Russian protection against outside interference. The Russian government meant to take full advantage of Great Britain's current embarrassment in India. Ignatyev was to point to the subcontinent's fate when drawing the attention of his hosts to British designs on their independence. 'I am convinced', wrote the younger brother of Alexander II, referring to Khanykov's expedition, 'that it will have the most important consequences in preparing the way for future activity by us in the East and in denying to posterity the right to say that we stood with folded arms at a time when unfortunate India struggled to overthrow the hated English yoke.'[1]

Neither expedition accomplished much in political terms. Khanykov, who set out across the Caspian in March 1858, visited Herat, but had to abandon his proposed mission to Kābul. Dost Muḥammad had made an alliance with the British in January 1857 at the time of the Persian occupation of Herat. He had received badly needed arms and money, and he had been gratified by the speed with which his allies had compelled the Persians to evacuate Herat. Conversely, he had seen the Russians defeated by the British and unable to save the Persians. He was thus convinced of the superior power of the British and of the value of their alliance in advancing his own claims to Herat. He expressed his satisfaction by restraining his subjects from intervening against the British during the Indian Mutiny, at a time when such intervention could have been decisive. A Russian alliance held no attraction for him, and he refused to admit their emissaries. Had Khanykov been able to initiate negotiations with Dost Muḥammad, the Russian government would have faced the same kind of dilemma the British had once faced. In the 1830s the price to the British of an Afghan alliance would have been help in gaining Peshawar, and hence alienation of their existing ally, the Panjāb; its price to the Russians in 1858 would have been help in gaining Herat, and hence alienation of their existing ally, Persia. Khanykov's failure to reach Kābul was, therefore, of little moment, but the rebuff seemed to underline the strength of the British position in central Asia, and made seem all the more valuable Khanykov's showing of the flag on the Persian borders, the new information he brought back on the physical and political geography of the region, and the trading links he fostered there.

Ignatyev's mission to Khīva and Bukhārā between June and October 1858 was, on the face of it, more successful. He came near to securing a treaty with the khan of Khīva, and the amir of Bukhārā actually signed an agreement granting the Russian emperor's demands. The amir was encouragingly anti-British, hoped the Russians might help him conquer his neighbours, Khīva and Khokand, and feared that the Russians might, alternatively, help his neighbours to conquer him. Ignatyev him-

[1] Quoted by Rieber, *Politics of Autocracy*, 79.

self wanted Russian annexation of the khanates. Perhaps for this reason, he and his colleagues on the expedition did not expect the paper concessions to be honoured, and were unimpressed by the rather favourable prospects for a Russian diplomatic offensive in central Asia which this first attempt of his appeared to indicate. In any case, the immediate value of Ignatyev's expedition, like Khanykov's, was to remove the Russian government's ignorance of conditions in a region which had become of urgent concern to them. The same was true of Valikhanov's secret mission in 1858–9 to the restless Chinese border province of Kashgar.

The emperor and his advisers were agreed on the need to erect a barrier against the expansion of British power and influence right across Asia from the Black Sea to the Pacific. They were agreed in discarding the previous assumption that the existence of neutral territory between the two empires and belonging to neither of them was sufficient protection. The result of this complacency had been, according to Kovalevsky, that 'while we stayed peacefully and unconcernedly within our borders England advanced from India to Lahore, captured the latter, placed her agent in Afghanistan and extended her influence to Herat'.[1] But there was no agreement and much uncertainty as to the minimum risks required to create an adequate barrier. Alexander II was experimenting with peaceful penetration in central Asia, until his main diplomatic effort in Europe brought results. But, as the British had found in the 1830s, the slow and frustrating diplomatic process in Europe could be relieved by direct action in central Asia, whose principalities the expeditions of 1858–9 had shown to be temptingly weak and irritatingly unpredictable. Once the need to counter a threat had been accepted, it was a short step to conceding the need to conquer areas in which the threat might arise. In the British case the step had led to the first Afghan war and the annexation of Sind and the Panjāb. The missions of Khanykov and Ignatyev, by making the new interpretation of world politics look still more convincing, stimulated those of an imperialist temperament and enhanced their prospects of winning the emperor's support for an expansionist policy. Despite Alexander's order of priorities, he was to win a substantial slice of empire in Asia before he had regained the right to maintain his fleet in the Black Sea.

All this Russian military and diplomatic activity in Asia assumed continuing British expansion. In the circumstances this was a reasonable assumption. The Russians had to take into account not only the attacks

[1] Quoted by A. L. Popov, 'Iz istorii zavoevaniya sredney Azii', *Istoricheskie Zapiski* (1940), 204.

on Persia and China by Palmerston's government, but also the British electorate's decisive endorsement of its belligerent policies. In the spring of 1857 the government had been defeated in the Commons over the war with China, but parliamentary disapproval was not echoed by the voters, and at the ensuing election Palmerston was returned to power with an impressive majority. Yet those politicians who had unsuccessfully challenged Palmerston in 1857 persevered with a view of world politics which discounted any Russian threat to India and which was to become identified with the emerging Liberal party. Since the 1830s, Whig and Tory leaders had disputed whether the Russian threat was short-term or long-term and what should be done, in either case, to neutralize it. Soon the very existence of a Russian threat was to become a party issue despite ever more dramatic Russian advances in Asia. There was a British as well as a Russian reaction to the wars of the 1850s. The Russians had begun their systematic counter-offensive just when the reasoning behind British expansion in Asia was being undermined.

What helped to undermine it was mounting scepticism about the methods hitherto thought necessary to defend British interests in both India and China. After the Afghan war, military and civilian leaders in India had avoided policies which might lead to involvement in the politics of Kābul. At first, this had been natural caution in the wake of defeat, but it had gradually been elevated into a strategic doctrine of 'masterly inactivity'. Its most powerful advocate was Sir John Lawrence, ruler of the Panjāb. Its principal assumption was that the British could not add to their security by reaching out for new frontiers in central Asia. The existing frontier was as secure as any frontier could be if it came to a Russian invasion. Greater security against Russia could be won only by promoting conditions beyond the frontier unfavourable to a Russian advance. Ideal for this purpose would be an Afghanistan friendly to the British and hostile to the Russians.

In Lawrence's view there was but one way to obtain this. The Afghans, he argued, were determined at all costs to preserve their freedom and independence. Their friendship depended on the British convincing them by word and deed that they had no designs of any kind on Afghan territory, and that they would abstain totally from interference in Afghanistan's periodic succession struggles. Dost Muḥammad had eventually been convinced, with gratifying results when the British faced their great crisis within India in 1857. As long as neither he nor his successors were given any cause for complaint, their cooperation would be assured in any crisis the British might face beyond the frontier; for the only threat to their independence then would be Russia, whose encroachments they would naturally resist. They might invite to their aid a British army, confident of its withdrawal once the crisis was past. If they did not, the British could wait in their well-prepared positions for a Russsian army which would have already been mauled and harassed by hostile tribesmen as it struggled to keep open long lines of communication and to conquer British India's natural barriers of river and mountain. To secure such beneficial relations with Afghanistan, Lawrence himself would have been willing even to cede Peshawar to Dost Muḥammad and to withdraw behind the Indus. This particular proposal found little support, but his general policy was widely accepted by military and civilian circles in India and by politicians in London. Ironically, the Russian policy of countering an expected British advance by their own expansion got under way during the years 1864–9 when Lawrence himself was viceroy.

Nor did the recent British conflict with China necessarily presage further onslaughts by which the Chinese Empire was to be subjected to some form of British domination. To Muravyov and other Russians particularly interested in China, a clear pattern might seem to have been forming since 1839, but, in fact, official British opinion was hardening against demands of British merchants for still deeper involvement. After the treaty of Nanking, Sino-British trade had failed to boom in the way expected by firms like Jardine, Matheson and Co. Nor did it boom after the treaty of Tientsin. To the merchants it was obvious that restrictions imposed by the Chinese government must be responsible for their subjects failing to buy British goods on the scale once predicted. They urged continued coercion of the imperial authorities to secure a more generous interpretation of the terms of the treaty of Tientsin than either government had intended. The merchants' interpretation was challenged by a British official in a famous report, which attributed the disappointing volume of trade to the inability of British manufactured goods to compete with home products in the largely self-sufficient Chinese economy. Lord Elgin backed the conclusions of the Mitchell Report, and the board of trade convinced the foreign office of their validity.

British policy in the 1860s was designed to promote strict observance of the Treaty of Tientsin by its own merchants as much as by the Chinese government. British politicians and officials were satisfied with the results of the *Arrow* war. They believed that British merchants now had as fair an opportunity for legitimate trade as they could reasonably expect the use of British power to achieve for them. A stable political framework was also necessary for a flourishing commerce, and this would be impaired by any further British coercion. By 1862 British troops were even helping to suppress the Taiping rebellion to accelerate the restoration of imperial control. Despite eloquent mercantile protests, the British government had sensed the danger of going too far. They had no intention of being lured by a mirage of vast commercial profits into actions so destructive of imperial authority that the British would find themselves governing parts of China. That was the way their Indian empire had begun. The Russians would have been relieved to know that China was not meant to become a second India.

In addition to this shift in thinking about long-term strategy in India and China, there was the prospect that British foreign policy might come to be conceived in more pacific terms. Controversy over particular conflicts in the 1850s had led some politicians to a general reappraisal of the role of war in international politics. Since 1815 peace societies, under Quaker inspiration, had campaigned in Great Britain and the United States against the use of war as an instrument of policy. In February 1854 a Quaker delegation had secured an interview with Nicholas I in a direct bid to avert war. During the Crimean War the British peace movement was the object of popular ridicule and hostility, but its political influence grew rather than declined because, as distaste for the war developed within parliament, more politicians took seriously the proposals for mediation and arbitration in time of international crisis, which the peace societies had so long been urging. Though themselves stopping short of outright pacifism, Cobden and Bright had given their powerful support to the movement in the House of Commons. As long ago as 1835-6 Cobden's first pamphlets had inveighed against the prevailing Russophobia. Now Gladstone and his friends drew nearer to a cause with which they were temperamentally already in tune. Although future Liberal governments did not, under Gladstone's leadership, much alter traditional ideas as to the interests a British government was obliged to defend, they were much less ready to assume the existence of a threat to those interests until it was proved, and much more ready to try and deal with a proven threat by peaceful means. When, in 1885, the British and Russian governments were once more involved in a crisis comparable to that of 1853-4, Gladstone prepared for war, but at the same time proffered arbitration.

Around 1860, these trends were only dimly apparent, especially to the outside world. But even had they been fully appreciated, only a very sanguine Russian emperor would have allowed himself to be diverted from policies conceived as a counter to continuing British imperialism over the previous three decades. A pattern seemed to have been established. It might be illusory, it might change; but to be inactive when confronted by hard evidence of Great Britain's expanded territory, and of its military and economic superiority in relation to every state in Asia including Russia and China, would have required an iron nerve, a willingness to take risks, and a quite exceptional sense of control. For all the new trends did was to introduce an element of uncertainty and probable discontinuity into British policy-making. Lawrence's policy of 'masterly inactivity' also required an iron nerve; even its supporters might be panicked into abandoning it in face of a major crisis in central Asia. The policy itself was under constant attack. John Jacob, the ruler of Sind, had in 1856 presented a systematic case for advancing the British frontier to control Quetta and the Bolan Pass, so as to be able to strike more quickly and effectively when the need arose in the direction of Persia, Herat and central Asia. Jacob died in 1858, but Sir Bartle Frere and others continued to advocate a forward policy, which had a good enough prospect of adoption should masterly inactivity come to lack conviction. The China merchants, likewise, would continue to put their case with the same vehemence to successive governments, and it, too, might someday come to look convincing again. And belligerent politicians were just as likely to predominate in London as those with more pacific tendencies. Like the British in the 1830s, Russian leaders had to take one of two risks. An expansionist policy would risk disillusioning the pacifically minded among the British, and make more probable the pursuance of the forward policy the Russians feared. A policy of restraint would risk missing, perhaps for ever, the opportunity to turn the tables on the British in the next war, which might be in the very near future should British belligerence persist despite Russian restraint. A government which had just suffered the humiliation of unexpected defeat and isolation was likely to prefer the first risk. At any rate, this was the one they took.

Events of the 1850s had revived the Great Game, with the Russians this time making the running from the Caucasus to the Pacific. There was no plan of systematic conquest, but the need to anticipate the British everywhere in Asia was firmly established in the thinking of enough leading Russians to ensure that it would powerfully condition official reaction to future external events and policy proposals. But there were also signs in the 1850s that both governments might soon be conducting their rivalry in a context far more complicated and daunting than that provided by the states of Asia and the now quiescent colonies of the Dutch, the Portuguese and the Spaniards. The rising American empire of the United States and the rising French empire of Napoleon III had made significant interventions in Asia. The Russians had been the most persistent of the governments trying to persuade the Japanese to abandon their ancient seclusion. The British, by their 'opening up' of China, had done most to influence Japanese thinking on the matter. But it was the threatening American squadron of Commodore Matthew Perry in 1853-4 which 'opened up' Japan by securing the first formal treaty and the usual concessions for trading facilities and consulates. And 1858-9 saw the beginnings of the French empire in Indo-China, when a missionary campaign to get the backing of their government there finally succeeded, and Napoleon III's ships and troops attacked Tourane and Saigon.

These episodes signified success for American and French advocates of empire in Asia. The British record of prosperity at home and victory abroad invited imitation, and it did not at that time seem unreasonable to associate the success of the British with their empire, and especially with their Asian empire. With Napoleon III on the throne, it was natural for some Frenchmen to revive his uncle's dreams of oriental conquest. 'The Far East will soon be the theatre of great events,' wrote a former missionary to Napoleon III in January 1857. 'If the Emperor wills, France will be able to play an important and glorious role there.' And a commission set up by the emperor to consider the abbé Huc's arguments for a forward policy agreed the time was ripe for France to associate herself 'with the movement of progress, civilization and commercial expansion of which China was going to be the theatre'.[1] They urged a French protectorate over Annam. Perry's 'opening up' of Japan was a particularly dramatic step in the slow realization of an American dream of commercial empire across the Pacific which had been endorsed by Thomas Jefferson. A more grandiose version of the dream was currently being put into circulation by William Henry Seward, who expected the United States eventually to embrace Canada, Mexico and Alaska, and from its great continental base to dominate the markets of Asia, 'the chief theater of events in the world's great hereafter'. Such commercial supremacy would make America the greatest power on earth.[2] Nor were imperialist ideas of this kind confined in the 1850s to France and America. Even Austria had in these years its prophet of oriental empire, a very prominent one in the person of Bruck, who

[1] Quoted by R. S. Thomson, 'The diplomacy of imperialism: France and Spain in Cochin China, 1858–63', *Journal of Modern History*, vol. 12 (1940), 334–56.
[2] Quoted by W. LaFeber, *The New Empire. An Interpretation of American Expansion, 1860–1898* (Ithaca, N.Y., 1963), 24–32.

thought that the Habsburgs should aim not merely at an Austrian-dominated Mitteleuropa but at eventual control of the Dutch East Indies. And one early Japanese reaction to imperialist pressure was to envisage Japan itself in an expansionist role, beginning with the conquest of China.

Advocates of Asian empire from countries other than Great Britain and Russia were still few in number in the 1850s. It was uncertain how far their vision would come to be shared and implemented. With the British welcoming French cooperation against the Chinese and with news of rebellion against the British in India, it was natural for Napoleon III to respond to such ideas. That the expedition to Indo-China was unlikely to be an isolated incident seemed underlined by the appointment in 1860 as minister of marine and colonies of Count Prosper de Chasseloup-Laubat, an ardent propagandist of empire-building in Asia. Civil war and reconstruction meant that American imperialism proceeded more slowly than might have been expected, but enough leading politicians already accepted the doctrine for it to have at the very least a good chance of implementation. Seward himself became Lincoln's secretary of state in 1861. In the case of Japan and Austria, the vision was of a future too remote to be influential. But in all of these countries a working hypothesis about empire in Asia was available for policy-makers should events seem to reinforce its assumptions and make its adoption seem appropriate. The presence of other powerful competitors would then severely test the adequacy of Russian and British interpretations of world politics.

6

Alexander II's counter-offensive 1860–78

The interpretation of international politics adopted by Alexander II in the years after the Crimean War served him admirably for twenty years. Between 1857 and 1877 the Russian government experienced a remarkable run of success and good fortune in its conduct of foreign affairs. Two of the powers which had contributed most to the humiliation of 1856, Austria and France, suffered defeats even more humiliating, though the defeats were not inflicted by Russian armies. The third power, Great Britain, cut a rather poor figure during these years. Rebellion in the emperor's Polish territories was crushed with only a show of international protest, which emphasized the current impotence of the French, the British and the Austrians to exploit it. The crushing of rebellion in the Caucasus reduced the risk of foreign intervention in another sensitive area of the empire. In the wake of the quiet but spectacular advances in east Asia, much of central Asia was brought under Russian control with gratifying ease. The Black Sea clauses of the Treaty of Paris were renounced with only token opposition. The old conservative grouping of Romanovs, Habsburgs and Hohenzollerns was revived, and, within twenty-five years of the ill-starred Menshikov mission to Constantinople, Alexander II's armies were marching against the Ottoman Empire with good prospects of a diplomatic as well as a military triumph.

The remarkable burst of military and diplomatic activity in the immediate aftermath of the Crimean defeat had brought the Russian government striking gains in Asia. The gains were not promptly followed up, and there was something of a pause in Russia's Asian operations during the early 1860s. In 1861 and 1862 the emperor was too absorbed in supervising the massive changes within Russia which he had set in motion by the emancipation of the serfs to spare much attention for developments in either Europe or Asia. In the first half of 1863 the Russian government faced a major insurrection by the Poles, and by May of that year it appeared to Alexander II that the Poles might be backed by Napoleon III to the point of war, with the diplomatic support, at least, of the British and the Austrians. But the pause was short-lived. The Polish revolt collapsed, the anticipated French expedition to the Baltic coast did not materialize, and their attempts at a common front over the Polish question merely revealed the deep conflicts of interest between the French, the British and the Austrians. By July 1863 it was clear that there would be no European war over Poland. In November the Franco-British alliance broke down altogether over British refusal to support Napoleon III's plan for a European congress. By then, fresh Russian advances in Asia had already been authorized.

Both the threat of war and the receding of that threat could serve to bolster the case of those who urged a forward policy in Asia. Military arguments for giving Russia effective striking power in the only part of the world where the British might be rendered vulnerable to the emperor's armies were reinforced. 'In the event of a European war,' wrote the minister of war, D. A. Milyutin, at the time of his government's rejection of foreign demands about Poland, 'we must set especially great store by the occupation of [Khokand], which would bring us near to the northern frontiers of India and facilitate our access to that country. Dominating Khokand, we can constantly threaten the east Indian possessions of England. This is all the more important in that only here can we be dangerous to this enemy of ours.'[1] In 1863, Milyutin was prepared to advance on Khīva and the Amu Darya (Oxus) valley, in the event of the British joining a French attack on Russia. At the same time, the divisions among Russia's former enemies, the fading of any direct threat arising from the Polish revolt, and the preoccupation of the European powers by the autumn of 1863 with a possible Austro-Prussian war, suggested an opportune moment for the sort of strengthening of the Russian position in central Asia which had long been discussed.

At any time there was a good case to be made for military action to strengthen the Russian frontier in central Asia. Since the emergence of the Muscovite state, the steppe frontier east of the Volga had been an unstable and insecure affair of fortified lines, constantly threatening and constantly threatened by the nomadic tribes on whose lands the Russians had encroached. Russian caravans trading with the khanates to the

[1] Quoted by Popov, 'Iz istorii zavoevaniya sredney Azii', 211.

south risked attack; Russian frontier settlers risked enslavement in the khanates themselves. The need for a secure frontier to protect settlers and for a powerful military presence to protect commerce beyond the frontier was unquestioned. When and how the need was to be met was very much open to question because of the great diversion of resources and the effort likely to be required. The attempts that were made resulted from a combination of exceptional energy by the men on the spot and an unusual willingness on the part of the central government to countenance the certain expense and the risk of failure. The frontier had, therefore, been expanded and stabilized spasmodically. It had been advanced several hundred miles, for example, during the fourth decade of the eighteenth century at the expense of the Bashkirs. In the 1830s and 1840s the Kazakh steppe had been brought under effective Russian control. Two fortified lines now stretched out towards the settled khanates of central Asia. From the west, a line of forts had been established along the Syr-Dar'ya from its mouth in the Aral Sea to Ak-Mesjid, captured in 1853 and renamed Perovsk. From the east, the line of forts from Semipalatinsk was extended across the Ili to Vernoye, captured in 1854. It had been intended that these pincers should eventually close, giving Russia a continuous frontier from the Aral Sea to the Irtysh. During the ten years since the capture of Ak-Mesjid, the case for further expeditions to join up the six hundred miles gap had been acknowledged. But, during the Crimean War and after, there had always been more urgent calls on the state's resources.

By 1863, however, the essential conditions for a renewed burst of activity existed. There were men on the spot quite as energetic as Perovsky, the driving force behind the expansion in Nicholas I's reign. In St Petersburg there was greater will for empire-building because Alexander II saw expansion in Asia as an important contribution to rebuilding Russia's position in the world, not simply as part of Russia's ancient and unhurried search for settled frontiers. As soon as possible after the reconnaissances of Khanykov, Ignatyev and Valikhanov, the logical next step in central Asia was authorized. In February 1863, the finance minister, Reutern, and the foreign minister, Gorchakov, could still reasonably argue that the cost was too great and the international situation too delicate. But in the spring of 1863 Colonel Chernyayev scored cheap victories in the course of the reconnaissance expedition which had been authorized, and by the summer the Polish crisis had cooled. While both military and civilian opinion remained divided, Gorchakov now sided with Milyutin in the advice offered to the emperor. Before the end of the year Alexander II accepted the plan proposed by

Milyutin for closing the frontier during the course of 1864. It proved a simple and straightforward operation. In June 1864, after careful preparations, Colonel Verevkin led 1,500 troops against Suzak and Turkistān, while Colonel Chernyayev's force of 2,500 moved on Aulie-Ata. The two expeditions linked up, and the government proclaimed the establishment of a new Khokand Line under the command of Chernyayev.

Chernyayev now went beyond his instructions. In September 1864 he advanced to capture Chimkent, and subsequently he made an unsuccessful bid for Tashkent. This unauthorized initiative was variously greeted in St Petersburg with enthusiasm and dismay. His principal detractor was Gorchakov. The foreign minister had assumed that the purpose of these and similar expeditions was to obtain a secure frontier, and that this would be accomplished once the nomadic tribes had been conquered. The Russian frontier would then march with those of principalities whose rulers were in a position to enter into formal diplomatic relations with the Russian government. An eventual advance to the Arys, a tributary of the Syr Dar'ya, and the capture of Chimkent, had been accepted by the foreign and war ministries alike as contributing to a secure frontier in this sense. The capture of Chimkent had been merely premature. But in trying to take Tashkent, a Khokandese city of a hundred thousand inhabitants, Chernyayev was going beyond the needs of security. Once militarily involved in the settled oasis region of the khanates, Russia would be drawn deeper and deeper into Asia on new paths of expansion, each move requiring further conquests to secure it. For Gorchakov, Russia's interests required a clear, stable frontier adjoining diplomatically approachable states. This had now been achieved, at least in the region east of the Aral Sea.

Milyutin agreed with Gorchakov on the need for a clear policy to guide frontier commanders. He agreed, too, that maintenance of an ever lengthening frontier and responsibility for an ever-growing proportion of the population of central Asia were burdens the government should try to avoid. He therefore endorsed a foreign ministry memorandum prepared on these lines. But he disapproved of Gorchakov's informally defining the limits of Russian advance in his famous circular to foreign capitals of December 1864. In this, Gorchakov compared Russia's position in central Asia with that of the British in India, the French in north Africa, the United States in north America, and the Dutch in south-east Asia, all of whom had been 'irresistibly forced, less by ambition than by imperious necessity, into this onward movement where the greatest difficulty is to know where to stop'. Gorchakov claimed that the Russian government did know where to stop. Its security problem in central Asia had concerned 'half savage, nomad populations, possessing no fixed social organization'. The recent extension of the frontier had put Russia 'in the immediate neighbourhood of the agricultural and commercial populations of Khokand. We find ourselves in the presence of a more solid and compact, less unsettled and better organized social state, fixing for us with geographical precision the limit up to which we are bound to advance and at which we must halt.'[1]

Since the Russians did not, in fact, halt at the frontier of 1864, Gorchakov's circular was quickly discredited, and later Russian reassurances to the outside world were treated with scepticism. Ever since, the intentions of the Russian government at this time have been debated, with deceit, muddle-headedness, and weakness in face of military insubordination among the explanations offered for the failure of Russian deeds to correspond with Gorchakov's words. As to Gorchakov himself, there is no more reason to doubt the sincerity of his belief that the Russian frontier *could* be stabilized at that point than to doubt that of Peel twenty years earlier in believing that the annexation of Sind and the Panjāb would be avoided, or that of Hastings in assuming thirty years earlier still that the 1813 limits of British India would be preserved. Gorchakov was too experienced a diplomat not to appreciate the effect of making clearcut promises on the eve of their violation. He believed in the practicality of his frontier principle. On the other hand, he knew from Chernyayev's conduct that the frontier *would* be stabilized at that point only if Chernyayev and other ambitious soldiers were kept under control. By committing the Russian government publicly to observe clearly stated limits to its expansion in central Asia, he hoped, perhaps, that the expectations of foreign governments would curb any temptation Alexander II might feel to discard the principle he was at present willing to accept. If so, he failed. Conceding Gorchakov's sincerity of purpose leaves unsettled the intentions of the emperor himself, who alone could make decisions of this weight. Was subsequent Russian expansion his deliberate aim, or did he merely feel obliged to confirm the unexpected triumphs of border warfare?

It is possible to avoid the stark choice between a central government dragged reluctantly into unwanted expansion by ambitious frontier commanders, and a programme of systematic empire-building directed from St Petersburg. Had Gorchakov studied more closely the example

[1] Quoted by Firuz Kazemzadeh, *Russia and Britain in Persia, 1864–1914. A Study in Imperialism* (New Haven, Conn., 1968), 8–9.

of the British in India, which he cited in his November circular, he would have realized that their expansion had not been in response to the activities of 'half-savage nomad populations'. Peel had invoked his 'uncontrollable principle' to justify the conquest of societies very like the khanates, whose proximity Gorchakov expected to free his government from such 'imperious necessity' altogether. The khanates were turbulent, unstable, hostile to Russia and open to foreign intrigue. They would make it no easier for the Russians to feel secure on their new frontier than had the nomads on the old one. Milyutin understood better than Gorchakov that the advances already made would not solve the frontier's military problems. They would simply put the Russians in a more favourable position for dealing with them. He reluctantly accepted Chernyayev's explanation of the seizure of Chimkent as necessary for the proper securing of the gains he had been authorized to make. He also understood what acceptance of such 'necessary' insubordination would imply. 'Fine,' he remarked, 'but who will guarantee that after Chimkent Chernyayev won't consider it necessary to take Tashkent, then Khokand, and there will be no end to it.'[1]

By the 1860s Russia's position in central Asia had, as Sir John Malcolm had predicted, become much like that of the British in India in the early nineteenth century. Like India at that time, central Asia was an area of warring principalities. The three khanates, Khokand, Bukhārā and Khīva, were in a state of almost continuous war with one another, and with the nomads, who were an even greater threat to their security than to that of Russia. The Russians now replaced the nomads as the threat from the steppe lands, and the khanates were incapable of uniting to meet it. As Ignatyev had found on his mission of 1858, the rulers of central Asia were as likely to see Russia as a potential ally against one another as a threat to themselves. The Russians had already involved themselves in the region's struggles by their search for a defensible frontier. Although it was intended to leave the settled area alone, the army's natural preference for a frontier in a fertile rather than desert region meant some encroachment on lands claimed by and disputed among the existing rulers. Taking Ak-Mesjid (Perovsk) and joining the lines had meant the occupation of Khokand's outlying territories and the weakening of the khan's grip on towns like Tashkent, which the amir of Bukhārā also coveted. Whether they desired the role or not, the Russians had already made themselves the most potent force for change in an area of shifting frontiers and allegiances. Like the

[1] Quoted by D. Mackenzie, 'Expansion in central Asia: St Petersburg versus the Turkestan generals (1863–1866)', *Canadian Slavic Studies*, vol. 3 (1969), 293.

British in India, of course, they did have an alternative to exercising this power; they could simply gaze aloofly from behind well-defended frontiers at the spectacle of lesser states battling for supremacy over one another. This had been the course favoured at the turn of the century by many East India Company officials, and something of this sort was rather vaguely envisaged by Gorchakov in his circular. But, given the hypothesis about Eurasian politics favoured by Alexander II since the end of the Crimean War, the emperor could no more be indifferent to the struggles for power immediately beyond his own territories than could Wellesley in India during the Napoleonic Wars.

For most Russians officially concerned with international problems, it was a fixed point that the British would try to exploit the region's instability and strife and, by developing diplomatic and commercial links with the khanates, make their own political influence predominate. They thought it no coincidence that Afghanistan, an ally of the British and in receipt of British military and financial aid, had been vigorously pursuing territorial claims against Bukhārā. They also took it for granted that British policies must be frustrated, and that their own influence must flourish throughout central Asia. It was the means rather than the end which caused dispute. One uncontroversial method, used so effectively by the British, was the promotion of trade, especially as in the 1860s the raw materials and markets of central Asia were becoming of increasing value in themselves to the Russian economy. The convenience of developing the supply of raw cotton from relatively local sources was underlined by the Russian textile industry's difficulties during the American Civil War. But even trade could be promoted only by forceful diplomacy because the khans did not wish to grant the rights and privileges for Russian merchants which were demanded.

Again, the Russians found themselves faced with the same problem in relation to Khīva, Bukhārā and Khokand that the British had faced in relation to Sind, the Panjāb and Afghanistan. The emperor and his advisers were reluctant to embark on a policy of progressive annexation with all its added expense and administrative responsibilities. At the same time, they deemed it essential to have friendly, docile and cooperative neighbours, undisputedly linked to the Russian economic system and manifestly within the Russian political orbit. They would have preferred to create this situation by diplomacy rather than by war, with all its attendant risks of failure and international complications. But diplomacy could scarcely be successful unless the khans were as weak as the amirs of Sind had been in the 1830s, or strong enough to be taken seriously as allies and barrier states, like the Panjāb until the death of Ranjit Singh or Afghanistan during the later part of Dost Muḥammad's reign. And, as the British had found, even such favourable conditions tended to be temporary. The Russians confronted rulers who felt strong enough to defy Russian diplomatic approaches, but whom the Russians knew were too weak and unstable to be reliable neighbours. If normal diplomatic manœuvres failed, the Russian government would have to abandon its basic aims in central Asia or use military force to win compliance. The emperor made no bones about welcoming a belligerent course, provided it was successful. 'A glorious affair' was his terse reaction to the unauthorized capture of Chimkent, and he made an identical comment when Chernyayev later took Tashkent in defiance of orders from St Petersburg.[1] But perhaps, like their British counterparts, his advisers were reluctant to admit how dependent they were likely to be on local military action to implement their policy, and on local military advice as to how much action was 'necessary'.

The status of Tashkent underlined their dilemma. Tashkent, a large and important trading centre, had since 1808 been included in the dominions of the khan of Khokand; previously it had acknowledged the suzerainty of the amir of Bukhārā, and the present amir schemed to regain it. In practice, it was largely independent. Its leaders were well aware that their future might lie with the emperor of Russia or the amir of Bukhārā rather than the khan of Khokand, and they were divided as to what should be their policy in the current power struggle in central Asia. Roughly speaking, the religious leaders looked to Bukhārā as the principal centre of Islam in central Asia, and the mercantile community tended to look to Russia. Russian policy in the months after Chernyayev's unsuccessful assault was to encourage Tashkent's independence of Khokand. Loss of the town would weaken Khokand, and its capacity to disrupt Russian trade with Kashgar, which the recent treaty with China had given the Russians the opportunity to develop. Chernyayev's intrigues with pro-Russian elements in Tashkent were encouraged, with the aim of converting it into a Russian satellite. But given the amir's designs on Tashkent and the presence in the town of a pro-Bukharan group, Russian policy implicitly demanded military action by Chernyayev if it looked like being frustrated by Bukharan intervention.

When this happened in May-June 1865, Chernyayev seized the excuse he had been looking for to storm the town. This was contrary

[1] Quoted by D. Mackenzie, 'Expansion in central Asia: St Petersburg versus the Turkestan generals (1863-1866)', *Canadian Slavic Studies*, vol. 3 (1969), 293 n. 24, 299.

to telegraphed intructions, which he concealed from his subordinates, and his timing may have been influenced by the impending arrival of Kryzhanovsky, the new governor of Orenburg, who was thought to want the credit for such a spectacular blow himself. But, as with Chimkent, Chernyayev's action was no more than premature. It was in accordance with the spirit of official policy, which required that Russian influence in Tashkent should prevail over that of any rival; it violated only the letter of his instructions, which required that he should await sufficient reinforcements to avoid another repulse. Chernyayev rightly believed that success would be adequate vindication.

The storming of Tashkent left the government in St Petersburg still confused and divided as to how central Asia could best be controlled without actually incorporating it in the Russian Empire. Whether Tashkent should be annexed or not was still a matter for dispute. The Moscow–Tashkent Company was set up on government initiative and with government financial backing to strengthen the town's commercial interest in an intimate political relationship with Russia. Meanwhile, Chernyayev undertook further unauthorized measures, this time against Bukhārā, which brought about his downfall – but whose consequences, in effect, resolved the government's dilemma. Chernyayev tried high-handed diplomacy to convince the amir that he had no alternative to closer ties with Russia. When the amir, Muẓaffar al-Dīn, refused to be intimidated and replied in kind, Chernyayev, at the beginning of 1866, initiated hostilities.

War with Bukhārā was more than premature as far as the government was concerned, and Chernyayev's recall had been decided even before it started. But, although Chernyayev behaved clumsily, it is difficult to see how more skilled diplomacy could have given the Russian government what it wanted. The actual Russian demands were, admittedly, of a most modest kind, commercial in character, and not infringing the amir's sovereignty, but Muẓaffar al-Dīn could be under no illusion as to their significance. They were the thin end of the wedge, like the first British treaties with, say, Sind, and would be followed by increasingly onerous demands which it would be increasingly difficult to resist. He preferred to fight for his independence as the khan of Khokand had done, rather than voluntarily surrender it by degrees; and there was enough hostility to Russia and self-confidence among leading Bukharans to ensure resistance even had he himself responded differently. The emperor wanted Russian predominance to be established in the near future, and on a lasting basis. Diplomacy without a show of force was unlikely to achieve this. By his persistent insubordination and especially by committing the government to war with Bukhārā, Chernyayev demonstrated that war could bring the desired result quickly and cheaply, that the military risks were negligible, and the international consequences not much less so.

When the war started this was far from clear to the emperor and his advisers. Despite easy victories they exploited them cautiously. Chernyayev had encountered an initial setback before his replacement, but his successor, Romanovsky, defeated the Bukharan army in May 1866, and took the opportunity of seizing the Khokandese town of Khojand as valuable in operations against either Bukhārā ot Khokand. Khojand was annexed, although the khan was not currently in conflict with Russia, and it was decided that war conditions required the ending of the anomalous position of Tashkent, also by annexation. After unsuccessful peace talks the war against Bukhārā was renewed in the autumn of 1866, and once more the Russians were victorious. The whole of 1867 was taken up with abortive negotiations. The negotiators got so far as to agree on a draft treaty, but the amir stalled over its ratification. Meanwhile, the Russians consolidated their gains in central Asia since 1864 by creating a separate administration for Turkistān, based on Tashkent, with General von Kaufman as its first governor-general. The amir tried to organize a coalition of central Asian rulers against Russia. He failed, but despite this, and despite the probability of further defeat, he faced rebellion if he did not reopen the struggle. In the spring of 1868 a holy war was proclaimed. The two armies faced each other on the river Zarafshān, which the Russians forced in May 1868, and went on to capture without a fight the legendary city of Samarqand. The Bukharans then made a stand, but were routed. This time the Russian victory was decisive, and peace was quickly made in the summer on 1868. At the beginning of the year the khan of Khokand had also accepted the terms demanded by the Russian government.

The actual terms conceded by the rulers of Khokand and Bukhārā in 1868 were not in themselves severe. Apart from a war indemnity imposed on Bukhārā and recognition of recent Russian annexations, the treaties allowed Russian commercial agencies to be set up in each of the khanates and enabled Russian merchants to trade with greater freedom and security. A fixed duty of $2\frac{1}{2}$ per cent ad valorem on imports was agreed. Samarqand, of great strategic value to an army overawing the town of Bukhārā itself, was to be temporarily occupied by the Russians. The Russian government could claim that both khanates remained independent states, as Gorchakov's circular had forecast they would. But their capacity for independent action beyond their frontiers had received a fatal blow by the repeated demonstrations of Russian military superiority. At last the Russian government had stumbled upon, or rather had been shown by the initiative of its frontier commanders, the means of realizing its policy in central Asia: the annexation of enough key bases and areas to ensure a commanding position in the event of further war; just enough military operations to convince neighbouring rulers of the hopelessness of resistance; and treaties symbolizing the new relationship of such modest provision as to deprive the British of their most obvious grounds for protest.

It was already clear, however, that Gorchakov's circular had been unwise. The Russian government had shown notable restraint in negotiating with the rulers of Khokand and Bukhārā. Limitations on their freedom in the conduct of foreign relations, the usual badge of protectorate status, had not been insisted upon. But the khanates had shrunk both in size and status. The temporary occupation of Samarqand ended in annexation, as had that of Tashkent and Khojand, and no one seriously doubted the khanates' future helplessness in relation to Russia. The impression Gorchakov had given of a new and final Russian frontier, leaving the khanates untouched save for occasional punitive expeditions and the intangible transmission of Russian civilization, had been dispelled in such a way as to make the whole memorandum look deliberately ambiguous and misleading. The Russian government did not, therefore, get the credit for restraint in the hour of victory which it might otherwise have enjoyed, though it is possible, of course, that the restraint would have been less had the circular not raised foreign expectations. But there was no doubt that the discrediting of the circular by events so soon afterwards could be exploited by those in Great Britain and India wishing to reactivate alarm about Russian expansion in Asia.

Nevertheless, reaction in Great Britain was slow to take effect. There were some resemblances between the 1860s and the years which had witnessed the first great British scare about a Russian threat to India. As well as the dramatic Russian gains in Asia, there was another Polish revolt and its repression to generate anti-Russian feeling. In two articles for the *Quarterly Review* in 1865, Sir Henry Rawlinson, like a latter-day Evans, placed the Gorchakov circular and the recent Russian expansion in historical perspective, prophesied the direction of future expansion, educated his readers as to the complex political and military geography of central Asia, and urged the need of a more active policy by the British beyond their Indian frontiers. But there was, as yet, no revival of Russophobia. As around 1830, agitation for parliamentary reform competed strongly for public attention, and other events abroad like the American Civil War and the dramatic crises involving Prussia were more compelling than remote and relatively small-scale wars in central Asia, whose effects were by no means obvious to a new generation. 'To those who remember the Russophobia of 1838-39,' commented Rawlinson in the first of his two articles, 'the indifference of the English public to the events now passing in Central Asia must appear one of the strangest instances of reaction in Modern History.'

But public opinion had been slow to take alarm in the earlier period for much the same reasons. The main difference lay in government attitudes. Ellenborough and Wellington had responded relatively quickly in 1828-9, and Palmerston in 1832-3, to an essentially new interpretation of unexpected events. Ministers in the 1860s watched instead the unfolding of developments long predicted, most of them remembered the crises of the 1830s, and they were fully aware of the possible implications of Russia's forward policy. But they were no longer clear as to what should be done about it. Memories of the Afghan war and the Crimean War stimulated no desire to risk similar military adventures as a check to Russia. Direct aid to Bukhārā and Khokand was impracticable. Lawrence's views had calmed some of the fears about India, and as long as Lawrence remained viceroy there would be no demands from the man on the spot for prompt action. As long as Russian expansion was confined to Asia other European governments had no interest in the matter, and, in any case, the period 1864-8 was not one in which a coalition against Russia would have been relevant to any other government's interests. The mood of the 1860s in British government circles – and there were four governments during the five years of Russian activity down to the treaty with Bukhārā – consistently favoured coming to terms with the Russian government by a deal over central Asia, rather than throwing down a challenge in the manner of Ellenborough and Palmerston.

So, despite the transformation of central Asian politics to Russia's advantage and despite the expectation of further amendments to Gorchakov's forecast, the British did not respond in the belligerent style which had occasioned the Russian forward policy in the first place. Too much scepticism had grown up as to the efficacy of extending still farther the frontiers of India as advocated by Rawlinson and his associates for it to seem an obvious response. What seemed the more obvious response at this time was to try to persuade the Russian government to make some more formal commitment to limit its advance than had been provided by the dubious reassurances of 1864. But ministers in London came up against two difficulties in attempting this. First, there was the natural difficulty of getting the Russian government to make such a commitment when it had no pressing reason for doing so. Secondly, the British had to make up their minds what limitation they were willing to put on their own activities in central Asia as a *quid pro quo*. And it was the second difficulty that proved the harder to resolve. There was general agreement among British leaders that Russia could not be allowed to advance into Afghanistan, which it was deemed essential to keep as a barrier between the two empires. There was profound uncertainty as to what sort of barrier the British wanted Afghanistan to become. A forward policy was out of favour, but Lawrence's view that Afghanistan should be treated as an entirely independent state diminished in appeal as the Russians advanced in its direction.

The problem emerged slowly as the British adjusted themselves to the scale of Russia's achievements. Lord John Russell, foreign secretary in Palmerston's government, had made the first approach in August 1865. He suggested an exchange of notes recording the firm resolve of the British and Russian governments to maintain 'the present state of possession in central Asia' and to respect the independence of Persia. Made just after the storming of Tashkent, when the Russian government itself would have been hard put to it to define what 'the present state of possession in central Asia' actually was, the proposal had no chance of success. It was met by a restatement of Russian aims as secure frontiers, regularized commerce, and peace. The reaction of the India Office to Russell's draft was more significant. They persuaded him to weaken the original wording so that there was no actual undertaking which might inhibit future viceroys from making frontier changes. A proposal more acceptable to both sides than the 'freezing' of existing frontiers emanated from Lawrence himself in 1867 when he suggested an understanding with the Russian government on a line beyond which they would not advance. In 1869, on retirement from his post, he wanted it made clear to the emperor that violation of such an agreed line would be automatically followed by war. Since the British thought in terms of the northern frontier of Afghanistan as such a line, and as the Russians were willing to regard Afghanistan as outside their sphere of influence, this seemed a good starting-point in the search for agreement.

Between 1869 and 1873 discussions took place in which Clarendon, and after his death in 1870, Granville, tried to persuade the Russian government to agree on what constituted the northern frontier of

Afghanistan. The principal dispute concerned Badakshān. Since the death of Dost Muḥammad in 1863 Afghanistan had undergone its customary succession struggle from which Shēr ʿAlī had emerged victorious. He proceeded to assert his control over those border areas whose allegiance had become uncertain. Badakshān was one of these. Its position made it of great strategic value to an army threatening Bukhārā, which disturbed the Russians, or to an army threatening the passes of the Hindu Kush, which disturbed the British. The local military superiority they had already won in relation to Bukhārā made it easier for the Russians to give way, and they wanted their imminent conquest of a third khanate, Khīva, to give rise to as little tension as possible. In January 1873 Gorchakov conceded the line which the British, without consulting the amir, had claimed for Shēr ʿAlī. Granville thus won a technical victory, but one which merely signified growing Russian confidence. Moreover, given the guarded terms in which Gorchakov accepted the British point of view, the Russians were not conceding very much. They gave themselves ample room to retreat if the British information about the lie of the frontier proved incorrect, which it turned out to be, or if the British failed to keep the amir under control, as they pointedly assumed it was within the British power to do.

This last proviso showed that the implications of a restrictive line were more awkward for the British than for the Russians. Violation of the line by, say, the Bukharans would amount to Russian aggression in the eyes of the British; but violation of the line by the Afghans would, it was clear, be regarded by the Russians as evidence of British hostility. This was the weakness of the otherwise clear and mutually agreeable concept, which had been implicit in the Russo-British conversations, of each empire exercising predominant influence over technically independent neighbours. Mayo, Lawrence's successor as viceroy, suggested to his own government in 1869 that Great Britain should claim the right of influence and punitive intervention in Afghanistan, Kalat, and Yarkand (eastern Turkistān); Russia in the khanates. The Russian government already exercised effective control over Khokand and Bukhārā; it was about to force the submission of Khīva. Its tier of compliant buffer states would then be virtually complete, though it would be unlikely to concede a British right to predominance in eastern Turkistān. The British Indian authorities were in an altogether less powerful position. They could control Kalat and the Bolan Pass, as John Jacob had pointed out in his advocacy of a forward policy; they had no immediate prospect of controlling Afghanistan or of doing much more than trying to counter Russian influence in eastern Turkistān.

Afghanistan was the real test of whether such a means of keeping the two empires apart and at peace in Asia would work. Both Lawrence and Mayo had given military and financial aid to Shēr ʿAlī once he had established himself, and he had shown himself willing to listen to British representations on border hostilities in areas important to Russia. But the British relationship with Kābul was not comparable to Russia's relationship with the khanates; Afghanistan was not a client state whose policies could be dictated from London or Calcutta. Yet if the British failed to control Afghan activities in sensitive border areas, the Russian government would have an excuse, should it be needed, for discarding previous assurances that Afghanistan was outside its own sphere of influence. On the other hand, if the British tried to force compliance on the amir, as the Russians had done with their neighbours, they would face a far tougher struggle and, in the event of failing again, might drive the amir into the arms of Russia.

The Russian position was strengthened by expeditions against Kulja and Khīva. One of the reasons for the Russians wishing to dominate Khokand had been to facilitate their commercial links with China in accordance with the treaty of Peking. After 1863 a rebellion by its Muslim subjects in eastern Turkistān had deprived the Chinese emperor of control over the area with which Russia hoped to develop contact. In the late 1860s a former Khokandese officer, Yaʿqūb Bey, who in 1853 had defended Ak-Mesjid (Perovsk) against the Russians, carved out an independent state based on Kashgar. He showed himself to be hostile to Russia and friendly to the British in India and to the Ottoman Empire. In 1870–1 his power seemed to be spreading to Kulja, important to the Russians in relation to their access to China. In 1871 Russian forces occupied Kulja, which put them in a good position to attack Kashgar. Yaʿqūb Bey accepted in 1872 the same sort of commercial treaty as had been imposed on Khokand and Bukhārā, though he was not brought under Russian control in the same way. Having achieved their immediate objective and countered the threat to Kulja, the Russian government could switch their attention back to a long-planned expedition against Khīva. A British mission obtained a similar treaty with Yaʿqūb Bey the following year and thus signified their intention of resisting Russian claims to predominance in Kashgar, but the fact was that the Russians could easily put an army in Kashgar and the British could not. And Kashgar, although separated from Kashmir by an impregnable mountain barrier and hence not itself forming part of a Russian invasion route to India, could be of crucial importance if the

Russians approached India across the Pamirs farther to the west. If friendly to the Russians, it could furnish all the supplies an invading army would need; if hostile, it could offer a fatal threat to their communications.

A favourable response over Badakshān had eventually been elicited from Gorchakov as part of his diplomatic preparation for the expedition against Khīva. The slaving centre of Khīva represented the same kind of obstacle to Russian security and commerce as the other khanates had done, and its subjection would open a shorter trade route to central Asia via the Volga and the Caspian. A trading station had been established in 1869 on the eastern shores of the Caspian in territory claimed by the khan of Khīva. In view of the failure of 1839, careful planning had been going on since 1870, and finally in May 1873 Khīva was conquered in a swift campaign. The peace treaty reduced the khanate to the status of a Russian protectorate, and transferred to St Petersburg control of Khīva's foreign policy. Khīva was, like Khokand and Bukhārā, substantially reduced in size; the Russian frontier was advanced to the right bank of the Amu Darya, and they controlled the east coast of the Caspian and the Ust-Urt plateau.

The way was opened for the obvious next stage in the Russian advance – Merv, near the ill-defined Persian and Afghan borders. Beyond Merv lay Herat, part of Shēr ʿAlī's dominions and the legendary key to India. The absorption of Merv was generally expected by British observers. Russian assurances that this was not so were unlikely to be taken seriously. Count Shuvalov had, after all, been sent to London expressly to convince the British government that the attack on Khīva would be a minor punitive expedition, and its conqueror, von Kaufman, had been warned to avoid any extension of Russia's frontiers. But, as usual, unanswerable military arguments emerged as to why such restraint was impossible, and similar arguments could be expected to emerge again. Not that any British political leader imagined an indefinite Russian advance with the aim of conquering India. But the massive extension of Russian power in central Asia meant that the aim of the late 1850s of preparation for a future war looked like being realized once Merv had been taken, the Persian and Afghan borders reached, and Herat had been brought into striking distance. Not only had Alexander II acquired for Russia a potentially valuable empire, but in a crisis originating in Europe or anywhere else, the British would know that if their government committed them to war they would have to fight off a direct threat to their Indian empire. Evans's vision of a Russian army approaching India via the Caspian and Khīva had come close to reality, even if it had taken nearly fifty years longer than he had expected.

The new Russian power in Asia was accompanied by signs that recovery in Europe was now complete. In 1870 the clauses of the treaty of Paris neutralizing the Black Sea were at last renounced. Austria and Prussia had long been willing to support the Russians on this; a circular had been drafted in 1866, but the emperor still hesitated to make the move. The collapse of France was deemed the appropriate moment. At the news of the surrender of Napoleon III at Sedan, Alexander II is said to have crossed himself and exclaimed, 'Thank God, Sevastopol is now avenged.'[1] The unilateral abrogation aroused more opposition from the British than had been predicted, but they were in no position to fight about it in isolation. Nor was Gladstone's government so minded. A conference in London the following year regularized the proceeding in a manner satisfactory to them. Then, between 1872 and 1874, a series of meetings attended by the German, Russian and Austrian emperors and their foreign ministers restored the conservative grouping of pre-Crimean Europe. It was still fragile, but from the Russian point of view it offered better prospects of security than any other diplomatic order. And Milyutin's earlier army reforms were capped in 1874 by sweeping changes which recognized some of the lessons of Prussian victories. It would take time to rebuild the Black Sea defences, to consolidate the Dreikaiserbund, and to restructure the army, but with solid military achievement in Asia, growing diplomatic success in Europe, and a more efficient social and administrative framework in Russia itself, Alexander II might claim to have presided over Russia's return to the ranks of the great world powers.

The events leading up to a new Russo-Turkish war in 1877 seemed to confirm the recovery of Russia's diplomatic and military strength, and to suggest, moreover, that Russian leaders had learned the lessons of the 1853-4 crisis. The new crisis originated in the summer of 1875 in the Turkish province of Herzegovina, where a revolt broke out and persisted despite Turkish efforts to quell it. Gorchakov and the Austrian foreign minister, Andrássy, cooperated to find some formula for a cease-fire and reforms to meet rebel grievances, and Bismarck promised German backing for any programme they agreed. The Dreikaiserbund was working effectively. When the Andrássy Note embodying their proposals got nowhere and the revolt spread, the three governments produced in May 1876 a fresh set of proposals

[1] Quoted by W. E. Mosse, *The European Powers and the German Question, 1848-1871* (Cambridge, 1958), 342-3, n. 7.

known as the Berlin Memorandum. Disraeli's government, which had replaced Gladstone's in 1874, showed its resentment at the initiative being held by the Dreikaiserbund by direct overtures to the Russian government, and by admonitory gestures as in the rejection of the Berlin Memorandum and the sending of a British squadron to Besika Bay. The crisis worsened with Serbia and Montenegro deciding on war against the Turks, revolt breaking out in Bulgaria, and upheaval in Constantinople, where two successive sultans were deposed in the summer of 1876. The breakup of the Ottoman Empire seemed once more at hand, yet the Russian and Austrian governments continued to see eye to eye. They agreed at Reichstadt in July 1876 on the various gains they would make according to the extent of the Turkish collapse, and on the terms they would insist upon if the Turks won. It was Serbia which collapsed, not the Turks, and a Russian ultimatum secured them an armistice. Alexander II publicly proclaimed his readiness for war if the Turks did not concede autonomy to the rebellious provinces despite their victory over the already autonomous Serbia. Partial Russian mobilization was ordered.

The Russian government was taking a bold initiative in a crisis which seemed to be taking more the shape of 1828 than of 1853. Echoes of the latter soon followed, only to be lost again. The Constantinople Conference, held at Great Britain's suggestion, found a formula for peace satisfactory to the European representatives. As in 1853, the Turks prevented the powers settling their own affairs peacefully at Turkish expense. They rejected the conference programme, and proclaimed their own new constitution for the Ottoman Empire. But it seemed less certain that they could divide the powers as successfully as in 1853. The British government faced strong anti-Turkish feeling at home owing to Turkish atrocities in Bulgaria, and the government itself was deeply divided. The chief regret of Lord Salisbury, British delegate to the conference and secretary of state for India, was that the conference's failure meant the fading of prospects for a deal with Ignatyev, the Russian ambassador at Constantinople, over central Asia, and for this he would personally have gladly sacrificed the Turks. As the threat of war grew, strains developed in the Austro-Russian alliance, but great care was taken this time to come to terms with Vienna over Austrian interests in the coming conflict. The Russian government finally went to war with the Ottoman Empire in April 1877 after unprecedented diplomatic preparations. Alexander II seemed about to exact his revenge for the events of 1853–6.

So far, the gratifying realization of his objectives abroad had vindicated those speculations about the future which had seemed so appropriate to Alexander II twenty years before in the aftermath of defeat. Interpreting events within the framework they provided had helped him and his advisers to exploit the many opportunities which came their way to strengthen the Russian Empire. Urged by some advisers to concentrate on Europe, by others to concentrate on Asia, the emperor had discovered he could have it both ways – the restoration of security in Europe and the acquisition of an empire of great strategic and economic value in Asia. Alexander's policy has often been described as vacillating between the extremes of advice offered by his foreign minister on the one hand, and his war minister on the other, but he appears rather to have been tentatively probing in a number of different directions to see how far he could safely go in measures to revive Russian power without provoking a premature war. He was ready enough to listen to warnings that the moment was not ripe for a forward policy, but whenever the moment did seem ripe he consistently backed the expansionists among his advisers. The assertion of Russian predominance by war and diplomacy in states adjoining his empire from the Balkans to the Amur was an essential theme of Alexander II's foreign policy, and down until 1877 he had calculated the risks and taken his chances with striking success.

7

The Russians and the British lose confidence, 1878-94

The working hypothesis which had served Alexander II so well between 1857 and 1877 identified Great Britain as his principal enemy in Europe and Asia; it assumed that this enmity could be neutralized by extending the area of Russian control in Asia, and by diplomatic action in Europe to end Russia's isolation and to deprive the British of allies. In the ten years after 1877, Alexander II and, after his assassination in 1881, his son Alexander III, continued to interpret events and take decisions broadly within this framework of assumptions, but each ruler suffered such major setbacks that by the late 1880s the way was open for fresh interpretations of world politics. Although the Russian armed forces continued to push back the possible limits of British influence in Asia by further dramatic advances, this was outweighed by alarming checks in Europe. Russian hopes of permanent freedom from attack through the Straits as a result of political changes in the Balkans faded. Alliance with the Habsburgs and the Hohenzollerns, which had been thought a necessary accompaniment to securing such changes and to isolating the British, weakened and eventually collapsed. The British were able to exploit Russia's embarrassments in the Balkans as some compensation for their deteriorating position in Asia.

The first check to the Russian leaders' certainty that they understood how to get under control the potential threats in the international situation came in 1878. Careful preparations for a war to give Russia once and for all that controlling position in relation to the Ottoman Empire which had eluded Nicholas I went wrong. The war itself had not gone according to plan. After its initial success in July 1877, the Russian army was prevented from making a rapid march on Constantinople by the prolonged defence of Plevna, which was not taken until December 1877. Nor was progress on the Asian front much faster, Kars not falling until November. Although this military setback simply postponed Turkish defeat, the heavy losses and angry frustration endured unexpectedly for so many months inclined Alexander II to listen sympathetically to Ignatyev and others, who mirrored the general mood in the country when they urged Russia's entitlement to a peace drastic enough to satisfy South Slav aspirations and to make sure that the Russians did not in future have to mount a full-scale war every time they deemed it necessary to intimidate the sultan. The assurances given to the Austro-Hungarian government seemed to have been left behind by events in which the Austrians had played a purely passive role. The warnings of Gorchakov and Shuvalov against a settlement unacceptable to the Austrians and the British failed to carry conviction as Russian forces approached Constantinople in January 1878. Even Gorchakov made no serious attempt to challenge Ignatyev's draft treaty when it was discussed at an imperial council the same month. In the last week of February the Russians occupied San Stefano on the Sea of Marmara, six miles from Constantinople, and the treaty of San Stefano was signed on 3 March 1878.

Serbia, Montenegro and Rumania were to become fully independent states, the first two considerably enlarged. Kars, Ardahan and Batum were among the substantial gains in Asia. But the central provision of Ignatyev's treaty was a large Bulgarian principality, whose borders were to reach the Aegean Sea, to run less than a hundred miles from Constantinople, and to be within easy military reach of Russia's own frontiers. It was to remain within the Ottoman Empire, but the Turks were to do little except receive tribute. The Bulgarians were to enjoy full autonomy, and, while they were to have a national militia, the Turks could quarter none of their own troops there and could move them through Bulgaria only under strict conditions. The Russian government was to supervise the establishment of the new regime and to occupy Bulgaria for up to two years. Ignatyev assumed that the new Bulgaria would constitute a Russian sphere of influence stretching almost to Constantinople, and depriving the Turks of any effective defence against Russian power. Had the terms been allowed to stand, Alexander II could have claimed a purely Russian solution of the 'Eastern Question', and a dominant position in western Asia to add to his triumphs farther east. In fact, he had to consent to their substantial modification, which restored the uncertainty and insecurity the war had been designed to eliminate.

Alexander II was, of course, aware that such a treaty would meet with British and Austrian opposition, but until April 1878 he was fully prepared to fight in defence of the settlement his armies had won. He intended that they should occupy Constantinople and seize the Bosphorus as the means of keeping British warships out of the Black Sea. Russian troops on the frontiers of Austria–Hungary were reinforced in preparation for war. The value of Russian conquests in central Asia in helping to counter British hostility in Europe was at last to be demonstrated. Turkish missions to Kābul in 1877, inspired by the British ambassador in Constantinople, had failed to mobilize Muslim hostility to Russia. Now Russian forces were to move towards India along the three invasion routes of Merv, Kābul and Kashgar, and General Stoletov was sent to Kābul to negotiate a treaty with Afghanistan, once declared outside Russia's sphere of influence. War looked the probable outcome of the crisis. In the previous summer, Disraeli's government had sent the British fleet to Besika Bay, and had threatened war if Constantinople were occupied; the warning had been repeated in December 1877, and their fleet had been ordered to pass through the Dardanelles in February. Cabinet divisions had made it difficult for Disraeli to follow the sort of bold, assertive policy which he saw as appropriate to a great Eurasian empire, but by the end of March the hesitant Derby had been replaced as foreign secretary by Salisbury, whose experience at the India Office had convinced him of the need to negotiate, but only from a position of strength. The Austrians were divided and hesitant about a final breach, but they too made ostentatious preparations to improve their bargaining position.

In the event, Alexander II backed down before convincing evidence that Russian resources were inadequate for such a war. He had not been deterred by warnings from his foreign and finance ministries, but he was now receiving military advice he could scarcely ignore from Milyutin, his minister of war, and from Totleben, Russia's most renowned soldier. Milyutin believed that a European war in defence of the San Stefano settlement would mean certain defeat; he had been willing enough to risk conflict with Great Britain alone by a forward policy in Asia, but not a conflict over the Ottoman Empire in which the British would be joined by the Austrians. Totleben gave detailed support to Milyutin's pessimism. The hero of Sevastopol had just been appointed commander-in-chief in place of the Grand Duke Nicholas, who had incurred the emperor's displeasure for failing to take Constantinople. Totleben's report of 9 May 1878 exposed the weaknesses in the case for seizing the Bosphorus and Constantinople as a means of neutralizing British hostility. The minefield which would be needed at the Bosphorus to keep the British out of the Black Sea was impracticable. The Turks had now recovered sufficiently to have a good chance of repulsing a Russian attack on Constantinople, and the effect of an unsuccessful bid could be serious for Russia's whole military and diplomatic position. Totleben was reluctant to risk sending reinforcements to the Austrian frontier until the Turks had evacuated the fortresses they still held in Bulgaria and until the Russians themselves had pulled back to Adrianople. The emperor ceased to share Ignatyev's assumption that the war had made Russia so strong in the Balkans and at the Straits that British and Austrian resistance could be discounted. He did not propose to preside over another Crimean debacle. Milyutin replaced Ignatyev as Alexander II's most influential adviser.

The Russian government's aim was now to keep as many of its gains as possible without provoking an extension of the war. Negotiations with Vienna and London had continued during the spring in the hope of a deal with at least one of the opponents of San Stefano. Talks with the Austro-Hungarian government had broken down, but Salisbury was willing for a direct deal with Russia in the manner of Canning and Palmerston. His proposals reached St Petersburg just when Totleben's gloomy report was being studied. A European congress at Berlin had been accepted in principle by the Russians since March, but they had wished its discussions to be confined to issues they acknowledged to be 'European', like the status of the Straits. They were now willing to modify the provisions of San Stefano sufficiently to bring the British to the conference table; the British were willing to limit their demands sufficiently to overcome Russian reluctance to discuss the settlement as a whole. Once again, the powers had in the last resort preferred diplomacy to the immense cost and extreme uncertainty of a European war. This time the Turks allowed them to do so.

It was the fact that twenty years after their Crimean defeat the Russians were still unable to face the prospect of a European war in defence of interests their government considered vital which made the congress of Berlin look a humiliating defeat to so many of them. A few months of warfare had brought Russia what would normally have been regarded as very impressive gains. Admittedly, the Bulgarian principality provided for in the treaty of San Stefano was reduced in size, and divided in such a way as to give the Turks greater power south of the Balkan mountains and control of their key passes. But northern Bulgaria was to enjoy autonomy, and the Russians, as Bulgaria's liberators, could hope to make it dependent on them sufficiently to bring Russian power much nearer to Constantinople and the Straits.

Southern Bessarabia, lost in 1856, had been regained. Their position in Asia Minor had been strengthened by the acquisition of Kars, Ardahan and Batum. Moreover, the threatening moves against India and the mission to Kābul, called off when the congress was arranged, had proved instructive military and diplomatic exercises. Russian commanders had run into difficulties, but at least they now had a better understanding of the problems they would encounter in trying to convey troops across the Alai Mountains and along the Amu Darya towards Afghanistan; the treaty signed with the amir lost its immediate importance as the threat of war passed, but, like the military moves, it was a further manifestation of Russia's growing capacity to endanger India's outer defences. And early in the crisis, though quite unconnected with it, a revolt against Russian predominance in Khokand had led to its formal annexation in 1876. In all, the eventful years 1875–8 had left Russia with greatly enhanced power and influence in both Europe and Asia, but what rankled was the realization that all these and the other achievements of Alexander II's reign had not been enough to restore Russia to its pre-Crimean preponderance in international politics.

A disturbing sequence of events in 1878–9 seemed to confirm that recent Russian expansion was to be offset by a weakening in the empire's overall position in the world. In the first place, the crisis had imparted to the British that spirit of belligerency which Rawlinson had found lacking in the 1860s. In the closing stages of the congress of Berlin, Salisbury made a declaration about the Straits. Its studied vagueness cast doubt on future British adherence to the principle of closure of the Straits to warships while the Ottoman Empire was at peace. The Russian government would no longer be able to feel secured by treaty against attack in the Black Sea in the event of a conflict with Great Britain over Asia which did not involve the Turks. The British government balanced its resignation to the sultan's loss of Kars, Ardahan and Batum by a guarantee of Asiatic Turkey, with the sultan allowing a British protectorate over Cyprus as a military and naval base to be used in giving effect to the guarantee. The Cyprus Convention of 4 June 1878 was, moreover, part of a wider policy envisaged by Sir Henry Layard, the British ambassador at Constantinople, and adopted by Salisbury. As the Ottoman Empire crumbled in Europe, a vigorous and reformed Turkish state was to be revived in Asia which would serve as a bulwark against any Russian drive towards the Persian Gulf and the Suez Canal. It was a new version of the old Palmerstonian programme, with a Euphrates railway project linking Baghdād to the

Mediterranean, and with military consuls appointed in 1878-9 to various points in Asia Minor to promote reforms. To the Russians and most other observers, including some enthusiastic British, the British government appeared to be bent on converting Asiatic Turkey into something like a protectorate. Layard himself did, indeed, hope for the sort of subordinate relationship accepted by the princely states in India.

A British forward policy had likewise been revived in central Asia. Salisbury had given qualified support to such a policy as secretary of state for India and, after 1878, as foreign secretary. The case for it had received recent publicity with the timely publication in 1875 of Sir Henry Rawlinson's *England, Russia and the East*. The arguments advanced by John Jacob for controlling the Bolan Pass had at last been accepted, and a treaty with the khan of Kalat had made possible the occupation of Quetta in 1876. The appointment of Lord Lytton as viceroy in 1876 signalized the triumph of the forward school. He went to India with instructions to get at least a temporary British mission received at Kābul, as a first step towards supervising the amir's relations with the outside world and ensuring the exclusion of Russian influence. Diplomacy between mutually distrustful representatives failed in 1877 to bring quick results, and Lytton was already convinced of the need for military action should diplomacy fail. He was determined that the Hindu Kush should become for all practical purposes the frontier of British India. The reception of Stoletov's mission at Kābul in July 1878 suggested that Shēr ʿAlī feared the Russians more than he feared the British, and that the advance of the effective Russian frontier south of the Hindu Kush was the more likely outcome. When a British mission was turned back at the Khyber Pass in September 1878, Lytton sent his forces to invade Afghanistan. They quickly occupied Qandahār and Jalālābād, Shēr ʿAlī fled to the Russians, and his son concluded in May 1879 the treaty of Gandamak. By this agreement a permanent British representative was to be stationed at Kābul, Afghan foreign policy was to conform to British wishes, the British were to retain control of the Khyber Pass and other key frontier areas, and they were to pay the amir an annual subsidy. Afghanistan, whose ill-defined northern frontiers lay close to the still unsettled frontier of the Russian Empire, had acquired a dependent status similar to that of Khīva and Bukhārā.

The Russians had provoked a new British drive in western and central Asia which they were ill-equipped to counter. Germany was now looked upon as a dangerous potential enemy as well as Austria-Hungary and Great Britain. Bismarck had made it clear during the recent crisis that the German government would not back Russia against Austria-Hungary. Although he also refused to promise the Austrians aid against Russia, and although he tried to help the Russian delegates as much as possible at the congress of Berlin, the Russian government was disappointed and suspicious. Observers in St Petersburg tended now to think more of the consequences of future German enmity than of what might be gained from a German alliance. Milyutin, who favoured a restoration of the three emperors' grouping, nevertheless took precautions on the frontier to provide against Germany's greatly superior capacity for rapid mobilization and concentration of forces. In doing so, he confirmed Bismarck's growing belief in an anti-German war party in Russia, while Bismarck's manifest resentment was in itself alarming to the Russians. Disputes over the execution of the Berlin settlement sustained an atmosphere of crisis until 1881. Bismarck seems to have convinced himself in 1879 that a Russian threat existed. His moves to counter it included proposals for a defensive alliance with Austria-Hungary in August, and sounding the British government in September as to their attitude in the event of a Russo-German breach. Saburov's mission to Berlin in September 1879 to try and restore the Dreikaiserbund or secure an alliance with Germany failed and, although it somewhat reassured Bismarck as to Russian intentions, the Austro-German defensive alliance against Russia was signed in October 1879. The breaking of its ties with both Berlin and Vienna left the Russian government isolated in Europe.

Even the Russians' unbroken run of success in extending their frontier of power and influence in Asia seemed to have come to an end at this time. The nomadic and warlike Tekke Turcomans proved far more difficult to bring under control than the feeble forces of Khīva and Bukhārā, and in September 1879 they defeated a Russian force sent against them. In the same month the Russians scored an apparent diplomatic triumph with the signing of the treaty of Livadia with China. The Chinese emperor's forces had regained control of Kashgar in 1877. The Russians had no further excuse for the occupation of the Ili area, and the Chinese government opened negotiations on the matter in 1878. The treaty, as it stood, returned Ili but gave the Russian government control of the passes through the Tien-shan mountains, without which the Chinese could not defend it. The Chinese government repudiated the agreement, sentenced its negotiator to death, and made extensive military preparations. Instead of a diplomatic triumph, the Russian government found itself on the brink of war in Asia over a relatively inessential area, and at the moment when they were isolated in Europe and grappling with the persistent Turkish crisis.

Events between 1880 and 1885 assumed, however, a more reassuring pattern, and the alarming developments of 1878–9 did not provoke a fundamental reappraisal of Russian foreign policy. For one thing, the British forward policy quickly faded. In the same month as the Russian defeat at the hands of the Turcomans, Sir Louis Cavagnari's mission, who had been sent to Kābul in fulfilment of the treaty of Gandamak, was massacred. A prompt military response had brought General Roberts's army to the Afghan capital by October 1879, but the British were, as in 1842, not prepared to accept the huge cost and bloodshed which would have been required for a permanent occupation of the country. With annexation ruled out, the only alternative was to rely once more upon the uncertainties of a deal with the ruler of Kābul. Abdur Rahman emerged in March 1880 from exile in Russia as the new amir; a new British government took office the following month under Gladstone, pledged to reverse the Afghan policy of its Conservative predecessor. In practice, it adopted a compromise of the kind Disraeli and Lytton themselves would probably have felt obliged to accept. The British representative in Kābul was in future to be an unobtrusive Muslim; Abdur Rahman was to be defended against Russian encroachments and given subsidies provided his diplomatic links were confined to the British; and the British retained control of the Khyber Pass and other strategically valuable points, while abandoning Qandahār.

On the face of it, most of the Gandamak terms had been preserved, leaving Afghanistan's status still comparable to that of Khīva and Bukhārā. Cavagnari had been avenged, and some remarkable military operations by Roberts had demonstrated British striking power. But, in practice, the British were obviously not in a position to control Afghanistan in the direct and unequivocal way in which the Russians controlled Khīva and Bukhārā. Treaty terms apart, the rulers of Khīva and Bukhārā accepted Russian direction because they were militarily helpless. The ruler of Kābul was bound only by treaty and by fear of a military retaliation which he knew the British would hesitate to mount for a third time. He would side with the British against the Russians only as long as he found it in his interest to do so. The British forward policy had failed in central Asia, and Great Britain had a government anxious to discard it altogether.

Gladstone's return to power was reassuring to the Russian government in other ways. His speeches made clear his belief that the Russian threat to British imperial interests was greatly exaggerated. He believed that this and all other problems dividing European governments could be solved as they arose by informal consultation, provided there was a spirit of compromise and a willingness for mutual concession. He aimed at a new concert of Europe, in which tensions could be relaxed and a permanent basis for peaceful cooperation established. If his policy was in practice a good deal more combative than such a programme suggested, at least it was not directed against Russia. He had praised Russia as liberator of the Bulgarians, and he thought rather of coercing the Turks in the cause of reform than of making them an efficient bulwark against Russia. British relations with the Ottoman Empire deteriorated during these years, though Salisbury, too, had shown little sympathy for the Turks and, by the time he left office, had lost any faith he might have had in their capacity to realize the visions of Layard and others. The open hostility Gladstone had displayed to Austria before coming to power was also gratifying to the Russians. It did not prevent continued Austro-British cooperation, which the Austrian foreign minister, Haymerle, preferred to renewing the Dreikaiserbund, but conviction grew in Vienna during 1880 that Gladstone's zeal might bring about the Ottoman Empire's collapse to Russia's advantage. Moreover, a Russian rapprochement with Great Britain and, perhaps, Germany might lead to Austrian isolation. Bismarck was already less inclined to worry about a potential Russian threat, and since March 1880 he had agreed in principle with Alexander II that the three emperors' grouping should be restored. The Austro-Hungarian government reluctantly decided that the curbing of Russia would have to be attempted from within a renewed Dreikaiserbund. In September 1880 serious negotiations began among the three powers.

The treaty of 18 June 1881 restored the grouping of the three empires, this time by a formal alliance. It was an alliance founded on mutual suspicion rather than common interest. Each government believed the alliance offered the best chance of exercising some control over the potentially dangerous activities and aspirations of its neighbours. The Russian government also got, as its share of the bargain, a greatly enhanced sense of security in relation to the British. The Austrian and German governments were not to oppose the union of the two Bulgarian principalities, created by the congress of Berlin, into a single state. As long as their influence counted most with the Bulgarians, the Russians would then have an admirable forward base, close to the Straits, as their delayed reward for defeating the Turks in 1877–8. In addition, should the Turks ever be tempted to open the Straits to British warships bent on attacking Russia, the three governments proposed to threaten the sultan with further dismemberment of his empire. And, in the event of a Russo-British war, the other two powers would remain neutral. Gladstone's policies had not only relieved the Russian government of a good deal of anxiety over central Asia and the Ottoman Empire but had, indirectly, helped Russia to emerge from isolation.

By the time the Three Emperors' Alliance had been concluded Russia's fortunes in Asia had also revived; the unexpected threats to security from such contrasted opponents as the Chinese and the Tekke Turcomans had been ended. The Russians had faced the choice of renegotiating the treaty of Livadia or going to war with China; although both sides made belligerent gestures, the Chinese alone were in earnest. By a new treaty of St Petersburg in February 1881 the Russians abandoned the Tekes valley and the Talki and Muzart passes, worth a war to the Chinese emperor but not to Alexander II, especially in the midst of a European crisis. The Russian government retained various commercial privileges, received financial compensation, and kept a substantial amount of territory west of Ili. It was a settlement which satisfied both parties. The Chinese had scored an impressive diplomatic victory, and the Russians had escaped a war they could not afford without impairing the security of their central Asian empire. And just at the time peaceful diplomacy was disposing of the Ili affair, the Tekke Turcomans, who had inflicted a humiliating defeat on a Russian force in 1879, were being ruthlessly destroyed by war. Their stronghold at Gök-Tepe was stormed by Skobelev's army in January 1881 after a fierce struggle lasting forty days, and Skobelev ordered the massacre of the entire male population. All in all, it appeared that Alexander II had presided over Russia's recovery from its most dangerous international crisis since the one he had inherited in 1855.

Russia's international position seemed, indeed, to have been restored to that enjoyed in the early 1870s when Russia's expansion in Asia and its relatively favourable situation in Europe had put the British on the defensive. That this was so received confirmation in the series of events which culminated in the Panjdeh crisis of 1885. After the fall of Gök-Tepe, independent Turcoman groups survived only in the area centred on Merv. Merv lay between the effective frontier of Russia's empire and the ill-defined boundaries of Persian and Afghan power. Russian absorption of Merv was expected by all observers. As usual, there was uncertainty among the Russians themselves as to the form their control should take, complicated by rivalry between the authorities in Tashkent and Tbilisi (Tiflis) as to which should exercise control. Rival factions in Merv itself debated how best to avoid being controlled at all. In 1881, the khan of Khīva was invited to send a governor, in the hope that this would satisfy the Russians as to Merv's orientation while leaving the

Turcomans there to their own devices. The emperor's representatives in Tashkent encouraged this; so did the Russian foreign ministry, which preferred such indirect assertion of influence. A governor was sent, and the Turcomans were told not to enter into relations with the British, the Persians or the Afghans.

Since a Khīvan governor had little prospect of dominating the Turcomans on Russia's behalf, their relationship to Russia would have been much like that of Afghanistan to Great Britain. But their continued turbulence gave the authorities in Tbilisi, who had initiated the conquest of Gök-Tepe, a pretext for military operations against them at the end of 1883. With the connivance of a friendly faction within Merv, the oasis area was occupied and annexed in March 1884. Russian troops were at last approaching the border of Afghanistan. If Russian forces centred on Merv encroached on Afghan territory, the British might feel obliged to assist in its defence, precipitating the long-awaited confrontation between British and Russian armies in Asia. The Russian government agreed, therefore, in May 1884 to a British proposal for delimiting Afghanistan's north-western border. While the work was in progress, Russian and Afghan troops clashed at Panjdeh on 31 March 1885.

The Panjdeh battle, in which several hundred died, was one of those mysterious frontier incidents responsibility for which is difficult to pin down. There is some evidence to suggest Afghan provocation, with British officers on the spot encouraging Afghan occupation of Panjdeh as the only way of staking their claim to a disputed area. But the clash bore out alarmist predictions about Russia in such dramatic form that even Gladstone, though continuing to believe in Russian willingness to compromise, felt obliged to take strong precautions. His government asked parliament for war credits; the viceroy, Lord Dufferin, prepared to move twenty-five thousand troops to Quetta; and the navy was ordered to occupy Port Hamilton in Korea, from which operations against Vladivostok could be mounted. Nor were these simply gestures to make British protests look convincing; even before the Panjdeh clash, the British cabinet was agreed that a Russian attack on Herat would mean war. And the measures carried a certain risk of precipitating what they were aimed to avert. British forces could not be transferred over five hundred miles from Quetta in time to prevent an attack on Herat if one were imminent, while if the Russians had no such plan a British advance might convince the emperor that war was inevitable, and a Russian occupation of Herat necessary to winning it. But the whole sequence of events in central Asia since the 1860s now looked a coherent pattern even to the most sceptical, and an advance on Herat seemed the logical next step after the incorporation of Merv and Panjdeh. After the battle for Panjdeh, war was thought by the British to be as likely as not, to the extent that official announcements of the outbreak of war were printed in readiness. Gladstone's government could only hope that the Russians would not think Herat worth the general war which the British ambassador in St Petersburg was instructed to threaten. And Gladstone, in keeping with his views on international behaviour, proposed arbitration as a way out of the crisis.

In retrospect, a Russo-British war in 1885 was unlikely in the extreme. A war with Great Britain for the sake of Herat would have made no sense in the context of the general policy which the Russian government had pursued since the end of the Crimean War. The central purpose of the advance through central Asia had been to put Russian forces in a position where they could attack the British at their most vulnerable point in the event of war, and, above all, by this implicit threat to make the British government less ready to go to war in another crisis of the 1853-4 kind. This they had now achieved by reaching the border areas of Persia and Afghanistan. Their frontier with these buffer states had still to be defined, and they naturally pressed for as advantageous a line as possible in territories where suzerainty had been uncertain and liable to frequent change. But to push this process to the point of persuading even such a sympathetic government as Gladstone's that India was in danger and war the only remedy would have been absurd. Not that Gladstone's belligerent moves and clear warning were wasted. Without them, the Russian government – perhaps not in 1885, but later – might have been tempted by its defencelessness and proximity to bid for Herat as the ideal forward position from which to threaten British India in time of crisis. But the Russian government would have ordered a march on Herat in 1885 only if the British had looked like opting for war regardless. Both Gladstone and Salisbury, who inherited the crisis with a change of government in June 1885, had too much sense of control for their response to suggest any such thing. So the Russian emperor could halt his forces, accept the principle of arbitration, and take his time about it all as befitted his position of strength.

For the Russian position was undoubtedly very strong compared to that of Great Britain. Their forces could move forward to occupy Herat, and the British knew there was nothing they could do immediately to prevent it. The Russian position would soon be stronger still with a rail link to Merv from their Caspian line. A crisis, moreover, could be confined, militarily speaking, to Asia. In 1878, the Russian government had planned an Asian riposte to a British threat in Europe; now, the only British war plan in the event of Russian troops taking Herat was to strike through the Straits at Russia's possessions in the Caucasus. But Russian diplomacy had made this difficult if not impossible to accomplish. In accordance with their treaty obligations of 1881, Russia's allies warned the sultan of the consequences to his empire should he allow British warships through the Straits while Turkey was at peace. The British would have been hard put to it to initiate and sustain a war in the Caucasus in face of Turkish resistance to their using the one and only line of communication. Even without the representations of Germany and Austria, 'Abd ül-Ḥamīd's resentment of British pressure on him in 1878 and after made him an unlikely accomplice.

In addition to these basic disadvantages, the British were currently engaged in military operations in the Sudan, and Gladstone's cabinet was divided as to whether the campaign should be called off and the forces there sent to India. The British were at odds with the French over Egypt, and with the Germans over other African issues. There was some truth in Salisbury's jibe that the Liberal government had 'at least achieved their long desired "Concert of Europe". They have succeeded in uniting the continent of Europe – against England'.[1] Salisbury himself, on taking office in June 1885, promptly tried to end British isolation by an informal approach to Bismarck, his emissary, Sir Philip Currie, going so far as to offer the Germans an alliance. This was, presumably, to convince Bismarck of the seriousness of Salisbury's long-term desire for improved relations, for there was no hope of such an offer being taken up on the eve of a possible Russo-British war. The approach had little relevance to the Panjdeh crisis, unless Salisbury hoped that his expressed determination in the event of war to force the Straits whatever the consequences would be transmitted to the Russians, and make them hesitate to move on Herat. But Alexander III had no interest in driving the British to such desperation; it was enough to know that Russian conquests and diplomacy had made war a desperate undertaking for any British government.

The Russian government took its time over settling the details, and kept the British on tenterhooks throughout the summer. But Afghan willingness to abandon Panjdeh, and their determination, on the other hand, to retain Zulfiqar and the pass linking north and west Afghanistan with Khurāsān, constituted a formula acceptable to the Russians since April. When it became clear that the British had kept their nerve and

[1] Quoted by Lady Gwendolen Cecil, *Life of Robert, Marquis of Salisbury*, 4 vols (London, 1921–32), III, 136.

would concede nothing more without war, Alexander III's ministers wound up the affair with a protocol early in September. The Afghans kept Zulfiqar, the Russians kept Panjdeh, and general agreement was reached on Afghanistan's frontier between the Amu Darya and the Hari-Rud. The settlement came as a relief to the British, but it did not solve the problem of their growing vulnerability in Asia. Not only did much uncertainty remain as to Russia's frontiers with Persia and Afghanistan, but the attitudes of both countries in future Russo-British crises could not be predicted. As long as they were potential allies – or victims – of Russia, the British could not feel secure, and they had no reason to believe that the Russian advance in Asia had ended. And the underlying fear that Russian intrigue might fatally weaken British prestige and authority within India itself was reinforced by the crisis. The Russians appeared to have recovered fully from the shock to their self-confidence delivered by the events of 1878–80, and the Panjdeh affair had clearly demonstrated their new-found strength in relation to Great Britain.

But there was a fundamental weakness in Russia's position which the circumstances of the Panjdeh crisis had concealed. The conduct of the emperor's allies had been impeccable because the crisis had been confined to Asian matters in which they had no direct interest. The Russians had secured themselves in Asia by solid conquests, and were arguably at an advantage there in a localized war with the British alone. But the British government had the power to extend an Asian war to Europe, where it was unlikely to remain a purely Russo-British duel. If Salisbury had carried out his threat to make war by forcing the Straits against both Turkish and Russian opposition, the whole 'Eastern Question' would have been reopened. The Austrian government would then be too much concerned with defending its own interests in face of a possible Ottoman collapse to have much time for those of Russia, and might, indeed, be glad to see them weakened. The military advantages might still lie with Russia, but it would be of little consolation to compel the British, by threatening India, to call off their Black Sea offensive if the British had already wrecked the fragile security afforded to Russia in the Balkans and at the Straits by the Dreikaiserbund. And not only was the Dreikaiserbund a fragile association in any crisis involving the Balkans and the Ottoman Empire, but the Russians had as yet failed to make the most of the Austrian concession over Bulgaria which had been part of the bargain. They had not yet succeeded in making Bulgaria a dependent ally on their European frontier as they had Khīva and Bukhārā on their Asian frontier. A controlling position in Bulgaria would enable the Russian army to strike quickly at the Straits in time of crisis. Restricted to more subtle methods than in Khīva and Bukhārā, they had alienated important groups whose cooperation was essential to their success, and the emperor made obvious his dislike of the ruler, Alexander of Battenberg. There is nothing to suggest that the Russian government had any intention of pressing the Panjdeh crisis to the point of war, nor that they came to terms for fear of war. But there is no doubt that war would have been as unattractive an option to them as to the British.

Between 1885 and 1890 the weakness in Russia's position again became more pronounced than its strength. Alexander III and his advisers suffered a series of shocks which revived and reinforced the sense of alarm experienced in 1878-80. In September 1885, a few days after settling the Afghan dispute, the Russian government learned of a coup by which the Bulgarians had ended the division of their country provided for by the congress of Berlin. Something approaching the big Bulgaria, planned by Ignatyev and anticipated by the Three Emperors' Alliance, had come into being. But growing Russo-Bulgarian hostility meant that it was not currently in Russia's interest; this big Bulgaria would be a barrier, not a bridge to Constantinople. The British government, on the other hand, now naturally supported the unification, and the Austrian government felt that the Serbs, whom they had succeeded in making a dependable ally, were entitled to compensation. The latter question was settled simply enough by a Serbo-Bulgarian war which the Bulgarians won. The Austrians intervened to save the Serbs, but the Russians were frustrated from forcibly bringing the Bulgarians under their control by British and Austrian opposition. Alexander III refused to renew the Three Emperors' Alliance, and in 1886-7 the Russians tried to get their way by intrigue and diplomatic pressure within Bulgaria. They got rid of Prince Alexander, but the Bulgarians selected another ruler unacceptable to Alexander III. Bulgaria was still lost to Russia as a forward base.

In addition to this, the Russian government got wind of a British-led grouping of powers to combine against Russia should the latter attempt to alter the distribution of power in areas adjacent to the Mediterranean. The Mediterranean Agreements of 1887 between the British, Italian and Austrian governments ended British isolation, and raised again the spectre of a coalition too powerful for Russia to risk challenging. The grouping was secretly encouraged by Bismarck. With both the breakdown of the Dreikaiserbund over Balkan questions, and dangerously heightened tension between France and Italy, Bismarck needed the

British to support his partners in the Triple Alliance. The Mediterranean Agreements provided this, and helped restore the deadlock in Europe which constituted his formula for prolonged peace. Since it was in the Russians' interest to modify the status quo in the Balkans, not preserve it, they tried to regain the freedom of action conferred by the defunct Dreikaiserbund through a direct deal with Germany alone. The Reinsurance Treaty of June 1887 recognized Russia's right to dominate Bulgaria and its right to seize Constantinople and the Straits should the Russian emperor deem it necessary. But even German support was short-lived. After Bismarck's dismissal in 1890, the German emperor William II declined to renew the Reinsurance Treaty, and in the same year he concluded a spectacular African agreement with Salisbury. The upshot of all this was that Great Britain, although vulnerable in Asia, was more secure in Africa and had become associated with the Triple Alliance powers so intimately as to suggest that its formal adhesion was imminent. It was the Russians who were now isolated in Europe. Their attempts to win security on their unstable Balkan frontier had aroused opposition for the British to exploit. Russia's counter-thrust in Asia had itself been effectively countered.

The post-Crimean interpretation of international politics had brought rich rewards; operating within its framework of assumptions the Russians had won security in Asia against any future British threat, and the power to threaten the British themselves in India. Because of these Asian conquests, the British were dangerous only as members of a European coalition; but, because of Russo-Austrian antagonism in the Balkans which no paper agreement could apparently resolve, the British were only too likely to be able to act as members of such a coalition. German friendship had faded, and with it any hope of pressure on Austria-Hungary to exercise restraint. The worst might not happen, but the possibility of an isolated Russia again facing a coalition with which neither the Russian army nor the Russian economy was strong enough to cope would, for the time being, inhibit the Russian government from acting confidently to protect its vital interests. The Bulgarians had to be left alone, and Alexander reconciled himself to a cautious policy which did nothing to relieve a fundamental sense of insecurity. It was the sort of sequence of upsetting events to shake official faith in accepted interpretations of world politics. By 1890 there was a climate of opinion in Russia receptive to new speculations about the future and fresh formulas for shaping it.

Russian political literature in the late nineteenth century was, like that of every other major power, rich in speculation about the nation's 'destiny' in world affairs. But Alexander III was not the sort of man to respond to the more lurid and dramatic of these ideas. He had preferred the plain commonsense arguments with which Giers had justified his policies, and the coolness with which he executed them. 'Giers n'est pas un homme à s'emballer', he remarked in March 1887, 'la prudence est sa qualité la plus précieuse.'[1] These words were addressed to Mikhail Katkov, one of the greatest of Russian journalists, and spokesman for a rival policy which was preferred by some of Alexander III's advisers. Katkov had formerly accepted the argument that, in an age of subversion and revolution, Austria and Germany were Russia's natural allies, and that, although Austrian and Russian interests would conflict and although Germany was dangerous and untrustworthy, formal alliance with them offered the best chance of keeping their anti-Russian tendencies under control. The Bulgarian crisis had changed his mind. In 1886–7, through his influential *Moscow Gazette* and through correspondence and interviews with Alexander III and his advisers, Katkov tried to shake official faith in the Dreikaiserbund. Russian diplomatic setbacks over Bulgaria had stemmed, in his view, from misplaced reliance on the German government. The alliance was far more beneficial to Germany than to Russia; its effect, he claimed, was to boost the power of an overmighty neighbour and potential enemy. Russian interests would be better served by the improvisations open to a power free of such ties. Down to 1890 Alexander III continued to find Giers' policy the more convincing as a means of controlling the international situation, as long as the German government was still willing to support Russia in a crisis involving the Straits, and he was angered by Katkov's revelation of secret details of the Three Emperors' Alliance as part of his newspaper campaign. But he was in tune with the nationalist sentiments which found such eloquent expression in Katkov's journalism, and, when Giers' policy was fatally undermined by German refusal to renew the Reinsurance Treaty and growing British links with the Triple Alliance powers, Katkov's way of thinking was the obvious alternative to the emperor.

Katkov himself died in 1887, and some of those who pursued his denunciation of the German connection went a good deal further in their anti-German feeling and in the policies they advocated. Katkov's 'free hand' for the Russian government in international affairs would have facilitated an understanding with France. By 1890 an actual alliance with France to check simultaneously the British and the Ger-

[1] Quoted by B. Nolde, *L'alliance franco-russe. Les origines du système diplomatique d'avant-guerre* (Paris, 1936), 458–9.

mans had obtained widespread backing in official and military circles. Alexander III, despite his dislike of France's republican form of government, became convinced that Germany was a major danger to Russia, and that only some ostentatious sign that Russia was in league with France would inhibit the Triple Alliance powers and Great Britain. The French government, for its part, had been angling for a Russian alliance to end its isolation. It had made all the usual indirect signals of its willingness; for example, it had, in contrast to Germany, helped to meet the urgent Russian need for foreign loans.

In July 1891, Alexander III at last decided that the time for a show of intimacy between the two powers had arrived. A courtesy call of the French fleet to Kronstadt was turned into a Francophile demonstration; the news that the emperor had stood bareheaded while the Marseillaise was being played was in itself sufficiently bizarre to impress foreign opinion that something momentous was afoot. An impression of this kind was all that the Russian government really needed, but the French were unwilling to sustain the impression without some paper agreement. An exchange of notes followed in August 1891, providing rather vaguely for consultation if either should be threatened. It took another year before the French were able to arrange staff talks. But Alexander III, although accepting the need to haggle about specific military action, was in no doubt as to what should henceforth be Russia's policy in the event of a Franco-German war. 'We really must come to an agreement with the French,' he told Giers in March 1892, 'and, in the event of a war between France and Germany, throw ourselves immediately upon the Germans so as not to give them time to beat the French first and then turn on us.'[1]

French and Russian military leaders drafted a convention in August 1892. If France were attacked by Germany, or by Italy supported by Germany, Russia would throw 700,000–800,000 troops against Germany. If Russia were attacked by Germany, or by Austria supported by Germany, France would put 1,300,000 men in the field against Germany. This arrangement would stand as long as the Triple Alliance existed. The Russians still hesitated to commit themselves so precisely, and when in the autumn of 1892 the Panama scandal threw French politics into confusion they had good enough reason besides for postponing ratification. But finally, in October 1893, the Russian fleet was welcomed so spectacularly at Toulon as to leave no doubt in the minds of foreign observers that the Franco-Russian alliance was an accom-

---

[1] V. N. Lamsdorff, *Dnevnik 1891–1892* (Moscow and Leningrad, 1934; repr. Paris and The Hague, 1970), 299.

plished fact, even though an exchange of letters formally recording the secret military arrangements did not take place until December 1893 and January 1894. No joint military action against the other common enemy, Great Britain, was planned because the French had no intention of involving themselves in war over Russo-British quarrels in central Asia, while the Russians did not intend to fight for France's African interests.

The arrangements perhaps seemed relevant enough to each ally's quarrels with the British. The Germans would not risk a two-front war for the sake of British imperial interests or for Constantinople, and their partners in the Triple Alliance would hesitate to act without German support. But since the Germans would not have risked war with Russia for British imperial interests in any case, the deterrent effect of the Franco-Russian alliance must have been very slight. It is likely that Alexander III was over-reacting to the temporary setbacks of the late 1880s by going the length of a full military alliance with France. Balkan politics were changeable enough for the Russians to hope they would change to their advantage; the British link with the Triple Alliance was limited and precarious. An equally limited and precarious link with the French would have served Alexander III's purpose in such a fluid situation.

8

The end of the Great Game, 1894–1908

During the ten years prior to the outbreak of its war with Japan, the Russian government was, indeed, able to carry out its policies under much more favourable conditions than was that of Great Britain. The anxieties of the recent past, which had bred the Russian desire for a French alliance, had lost their basis by the end of the century. British relations with the Triple Alliance did not become more intimate, as the Russians had feared they would. On the contrary, the Austrian government, after failing to persuade the British to extend their commitments, declined in 1897 to renew the Mediterranean Agreements, and agreed with the Russian government that Balkan questions should be put into cold storage. By 1896, the Bulgarian government, whose hostility had been so disturbing to Alexander III, was on friendly terms with his successor. When the new emperor, Nicholas II, visited Great Britain in 1896, Salisbury hinted that ultimate Russian possession of the Straits would not necessarily be opposed by the British in the event of Ottoman collapse, though they would oppose the Russians bidding for them in advance. The Russian hold on Persia was tightened in these years, and a comparable relationship with China was being actively prepared. Their ability to threaten India, whether by direct invasion or by blows at British authority through intrigue and ostentatious advances towards the frontier, was enhanced as plans for a new strategic railway from Orenburg to Tashkent got under way.

The British position, by contrast, continued to deteriorate. Earlier visions of political ascendancy in Asia had long been discarded. They had turned on plans for dominating central Asian markets, for mobilizing an anti-Russian coalition of Asian rulers, for strengthening the Ottoman Empire as a barrier to Russian expansion. Plans of this kind had been abandoned. The British were only partially in control of the political units on their side of the Hindu Kush. And in 1892 the traditional plan of striking at Russia's Black Sea coasts in the event of war was put into question. Military and naval intelligence chiefs advised that British forces could not beat the Russians to Constantinople except under improbably favourable circumstances. Although Salisbury himself was sceptical, his cabinet colleagues in 1895 refused to back him over sending the fleet to the Straits in time of crisis. A war with Russia over Asian questions would in future be fought in Asia, and its aim would be primarily defensive: the protection of India from attack. It was the Russians who now seemed well placed to bid for political ascendancy in Asia.

At the same time, there was some prospect of Russo-British rivalry becoming a less dangerous element in international politics. Alexander III was too conscious of his country's economic and financial weaknesses to risk a war which might be lost on their account. Successive finance ministers had struggled to eliminate them, and the latest attempt by Vyshnegradsky had collapsed with the great famine of 1891. The emperor backed the new finance minister, Sergei Witte, in his drive to industrialize Russia rapidly. A programme of public works, especially railways, would stimulate private enterprise to exploit Russia's vast resources; the result, it was hoped, would be that prosperity and economic independence whose absence had been such a limiting factor in the conduct of Russian diplomacy and war. The 'Witte system' required a period of peace. In Europe, the Franco-Russian alliance made this probable enough, and in Asia Russian policies were relatively restrained. Imperialist activities were fostered by Witte as part of his economic policy, and Russian influence was, indeed, promoted as actively as ever among weak Asian neighbours. But Witte's methods were those of economic penetration, familiar in form but employed with a new zest and efficiency. Military expansion continued in central Asia as Russian commanders pursued their search for the most advantageous frontiers in little-known and turbulent regions, but Alexander III and his ministers kept the predictable clashes with British interests under control.

Nor were the British likely to respond in panicky or belligerent fashion. Salisbury's forward policy had always been a rational and moderate one, in no way representing a spirit of alarmism. He wanted to see the military frontier advanced to points from which buffer states could be supported and volatile tribes controlled. In the 1870s he had backed the advance to Kalat, from which Sir Robert Sandeman had gradually brought Baluchistan under control; in the 1890s he urged the

Indian authorities to build a railway to Sīstān, a region of semi-independent tribes between Persia, Afghanistan and Baluchistan, possession of which could frustrate an attack on India and make military aid to Persia feasible. The Liberal government of 1892–5 made no change in this basically defensive strategy. In China and Persia Salisbury's instruments of policy were, like Witte's, primarily economic and diplomatic. While such long-term calculations shaped both Russian and British policies in Asia disputes were unlikely to reach a dangerous level.

The relatively quiet settlement of the Pamirs crisis, potentially almost as explosive as that of Panjdeh, was significant. Having advanced their frontier with the Afghans as far as possible for the time being, Russian soldiers and explorers were probing the high plateau of the Pamirs, where there existed a sixty-mile gap of unclaimed territory between Afghanistan and China. Beyond lay various passes through which, explorers reported, at least small forces of invaders might cross the Hindu Kush either way in the event of a Russo-British war. The passes were controlled by tribal rulers whose constant warfare with one another made their control precarious and necessitated intricate diplomacy on the part of British and Russian agents seeking their cooperation. In 1889 small forward parties led by Gromchevsky and Younghusband had encountered each other in the Pamirs, and when in 1891 Younghusband met another Russian force he was told that the Pamirs had been annexed. He was expelled from the area, and another British officer was arrested for trespassing on Russian territory. The British government secured an apology, and sent troops into key areas to subdue hostile tribes and to resist any attempted Russian encroachment through the passes. But their encouragement of Afghan and Chinese advances to close the gap altogether received a setback in 1892 when a fresh assertion of Russian power forced both instead to withdraw, thus widening the gap to nearly a hundred miles.

There was no doubt that the Russians could effectively occupy the gap and establish a frontier on the Hindu Kush, and that the British could not prevent them. A formal claim to such a line was made by the Russian government in 1893, and French provocation of a crisis over Siam during the negotiations which ensued suggested to many observers a concerted attack by the new allies on the British empire in Asia. But the Russian government was prepared to modify its pretensions slightly and to accept a formula which the British worked hard to produce. The Afghans were persuaded to make an exchange of territory farther west demanded by the Russians, and the latter contented themselves with a frontier line in the Pamirs region which fell short of the Hindu Kush. The territory between this line and the Hindu Kush was to be administered at British expense by the Afghans. A boundary commission was to decide details of the new frontier as far east as China. The Russians were sufficiently confident of their local superiority to concede such a flimsy barrier; the British were sufficiently aware of their weakness to find reassurance in Russian willingness to negotiate a clearly defined frontier at all. The settlement thus reflected mutual acknowledgment of the current state of power in this part of central Asia, and mutual reluctance to risk war in the course of modifying it.

Reliance on economic methods to influence the international alignments of Persia and China meant that the heightened sense of rivalry between the British and the Russians in these countries did not in itself threaten imminent conflict. In Persia economic imperialism had been slow to win the active support of the Russian and British governments until both were convinced it was politically advantageous to them. In 1872, Baron Julius de Reuter had obtained an extraordinarily wide-ranging concession to exploit Persia's mineral resources and forests, to build railways and canals, and to establish banks, but Gladstone's government refused Reuter the backing he needed. Salisbury's policy of keeping Persia a buffer state, hopefully more friendly to the British than to the Russians, made him look more kindly on such activities, and in 1888 the appointment of Sir Henry Drummond Wolff to Tehran brought vigorous moves to give the British political and commercial domination of central and southern Persia. After the Panjdeh crisis the Russians, too, stepped up their activities in Persia, appreciating the value of its eastern province of Khurāsān as a base in a future Russo-British war. They had not fully exploited the commercial clauses of the treaty of Turkomānchāy, which had looked so ominous to the British in 1828. Legal and cultural barriers to Russian merchants had remained considerable because their government had not thought it worth while exercising its influence to remove them, and Russian trade with Persia had consequently been small during most of the nineteenth century. With the shah's capital in striking distance of the Russian border and far from British ships in the Persian Gulf, the Russian government had felt sufficiently in control of its neighbour for the purposes of defence. Many Russians now began to urge a challenge to British influence in Persia generally, and aspirations to bases on the Persian Gulf and the Indian Ocean were voiced. The Russian government vigorously promoted trade as a means of consolidating and extending its political influence, and took up the new British economic challenge.

The end of the Great Game, 1894–1908

On his arrival in Tehran Drummond Wolff had quickly secured the opening of the Kārūn river to foreign ships and the establishment of a British-sponsored Imperial Bank of Persia, but Russia's representatives successfully organized resistance to his attempt to get the important tobacco trade into British hands. In 1894, Witte took over a failing Russian private bank in Tehran, and built it up as a rival to the British institution there, and he backed a major road-building project by a Russian entrepreneur in northern Persia. But both sides were tentative and cautious, concerned to measure the effect of their moves and ready to draw back. In 1890, after lengthy debate, Alexander III's ministers recommended postponing support for a concession to build a railway from the Caspian Sea to the Indian Ocean as too uncertain in its political consequences; and Drummond Wolff and his successors were already thinking of mutually agreed spheres of influence in Persia as a possible future arrangement.

The same long-term policies were pursued by both governments in China. The Russian government was the more ambitious in conceiving its ultimate role in China. Witte took up with enthusiasm the long-planned and recently launched project of a Trans-Siberian Railway, seeing it as a boost for the heavy industry by which he hoped to galvanize Russia's economy, as giving Russia the edge in the growing competition for the trade of China, Japan and Korea, and as facilitating support for Russian naval and military power in east Asia. He expected a close economic alliance with China to bring about at least the predominance of Russian political influence at Peking. In asserting Russian influence he was prepared to use adventurers like Badmayev, who in 1893 had plans for stimulating, in the course of his trading activities, a revolt against the Manchu dynasty and its replacement by the tsar. Witte held out to Alexander III the prospect that, if Badmayev succeeded, 'from the shores of the Pacific and the heights of the Himalayas Russia would dominate not only the affairs of Asia but those of Europe as well'. The emperor was sceptical, regarding Badmayev's plan as 'so new, unusual and fantastic that it is hard to believe in the possibility of success', but Badmayev eventually got a treasury loan to finance his commercial enterprises in China. His programme was clearly very long-term, if serious at all, and he himself expected only 'gradually to approach the contemplated aim'.[1] The Badmayev episode, trivial in itself, has become celebrated as indicating the domination of east Asia as the ultimate Russian goal; so it was, but Alexander III and his advisers

---

[1] Quoted by B. A. Romanov, *Russia in Manchuria, 1892–1906* (Ann Arbor, Mich., 1952; transl. from Russian), 45–8.

were aware that eagerness for quick results could be counter-productive.

For this reason, Salisbury's aims in China, while far more limited, were compatible with those of Russia for the foreseeable future. Salisbury accepted that both the primitive parts of the world and its declining empires and principalities would gradually fall under alien control in some form or other, and that the current rapidity of economic development in countries like Germany, America, Russia and Japan was likely to accelerate the process. But he saw no reason why the process should not be by peaceful agreement among the governments of the most powerful states. His African treaties with Germany, France and Portugal had shown the way by marking out in advance the regions in which the various governments wished to see the economic activity of their own nationals predominate. He encouraged Russian economic penetration of China on the grounds that there was room in Asia for all the major industrial powers to claim that some particular area should be specially profitable for their businessmen and financiers. Like his predecessors in the 1850s he had no inclination whatever for assuming the functions of government in these areas, and thus turning China into another India. He came to terms with the French in 1896 over south-west China, and he hoped the Russian government would recognize that the Yangtse valley was reserved for British enterprise as willingly as he accepted that northern China was reserved to that of Russia. The Russians were unwilling, as in Persia, to commit themselves formally to sharing when they could still aspire to control the whole, but their immediate aims were confined to the north. As long as the Trans-Siberian Railway was still being built, and probably for much longer, Russian and British policies in China were as unlikely as in Persia to bring about direct conflict between them.

Economic imperialism of this kind was a slow process in which the risks of war and the costs of annexation could be largely avoided. The Great Game had entered a less hectic phase, but the essential ideas which had governed it were unchanged; each power still regarded the other as the central threat against which it had to guard in Asia, and each government still regarded some sort of control over the countries lying between the two empires as the best means of countering the threat. Down to the mid-1890s the so-called 'new imperialism' had scarcely affected the pattern of Russo-British rivalry. It is, of course, disputable whether the novel features discernible in imperialist activity in the late nineteenth century amounted to a new imperialism, or whether they simply meant more imperialism of the familiar kind. But three of these developments did have potentially great importance for the future formulation and conduct of British and Russian policies in Asia.

First, there was the proliferation of ingenious financiers and concession-hunters in the capitalist economies of the day. Although the Russian and British governments remained rather aloof regulators of the activities which these groups generated abroad, they did have now at their disposal, as events in China and Persia had shown, additional and more effective instruments of economic imperialism than before. Indirect control of their weaker neighbours in Asia had normally been the form of frontier security preferred by both governments; war and annexation had often resulted because the means of exercising informal empire had proved inadequate. The willingness of rulers like the shah of Persia and the Chinese emperor to negotiate large loans and concessions made possible a much greater measure of control by financial strings and sometimes by the introduction of troops to guard railway, mining and other concessions. This development facilitated the sort of long-term economic competition, easily regulated at government level should direct conflict threaten, which both Salisbury and Witte favoured.

The second development was the increasing number of governments involved in large-scale imperialist ventures. The case for empire as a source of national wealth had been widely argued in the 1850s, and advocates of systematic empire-building had multiplied in the following decades. The German, Italian, American and other governments had been at least fitfully interested, as the partition of Africa and the competition for Pacific islands had shown. In the long run this would transform the context in which Russo-British rivalry operated. But apart from France's still rather limited empire-building in Indo-China, the mainland of Asia was as yet little affected by such additions to the ranks of the imperialists. Neither of these developments, therefore, had by 1894, when Alexander III died, altered the basic picture of a continent dominated by two great empires constantly probing to extend the area they controlled.

The third development was a reinterpretation of international politics in the world as a whole, a world in which imperialism had achieved such startling prominence. The future was seen in very different terms from the rather leisurely extensions of empire envisaged by men like Salisbury and Witte. The world situation was pictured as posing urgent problems which required drastic action and a readiness to use force. A great and growing popular literature had tried to apply the findings of biological, historical and social science in explaining various dramatic changes witnessed in the nineteenth century. The changes for which a unified explanation was sought included the rapid spread of industrialization, the striking extension of empires, and the prominence of western civilization in the scientific and technological triumphs with which the changes were associated. Two closely related assumptions suggested to many observers an explanation of contemporary international dissension. In the first place, it was thought that apparently unconnected crises between states in different parts of the world should be seen as a whole and in terms of a dynamic theory of history, which was derived from or supported by the theory of evolution. Conflict between nations was, in this view, a natural process testing the fitness of societies to survive. The defeat of the less fit would be beneficial to the species, the less fit being currently those peoples unable to resist the power of the West, later perhaps the weaker empires of the West. International conflict could thus be represented as natural and salutary, a welcome challenge rather than a peril to be avoided. 'All around us now is strife,' declared the American naval strategist Alfred Thayer Mahan, one of the most influential of the writers who did welcome the challenge; ' "the struggle of life", "the race of life", are phrases so familiar that we do not feel their significance till we stop to think about them. Everywhere nation is arrayed against nation; our own no less than others' (1897).[1] Secondly, the political and economic unit seen as appropriate to the fit in proving their cultural superiority was an empire, whether formal or informal, providing access to the raw materials and markets required for the thriving industrial economy which had come to be recognized as vital for political and military strength. '... the course of world history in the twentieth century', the German economist Gustav Schmoller had prophesied in 1890, 'will be determined by the competition between the Russian, English, American, and perhaps the Chinese world empires, and by their aspirations to reduce all the other, smaller, states to dependence on them.'[2]

These assumptions about international politics in the late nineteenth century were not in themselves unreasonable as either an interpretation of the present or as a speculation about what the future might hold. Given the vast accumulation of power which capitalist and industrial development was putting at the disposal of an ever-widening circle of governments, and given the human record in using power to acquire resources and to reduce weaker neighbours to a state of dependence,

---

[1] Quoted by R. Hofstadter, *Social Darwinism in American Thought*, rev. ed. (Boston, Mass., 1955), 188.
[2] Quoted by F. Fischer, *Germany's Aims in the First World War* (London, 1967; transl. from German), 9.

The end of the Great Game, 1894–1908

prophecies of conflict and competition on a global scale were in no sense outrageous. Nor did thinking in these terms necessarily foster the prophesied conflicts and create an atmosphere favourable to war as their solution. It could equally serve to underline the risks of this unprecedented capacity for war unless it was used with restraint. But much of the writing, commonly if misleadingly labelled social darwinist, conveyed this interpretation in emotive and extravagant language, liable to induce a mood of brutal arrogance in those who identified themselves as the fit, and a dangerous belief in inevitable and impending war in political leaders endowed with a sense of drama. Until the 1890s the world's governments had been little influenced by these ideas in their conduct of international policy. But this third element in the 'new imperialism' was potentially the most dynamic as far as the Great Game was concerned. Between 1894 and 1898 imperialist initiatives by the Japanese, the German and the American governments significantly modified the distribution of power in Asia, and the new interpretation played some part in determining the German and perhaps the American decisions. Whether the Great Game would remain an acceptably protracted and relatively peaceful process or whether it would acquire emergency status requiring precipitate action depended on how Russian and British leaders interpreted this dramatic sequence of events.

In July 1894 the Japanese government decided on war with China. Since 1868 power in Japan had been in the hands of men who believed that their country's independence could be secured only by westernization, by adopting the techniques of government and war which had made the states of Europe and north America formidable enough to threaten, limit or destroy the independence of every state in Asia. They believed, too, that even rapid westernization would leave them insecure if their immediate neighbour, Korea, was hostile or controlled by a hostile power. They hoped for the emergence of a modernized Korea, independent of China and the western powers, and friendly to Japan. As with their westernization programme, they accepted that a long haul would be necessary for success. By the early 1890s it was becoming clear that their patience was unlikely to be rewarded in Korea. A forceful Chinese representative in Seoul, Yüan Shi-k'ai, was exercising the kind of influence over the Korean government to which the Japanese aspired, and, as the Chinese grip tightened, the commencement of the Trans-Siberian Railway suggested that another powerful rival would be bidding to control Korea within a few years. A conciliatory, waiting policy seemed to have failed, and both liberal and reactionary groups within Japan were demanding bolder measures.

In the summer of 1894, the Japanese government reluctantly decided to risk war. The Chinese government had responded to a Korean request for military aid in suppressing a rebellion. Japanese forces were sent to ensure some balance of power, and Chinese cooperation in modernizing Korea was demanded as the price of Japanese withdrawal. A local war with limited aims ensued. As rulers of an island power off the Asian mainland, Japanese leaders felt about Korea much what the British felt about Belgium, and they sometimes contemplated a Great Power agreement on Korea as a source of security. But they were now aiming at the sort of semi-protectorate status for Korea which the Russians and the British had often favoured for states beyond their frontiers. Korea was to be independent, except in so far as it would rely on Japanese strength alone in ensuring its independence and in frustrating other foreign penetration. There was nothing new, therefore, about this Japanese imperialist venture; they had simply adopted the prevailing pattern of frontier behaviour by strong powers towards weaker, traditional societies. But the ease with which in 1894–5 the Japanese defeated China's forces in achieving their goal, and their demand for cession of the southern tip of Manchuria as a base from which to keep China in check, startled the other powers. The Russians, with French and German support, bullied the Japanese government into abandoning its mainland base, but this show of diplomatic strength was less significant than Japan's demonstration of military and naval strength against China. A new element of instability and uncertainty had entered international politics in Asia.

British and Russian assumptions about the future pattern of their competition for a controlling position in China were further unsettled in November 1897, when German troops were landed at Kiaochow in China's Shantung province. William II was one of the first political leaders to be profoundly affected by social darwinist ideas in his formulation of policy. By 1894–5 he had been convinced by current arguments that the British, American and Russian empires would soon come to dominate the world's markets and resources, and that the Germans would have considerably to extend their exercise of power in the world beyond Europe if they were not to be squeezed out. He had also found convincing the arguments of Mahan and Tirpitz as to the role of a big navy in such a bid for political and economic power on a global scale. In January 1896, speaking on the twenty-fifth anniversary of the establishment of the German Empire, he had announced that his government would henceforth pursue a 'world policy'. During 1896 and 1897 he was working on plans to make Germany a great naval power, and in November 1897 Tirpitz's naval bill was presented to the Reichstag. The move against Kiaochow in the same month had long been under consideration. Since 1895 William II had been set on a naval station in China as one of the overseas bases Germany would require in its new role. By the summer of 1897 Kiaochow had been selected as suitable. In November the murder of two German missionaries in Shantung offered a convenient pretext for a show of force, and the German squadron in Chinese waters was ordered to Kiaochow to demand compensation as a first step towards gaining control of it. 'Thousands of German Christians will breathe easier', the emperor told his foreign minister in the tones of belligerent and highly charged emotion with which international problems were coming to be discussed, 'when they know that the German Emperor's ships are near; hundreds of German traders will revel in the knowledge that the German Empire has at last secured a firm footing in Asia; hundreds of thousands of Chinese will quiver when they feel the iron fist of Germany heavy on their necks; and the whole German nation will be delighted that its government has done a manly act.'[1] In March 1898, the Chinese government agreed to a ninety-nine-year lease of Kiaochow, a fifty-kilometre neutral zone around the leased territory, and railway and mining concessions in its hinterland.

The American annexation in 1898 of Hawaii and the Philippines was less obviously relevant to the politics of mainland Asia, but it neatly met the expectations of those whose demographic and other calculations had led them to predict a major role for America in world, and especially Asian, affairs. The Americans were admittedly no newcomers to the quest for territorial and commercial empire in the Pacific. They had led the way in opening Japan to foreign trade, they had followed the British lead in treaty-making with the Chinese, their influence predominated in Hawaii, they had shared control of Samoa with the British and the Germans since the 1870s, and they had acquired a number of islands as naval bases. By the 1890s some influential Americans were demanding swifter and more systematic action, and their views were strongly represented in the cabinet of William B. McKinley, when he became president in 1897. There were members of the business community who aspired to a greater commercial empire of the traditional kind, and simply wanted a more integrated trade route to the China market, about which they entertained the same vast expectations as had the British and the Russians; and there were advocates of the 'new' imperialist

[1] Quoted by W. L. Langer, *The Diplomacy of Imperialism*, 2nd ed. (New York, 1956), 452.

thinking, like Theodore Roosevelt, Henry Cabot Lodge and Captain Mahan, who wanted in addition a Pacific network of coaling stations and naval bases as part of their plans for a big navy and for the extension of American power and influence in the world which a big navy would allow. Hence when war with Spain came over Cuba in 1898 Roosevelt's orders, as assistant secretary of the navy, to attack the Spanish-owned Philippines once war was declared, though regarded as premature, were not countermanded. Spain was easily defeated and, after a lengthy public debate, the Philippines were annexed; the long-discussed annexation of Hawaii was finally put through in the same year; and Guam and Wake islands were taken. To many observers the lesson was clear; the weak and declining empires of China and Spain were falling prey to the young and vigorous powers of Japan, Germany and America, and they expected a process deemed natural and healthy to continue.

The Russians adjusted much more easily to these events than did the British. Russia's position in Asia was not obviously weakened by Japanese, German and American achievements. The accretion of American power was remote from the areas of Russian ambition. There had been Russian reluctance to see the Germans leasing Kiaochow, but at least they had not wanted it themselves. William II had consulted Nicholas II first, and it seemed reasonable to assume that German interests in China would remain subsidiary for the foreseeable future. Russia's main concern was with Japanese aggrandisement, Witte regarding the Japanese as dangerous contenders for control of China if allowed to go unchecked. There was dispute as to the appropriate reaction. The emperor initially preferred making a deal with the Japanese government to share east Asia, but his advisers persuaded him that Japan must be deprived of its foothold in Manchuria and that China's predicament should be used to bind its government closer to that of Russia. Hence the diplomatic intervention by Russia, France and Germany to modify the treaty of Shimonoseki in 1895 was followed by Witte arranging with French help for the payment of China's war indemnity, by the founding of a Russo-Chinese Bank – again with capital mostly from French sources, and in 1896 by a Russo-Chinese secret defensive alliance against Japan. Witte intended the bank to finance commercial and industrial enterprises, railway concessions and telegraph lines, as well as the bribes needed to secure Chinese consent to the Trans-Siberian Railway taking a short cut across Manchuria. This line, the Chinese Eastern Railway, would later be extended, it was hoped, by branch lines to the south, becoming the principal artery of trade for Manchuria and the means by which Russia could exercise military

The end of the Great Game, 1894–1908

pressure in Manchuria, on the shores of the Yellow Sea, and in relation to Peking.

In 1898, as compensation for the German gains, the Russian government got the lease of the Liaotung peninsula in Manchuria, with the relatively ice-free Port Arthur, of which they had in 1895 deprived the Japanese in the name of China's integrity, and they secured the right to build a South Manchurian Railway as a branch of the Chinese Eastern Railway. Moreover, Japanese blunders in trying to exercise the right to informal control over Korea, which they had won from China, opened the way instead to an upsurge of Russian influence. The Japanese government was reduced to negotiating limits on Russian activities in Korea, and trying to exchange recognition of Russian predominance in Manchuria for acknowledgment of their own right to dominate Korea. The Russians cut back their existing activities in Korea to win Japanese acceptance of the Port Arthur lease, but they declined any clear commitment as to Korea's future. Witte had in December 1897 defined the maximum Russian programme as a sphere of influence covering Mongolia, most of Manchuria, and Korea. Japanese and German actions had enabled Russia to take important steps towards its realization.

By the end of the century the Russians had also consolidated their already powerful position in Persia. The Persians had tried to escape. After the shah's assassination in 1896, the ministers of his successor, Muẓaffar al-Dīn Shāh, sought to reduce the country's dependence on Russia. When they needed a foreign loan in 1897 they looked first to European sources other than Great Britain or Russia. When this failed they tried to get a British loan, but financial circles in London regarded Persia as a bad risk and imposed stringent conditions. Salisbury understood the political implications of this attitude, but knew no way of remedying matters. 'Other nations can lend money: and we cannot,' he wrote. 'The House of Commons, which never would guarantee the debt of India, would positively refuse any advance to an impecunious Oriental Ally. Other nations will give it. It is hopeless to struggle against that disadvantage. The real friend is the friend from whom one can borrow.'[1] Witte offered friendship of this kind. He was more interested in the political conditions such a loan would carry than in ensuring it was a commercially worthwhile transaction. In January 1900, the Persian government at last accepted a Russian loan. The security for the loan was the customs revenue (except in the Gulf); the Persians were to pay off all other foreign debts; they were to borrow from no other

---

[1] Quoted by J. A. S. Grenville, *Lord Salisbury and Foreign Policy. The Close of the Nineteenth Century* (London, 1964), 300–1.

government until the loan was paid off; and they were to give no other government railway concessions for ten years. The terms were regarded by Witte as a powerful instrument not only for consolidating Russian control over northern Persia but for the possible extension of Russian influence into those areas of Persia in which the British had so far predominated. At the same time the Russian government was taking advantage of British involvement in the Boer War to announce its intention of opening direct relations with Kābul, and Russian forces on the Afghan frontier were ostentatiously strengthened. But most of Nicholas II's ministers felt little more could be done to exploit British embarrassments. They were sceptical of what other governments were really prepared to undertake in the continental league against the British Empire which was being talked of in European diplomatic circles. Russia's own financial problems and the strains of rapid industrialization meant that the sort of patient accumulation of power being practised in China and Persia was still the only practicable course.

In effect, the events of 1894-8 had not disturbed the basic assumptions of Russian policy, and although there was frequent and anxious debate as to what should be the next step the policy itself had proved markedly successful. Indeed, the Russians had been more successful than they had realized. It was the obvious and growing strength of Russia in Asia which helped make the British government so uncertain and divided in its own reaction to these and other events. The British government had to interpret a much more complex set of crises than the Russians. As well as recurring crises over the massacre of Armenians in the Ottoman Empire and over the apparently impending breakup of the Chinese Empire, the British had faced American hostility evidenced in President Cleveland's bellicose message to Congress in December 1895, German hostility shortly after in January 1896 when William sent a famous telegram to Kruger, the prospect of war with France over the Niger and the Nile in 1897-8, and war itself with the Boer republics in 1899. In such circumstances confusion and uncertainty within the British cabinet as to the adequacy of British policies was understandable. Two of its members, Salisbury and Joseph Chamberlain, did not share the confusion and uncertainty. They offered clear and sharply contrasting guides to the way events were shaping.

Salisbury saw no need for a fundamental rethinking of the policies he had pursued for so long. He was confident of handling the disputes with France over Africa, and he regarded China's crisis as long-term rather than urgent in its effects on relations between the other powers. He did feel compelled to accept one major change of policy. In 1895-6 he had feared the imminent breakup of the Ottoman Empire and Russian seizure of the Straits as part of the crisis engendered by the Turkish massacre of the empire's Armenian subjects. He had proposed the traditional British policy of keeping the situation under control by sending the fleet to the Straits, but the cabinet had preferred the service view that the Franco-Russian alliance and the enhanced naval power at its disposal had made such a gesture too risky. When the massacres were resumed in 1896, he tried unsuccessfully to come to terms with Nicholas II over joint coercion of the sultan, holding out hope of British consent to Russian control of the Straits should the Ottoman Empire collapse. But by October 1897 Salisbury was taking a calmer view of this question as well. It had become clear that the Ottoman Empire was not breaking up, and, given cabinet refusal to threaten force, he had come to regard 'the Eastern question as having little serious interest for England'. He proposed to concentrate instead on strengthening 'our position on the Nile and to withdraw as much as possible from all responsibilities at Constantinople'.[1] But this was a change in the means of protecting British interests which Salisbury could accommodate within his general framework of thinking along with other novel features in international politics; a free hand would enable him to improvise a response to each threat as it arose, and, although he anticipated general world tension as the competition for empire at the expense of 'dying nations' accelerated, he continued to see France and Russia as offering the most serious, but by no means insurmountable, threats to Great Britain's own empire.

Chamberlain thought differently. He saw the expansionist and belligerent policies of so many of the world's powers as a very real peril to the British Empire's trade and security. As colonial secretary he promoted the idea of some form of imperial federation as essential to prosperity and survival in a dangerous world. By the end of 1897 he had come to believe that in addition the British must choose their allies if the empire's position was to be secured in a period of global conflict. The China scramble confirmed him in his vision, and he saw the defence of Great Britain's interests in China as crucial to its position as a world power. He regarded Salisbury's policy of the 'free hand' as obsolete, and called publicly as well as within the cabinet for a drastic reappraisal of British foreign policy. In a speech at Birmingham in May 1898 he urged an alliance with Germany and closer relations with America, and in November 1899 he went still further in suggesting that 'the Teutonic

[1] Quoted by J. A. S. Grenville, *Lord Salisbury and Foreign Policy. The Close of the Nineteenth Century* (London, 1964), 94.

race and the two branches of the Anglo-Saxon race' should form a 'natural alliance' to guarantee world peace. Chamberlain's attempts to initiate alliance negotiations with the Germans were conducted clumsily and with little understanding of German attitudes, but his attacks on Salisbury's policy carried conviction with many of his cabinet colleagues who shared his alarm at international trends. The feeling prevailed that Great Britain's position as a world power was in jeopardy, confirming older fears for its relative decline as a trading and an industrial nation. Salisbury's sangfroid was interpreted as the inability of an old man of failing health to adjust his ideas to a changing world.

What perhaps clinched the belief of men like Balfour and Lansdowne that Salisbury's policy was inadequate was expert assessment of British military weakness, especially in relation to Russia. Service pessimism was nothing new. That the Russians could threaten India much more easily than the British could attack any part of the Russian Empire had been known at government level during the 1885 crisis. Since then the Russian strategic rail system to transport troops and their supplies to the Afghan border had been developing as predicted, while British capacity for retaliation at the Straits had been discounted by the admiralty since 1892. But it was the exposure of British military deficiencies in fighting the Boers which turned official minds to just how catastrophic might be the consequences of having to fight two major powers like the Russians and the French simultaneously. It was estimated that, when the Orenburg–Tashkent railway was completed in 1904, the Russians would be able to put an army of 150,000 to 200,000 men into Afghanistan and reinforce it at the rate of 20,000 a month; the British had less than 300,000 troops at their disposal in India for the tasks of internal security as well as frontier defence, and reinforcement from the homeland in the event of war would be limited and uncertain. Planners in the military intelligence division in August 1901 saw no prospect of defeating Russia except by concentrating the war effort against its French financial backers. This sense of helplessness in face of Russian power to strike at India grew in the years that followed as military estimates of the men and money needed to contain a Russian offensive rose still further. As the old prophecies of a Russian threat to India seemed about to be fulfilled at last, confidence in being able to meet it was lower than it had ever been within official circles.

Chamberlain's claim that current events pointed to a general world crisis which the British government could hope to control only as part of some grand alliance had, therefore, a good deal to recommend it. In retrospect, the evidence looks inconclusive. It was true that the British had prepared for war with the French in 1898, with mastery of the Nile valley at stake; on the other hand, the French government gave way without war, and without Salisbury's government requiring allies or having to worry overmuch about France's Russian ally. When in 1899 the British actually did get involved in war, with control of South Africa at stake, they found world opinion on the side of their enemies the Boers. There were attempts by the Russians to organize a continental league against them, and the British, initially coming close to defeat, had to concentrate so much of their strength in Africa that they would have been more vulnerable than usual to an attack in Asia by the Russians. Nevertheless, the British eventually won the war, the continental league came to nothing, and, when it came to the point, the Russians were not ready to risk their long-term plans in Asia by a gamble on war. Similarly, the Boxers' war in 1900 against the intrusion of foreigners in China, their siege of the legations in Peking, and the rescue of the legations by an international force, all seemed to suggest that the final disintegration of China was nearer at hand than Salisbury had believed; indeed, Salisbury had been reluctant to promote international action lest it precipitate a final partition. But the partition of China had not, in fact, ensued. Nor was the statistical picture of British military inferiority presented by war office experts quite as unanswerable as it looked. Salisbury, of course, had long distrusted 'experts' in fields where much was unpredictable or disputed; '(if) you believe the doctors, nothing is wholesome: if you believe the theologians, nothing is innocent: if you believe the soldiers, nothing is safe'.[1] He had, besides, good grounds for scepticism about Russia's real capacity for waging efficient war in conditions of persistent economic weakness and threatened revolution. He believed that a British government which kept its nerve could handle crises in such a way as to make Russian leaders hesitate to fight. He thought the threats which so alarmed his colleagues could be dealt with separately and without need of lasting commitments to other powers, provided the government took care not to have 'more than a limited area of heather alight at the same time'.[2]

Salisbury's attitude reflects a cool commonsense, which is more attractive in retrospect, but Chamberlain's criticisms looked the more convincing to most political leaders at the turn of the century. Moreover, while Salisbury's intellectual grasp of foreign politics was unaffected by age and ill-health, his personality was not such that he could impress the cabinet with the correctness of his views once doubts had

[1] Quoted by Cecil, *Life of Salisbury*, II, 153.
[2] Quoted by Grenville, *Lord Salisbury and Foreign Policy*, 122.

set in. In October 1900, in the course of post-election cabinet changes, Salisbury appointed Lord Lansdowne as foreign secretary, and his own influence on the conduct of policy steadily declined thereafter until his retirement from the premiership as well in July 1902. But although Chamberlain had convinced his colleagues that new ways of defending British interests must be found, his own rather optimistic vision of an integrated British empire confidently holding its own as member of some grand alliance did not prevail. Balfour, who was to succeed Salisbury as prime minister, and Lord George Hamilton, secretary of state for India, did favour full membership of the Triple Alliance as stabilizing Europe and making it too dangerous for the Russians and the French to risk war with the British beyond Europe, but a divided and uncertain cabinet settled for the substantial modification of Salisbury's policy which Lansdowne, in effect, pursued between 1900 and 1905. Debate had exaggerated the degree of Salisbury's isolationism, and made the element of novelty in Lansdowne's actions seem greater than it really was. The so-called 'new course' resembled the policy of colonial settlements and regional pacts by which Salisbury, during his 1886–92 administration, had escaped from the dangerous isolation he had himself inherited in 1885. Lansdowne sensed still greater danger in 1900. In a world of restless, belligerent states and of scattered and thinly defended British possessions, he felt an urgent need of piecemeal measures to stop the situation from slipping altogether out of control. He went much faster than Salisbury would have gone in bidding for general settlements of overseas disputes so as to reduce defence commitments, and he went much farther than Salisbury advised in bidding for diplomatic and military partnerships to bolster British security in Asia. But he did not inaugurate the kind of diplomatic revolution envisaged by Chamberlain.

During 1901 Lansdowne was engaged in sounding or negotiating with the German, Russian, American, Japanese and French governments. Hopes of German support against Russian encroachments on China came to nothing, as Salisbury had predicted; the German government would accept no alliance confined to east Asia, and preferred to wait until the British felt obliged to commit themselves totally to the Triple Alliance. Soundings of the Russian government for a general settlement of disputes in Asia also came to nothing; the Russians saw no need to bargain. Other negotiations brought solid achievements.

In the first place, Lansdowne reduced British defence commitments in American waters. By the Clayton–Bulwer treaty of 1850 the British and American governments had agreed not to claim exclusive control of any canal that might be built linking the Atlantic and Pacific Oceans. The growth of their navy made a canal controlled by the Americans an urgent need, underlined by the experience of the war with Spain, and the American government sought the treaty's amendment. The British had been reluctant to assist in a development which would make more insecure than ever their empire in north America; since they had neither the means nor the will to prevent it, they tried to get American concessions elsewhere as compensation. Lansdowne cut short the proceedings by confining the negotiations to relatively minor matters, and conceding the essential American demand with good grace. The Hay–Pauncefote treaty of November 1901 tacitly acknowledged American naval superiority in the Caribbean as an established fact. Although the British war office continued to plan how it might conduct a war in north America, British governments would in practice rely on American restraint and a spirit of cooperation.

Secondly, vague talk of an alliance with the Japanese as Russia's other principal opponents in Asia changed to hard and successful bargaining. Lansdowne's tentative suggestion of an 'understanding' in August 1901 met with a sufficiently favourable response, and he presented a draft treaty of alliance in November. A formal and public alliance between the two governments was signed in January 1902. The terms meant that if either signatory got involved in war with one other power, such as Russia, its ally would remain neutral; but if the enemy was joined by a second power, such as France, the allies would both fight. The alliance would strengthen the hand of each in negotiating with the Russians, and enhance prospects of winning a war should diplomacy fail. Moreover, naval cooperation in peacetime would make for economies. Thirdly, talks in 1901 with the French led, though much more slowly, to a settlement in 1904 of many old overseas disputes between the two countries, and hence to a lessening of the risk of war.

Lansdowne's contributions to imperial security did not dispel the mood of doubt and anxiety which gripped the cabinet as a whole. Their confusion and uncertainty was apparent in their attitude to Younghusband's Tibetan expedition of 1904. Tibet had only recently begun to figure in Russo-British rivalry. It did not have the significance for India's north-east frontier that Afghanistan had on the north-west because Buddhist Tibet was not a warlike and unstable society, and because it was remote from Russia's own imperial frontiers. It had acquired significance because Tibet was claimed by the Chinese to be part of their empire, although they exercised no effective rule over it, and Tibet was among the Chinese provinces which Nicholas II aspired to control. Rumours of Russian intrigues in Lhasa and of overtures to Peking had convinced the Indian authorities that a Russian protectorate was in the offing, and it was difficult to see the value of Tibet to Russia except as a base against India.

The viceroy of India since 1898 had been George Curzon, a man of outstanding energy and intellect and with exceptional knowledge and understanding of the politics of Asia. Curzon did not share the general sense of helplessness about Russian expansion. 'I will no more admit', he wrote in April 1899, 'that an irresistible destiny is going to plant Russia in the Persian Gulf than at Kabul or Constantinople. South of a certain line in Asia her future is much more what we choose to make it than what she can make it herself.'[1] He favoured a more robust policy towards the Persians and the Afghans, and in 1902 he proposed to counter Russian penetration of Tibet by a British mission which would negotiate directly with the Dalai Lama instead of with the Chinese government as hitherto. The cabinet feared spoiling the prospects of a general settlement with the Russian government and promoting the disintegration of China, but eventually in the spring of 1903 it authorized British participation in a conference with Tibetan and Chinese representatives to discuss long-standing boundary disputes with the British protectorate of Sikkim. The Tibetans refused to negotiate with the leader of the mission, Colonel Francis Younghusband. Although Balfour and his colleagues did not share Curzon's desire to force a submissive relationship on Tibet, they grudgingly allowed mounting intervention during 1903 and 1904 in which Tibetan resistance was overcome, and Lhasa finally occupied in August 1904. Younghusband interpreted his orders in the sprit of Curzon, and the terms he negotiated in the Tibetan capital excluded foreign powers, save by British consent, from gaining control of any of Tibet's territory or revenues, acquiring railway, mining and other concessions, or despatching agents to Tibet to represent their interests. A British agent, however, was to reside at Gyantse, on the road to Lhasa, visiting the capital itself if business required. An indemnity was to be paid over seventy-five years, during which time British forces would occupy the Chumbi valley, commanding the Lhasa road – from which all military obstacles to a British advance were to be removed.

Curzon's approval of the Lhasa convention of September 1904 found no echo in the British cabinet, which reduced the indemnity and the length of the British stay in Chumbi, and disclaimed even occasional representation at Lhasa. Controversy as to who was responsible for this

[1] Quoted by D. Dilks, *Curzon in India*, 2 vols (London, 1969–70), I, 124.

muddle has persisted ever since, but there is no disputing the most remarkable aspect of the affair. The British government had disavowed a highly successful mission lest the Russians should consider provocative British predominance in a country bordering India and far from Russia itself. It was a measure of how far the Great Game had swung in Russia's favour.

Apprehensions as to the effect of Younghusband's expedition were high because his advance on Lhasa coincided with the opening phases of a war between Russia and Japan. Japanese alarm at Russian expansion was as great as that of the British government; their sense of urgency in seeking to check it was even greater. The Japanese, like the British, saw their position growing weaker as strategic railways consolidated Russian power on the mainland. The Genro, Japan's elder statesmen and the Meiji emperor's most influential advisers, wanted, like the British, an agreement with Russia about spheres of influence. They were willing to concede Russian predominance in Manchuria if the Russian government acknowledged Japanese predominance in Korea. There were, on the other hand, leading Japanese ministers and some members of the general staff who believed that the Russians would never accept such terms, that war was in the long run unavoidable if control of Korea was vital to Japanese security, and that Japanese prospects of winning such a war would sharply decline once the Trans-Siberian Railway was complete. In fact, the Russian government was not currently averse to such a deal, at least for the time being. There was considerable disagreement among Nicholas II's advisers as to the best means of developing Russia's already strong position in east Asia, but the Russian emperor accepted that war was inopportune because time was on Russia's side. But Russian diplomacy gave a contrary impression in its attempts to drive a hard bargain. War against the Boxers had given the Russians an occasion for a powerful military presence in Manchuria, and their promised evacuation by stages was delayed in 1903 while they extorted further concessions from the Chinese government. This intensified suspicion of Russia in Japanese governing circles, while in their negotiations with Japan in 1903 the Russians appeared so intransigent over Korea as to deprive Ito and the other Genro of convincing arguments against those who claimed the tsar was simply playing for time to release Russia from any need to negotiate at all. By December 1903 Japanese leaders were generally agreed that only war offered them any hope of containing Russia; at the same time, they regarded it as a desperate expedient for which their country was ill-prepared and which might well result in defeat.

The British cabinet had still less confidence in Japanese prospects. They agreed that the Russians would probably win. They differed, however, as to the likely consequences of a Russian victory and as to what should be their response to the war itself. Lansdowne wanted to avert a war in which the British could ill-afford to become involved for both military and financial reasons; he proposed to influence the Japanese government in the direction of a negotiated settlement. The chancellor of the exchequer, Austen Chamberlain, agreed that they should keep out of the war, but he did not want to discourage the Japanese from fighting when postponement would reduce still further their chances of victory; he hoped that a Russian government preoccupied by war would think it worth coming to terms with Great Britain. Selborne, first lord of the admiralty, thought that they would have to enter the war if the Japanese looked like suffering defeat, and his view was shared by the service chiefs. Balfour, on the other hand, believed a Russian mainland victory would be to British advantage; the Russians would cripple themselves financially in the process, and they would be able to sustain their newly won position only by permanently diverting much of their strength to east Asia.

Given such diverse views, it was not surprising that the British government's role was largely confined to cautious non-interference with events. It did not try to prevent war and, once war broke out in February 1904, it kept strictly to the letter of the alliance treaty in its observance of neutrality. The general settlement of overseas disputes hastily brought to a conclusion with the French within two months of the outbreak of hostilities emphasized how little the allies of either belligerent relished involvement. The British did momentarily resign themselves to war in October 1904 when the Russian Baltic fleet, making its way to the Pacific, attacked British trawlers on the Dogger Bank, but they were relieved when Nicholas II's expression of regret and promise of amends came just in time. It was only gradually that they realized that the events they were contemplating so helplessly had taken a reassuring turn for them. Russian prospects of victory had faded by January 1905 when Port Arthur finally fell to the Japanese, and a year of revolutionary upheaval began in Russia itself. As the Japanese triumph on land and sea reached its climax in the spring and early summer of 1905, an elated British government began to negotiate a new and wider alliance with Japan. This second alliance was concluded in August 1905. In contrast to the highly cautious and limited terms of its predecessor, the new treaty announced that the British and the Japanese would fight together if either got involved in war through

The end of the Great Game, 1894–1908 175

defending its interests in east Asia and India. This greater willingness by both governments to commit themselves to war in hypothetical circumstances recognized that a new balance of power was now possible in Asia. Russia might remain the greatest power in Asia, but after their failure against Japan alone the Russians would hesitate to risk war with Japan and Great Britain at once.

Russian policy in the immediate aftermath of defeat and revolution justified this optimism. While the emperor was striving to regain the authority he had lost within Russia during 1905, his ministers tried to secure the empire's interests in Europe and Asia by a more conciliatory diplomacy than they had practised in the recent past. Moreover, the main ambition of the foreign minister appointed in 1906, A. P. Izvolsky, was to persuade the other European governments to revise the Straits rule in Russia's favour, and he was only too willing to promote agreement on spheres of influence in Asia. Despite the outcome of the war, the Japanese and British governments were equally willing. The Japanese government had been glad to end the war on terms which gave it effective control of Korea and the lease of the Liaotung peninsula; at a time when a rapidly worsening crisis at home and Japan's spectacular naval victory in the straits of Tsushima had convinced Nicholas II that he must make peace, the Japanese generals were urging their own government to do the same. They believed that the war on land could not continue in their favour for long in face of an overwhelming build-up of Russian forces. Conscious of the narrow margin by which their victory had been won, Japanese political and military leaders were content to consolidate the sense of security it had brought. So in July 1907, the Japanese and Russian governments formally acknowledged one another's spheres of influence in east Asia – northern Manchuria and outer Mongolia in the case of Russia; southern Manchuria and Korea in the case of Japan. In the following month a Russo-British convention on similar lines was signed. Campbell-Bannerman's Liberal cabinet, which replaced Balfour's in December 1905 and was confirmed in office by the general election of 1906, found less ground for elation over the outcome of the war than had its predecessors. War office experts continued to regard British defences in Asia as wholly inadequate to meet a Russian attack, and saw no reason to believe the Russians would exercise restraint. The new government accepted the war office view of India's defences, but not the vastly increased expenditure and commitments recommended as the remedy. Instead, they hoped to cut imperial defence costs by a general settlement designed to still the Russian impulse for expansion.

There was little about the convention of August 1907 to suggest that it might mark the end of the Great Game. A deal with the Russian government as to spheres of influence in parts of Asia represented no dramatic shift in British policy, and need have heralded no more than a return to the long-term competition for trade and influence which had looked like prevailing in the early 1890s. The terms could be interpreted as a good or a bad bargain with equal force by observers in either country. The two governments agreed to certain restrictions on their behaviour in Asia. The Russian government undertook to send no agents into Afghanistan, to negotiate with its ruler only through the British authorities, and to forgo railway, mining and other concessions in the area of Persia closest to India, including Sīstān. The British government made a similar undertaking not to pursue influence by concessionaires in northern Persia, adjacent to Russia's frontiers, and not to use its exclusive influence in Afghanistan in a manner threatening to Russia. Neither government was to seek concessions in Tibet, to send its agents to Lhasa, or, Chinese suzerainty being acknowledged, to deal directly with the Tibetan government.

The effect of all these self-imposed restrictions would depend on whether the two governments would come to view them as a first step towards stable and amicable relations between neighbouring empires, as in the case of the Hay–Pauncefote treaty, or simply as a means of reducing the risk of war as they continued the struggle for a more favourable share of power and influence in Asia. Since the British government took the former view, and the Russian government the latter, it was not surprising that tension and antagonism persisted in the years that followed the convention. The restrictions still left plenty of scope for Russian expansion, while further revolutionary upheavals in Persia in 1909 and in China in 1911 offered still more. The Russians took their opportunities. Hence, despite the convention and despite the shock of military failure and of revolution, the basic fact of contemporary Asian politics had remained unchanged. Russian power was still on the increase and the British government had still found no means of halting it.

Yet the 1907 convention did happen to mark the end of the Great Game, even though it did not cause it to end. Around the turn of the century, when the old British interpretations were losing credibility, a radically different view of international politics had won important adherents. This saw the growing power of Germany and the naval and imperial ambitions of its emperor as likely to constitute in future the central threat to British security. It was a threat which would have to be neutralized by the British throwing their weight against Germany in the European balance of power; agreement with the French and Russian governments over old imperial disputes came to represent, in this view, not merely the reduction of British commitments, as Lansdowne had envisaged, but the opportunity of close cooperation with these traditional enemies against the enemy to come. This entirely new way of interpreting events was popular with certain foreign office officials and ambassadors like Francis Bertie, Charles Hardinge, Arthur Nicolson, Eyre Crowe and Louis Mallet. Few politicians were at first impressed, though Selborne took Tirpitz's naval programme seriously, and Chamberlain's disappointment at the German response to his alliance project had made him robustly anti-German by 1902. The new political leadership after 1905 was more susceptible to such arguments, especially as they took office just when an alarmist interpretation was becoming the most obvious way of explaining quarrelsome German diplomacy at a time of rapid German naval construction. Grey was, at any rate, sufficiently convinced of a latent threat from the Germans to pursue the recommended alignment with France and Russia, and even to allow precautionary staff talks with the French. The 1907 convention coincided, therefore, with the most radical reformulation of British foreign policy since the days of Ellenborough, Wellington and Palmerston. In the years that followed most British political leaders came to identify Germany, not Russia or France, as their principal antagonist in the world at large. German ambitions in Asia, too, especially in Persia and the Ottoman Empire, began to take on a threatening aspect. And after their humiliation in 1908–9 at the hands of the German and Austrian governments over the annexation of Bosnia and Herzegovina, the Russians were above all concerned to check any further extension of the central powers' influence in the Balkans and in the Ottoman Empire. The Great Game had lost its central role in British and Russian policy-making.

It might have regained its pre-eminence, but it did not. British and Russian preoccupation with Germany might not have endured for long. Nicholas II received conflicting advice during this period, in which the Russians experienced both a growing sense of danger and a persistent sense of weakness. The arguments for reviving close ties with their 'natural' conservative allies in an age of revolutionary agitation might have eventually carried conviction if some deal over spheres of influence in south-eastern Europe and western Asia had seemed negotiable. And British resentment of Russian activities in Asia was in turn resented, and seen as a sign that the traditional British threat remained strong despite the convention. On the British side, Grey had little interest in overseas questions, but he could not fail to be alarmed at the consequences of having left the Russians such a free hand. By 1914, northern Persia had for all practical purposes become part of the Russian Empire, occupied by Russian troops and with Russian consuls assuming governmental functions. Since the Chinese revolution of 1911, outer Mongolia retained only the most formal ties with Peking and was virtually a Russian protectorate; in 1913, it made an agreement with Tibet, which looked like an indirect instrument for Russian influence at Lhasa; and Russian activities in Sinkiang, the Chinese province bordering Tibet, had increased alarmingly. When in 1914 the government in India assumed a mediatory position between the Chinese and the Tibetans, who had taken advantage of the Chinese upheaval to get rid of the Chinese garrison, the Russian foreign minister, Sazonov, made it clear that recognition of more extensive British influence in Tibet would have to be purchased by such concessions as the acknowledgment of more far-reaching Russian rights in Persia, and the abandonment of Herat itself to the Russian sphere of influence.

This was on the eve of the 1914 war. The whole situation was very fluid. The Liberal cabinet was not irretrievably committed to the view of Germany as inevitably hostile and of cooperation with the Franco-Russian alliance as something to be preserved at all costs. Grey, indeed, made attempts at reconciliation with the Germans after 1912. The future alignment of Great Britain and Russia with other powers, and their future attitudes to one another, were quite uncertain. A sequence of crises in Asia around 1912–14 was as much on the cards as a sequence of crises in Europe. As it turned out, events in Europe were such as to convince most Russian and British political leaders that the German threat was the greatest they both faced. War with Germany finally became for them an obvious, if undesired, outcome of the Austro-Serb confrontation in the summer of 1914. With Russian and British armies fighting as allies to prevent German ascendancy in Europe, their own more leisurely contest for ascendancy in Asia was relegated to the background. The Great Game, cardinal to British foreign policy since the 1830s and to that of Russia since the 1850s, was manifestly at an end.

Conclusion

The British may be said to have lost the Great Game, but Russian capacity to exploit their defeat had been very limited. Since the 1860s the Russians had gradually undermined the ascendancy in western and central Asia established by the British during the previous three decades. By the end of the nineteenth century Russia was arguably the greatest single Asian power. The Russian Empire was no longer vulnerable to British invasion; the extension of British political and economic predominance over Russia's Asian neighbours had become improbable; and the weakest of those neighbours had been subjected instead to Russian control. Yet the Russians never enjoyed, any more than had the British, that political ascendancy in Eurasia as a whole which was essential to uninhibited exercise of the power they had secured in its Asian sector. It was the Germans who actually bid for such ascendancy, and came nearer to realizing it than any government since that of Napoleon I. Between 1914 and 1918 they proved their empire to be the most powerful in Europe, and the terms they imposed on the defeated Russians at Brest-Litovsk in March 1918 showed that their vague aspirations to world-power status had turned into a clearly formulated bid for unchallengeable ascendancy within the Eurasian continent. The survivors of the anti-German coalition, Great Britain, France and the U.S.A., just managed to frustrate this bid, so that by 1918–19 the British could look with satisfaction on the disappearance of both the old Russian and the new German threat. Moreover, to fend off possible German and Turkish moves against India in the aftermath of Russian withdrawal from the war, British troops had entered the Caucasus and the trans-Caspian areas, and British ships commanded the Caspian Sea. The Russian Empire disintegrated, and the Asian peoples conquered by the Russians in the nineteenth century were asserting their independence. The tier of buffer states friendly to the British, which so many British politicians had seen as the key to the security of their empire in Asia, seemed close to realization. The British appeared for a moment to have won the Great Game after all.

Not only did the moment quickly pass, but there was to be no resumption of the Great Game between the British and the Russians. The British cabinet, once the war against Germany had been won, was divided as to how much military effort should continue to be directed towards the border regions of the old Russian Empire, whether for improving India's defences or for undermining the prospects of bolshevism; predictably enough, in the aftermath of an exhausting war, their intervention in the Russian civil war was half-hearted and ineffective. The bolshevik regime not merely won the struggle for power within Russia, but gained control of the old empire's Asian territories. In effect, two great empires confronted one another as before, separated as before by highly unstable states of uncertain alignment, and now with additional reasons for mutual hostility. But the mutual antagonism of the British and Soviet governments was not to be central to either's policy-making. Although Soviet policies were sometimes to bear a superficial resemblance to those of tsarist predecessors, Soviet leaders interpreted events according to a quite different hypothesis, in which the British figured only as part of a worldwide threat by capitalist-controlled governments, and which included very distinctive assumptions as to the long-term means of ending the threat. British political leaders lacked such a clearcut interpretation of international politics, but for them the Soviet threat was likewise just one factor in a new and complex world. Indian nationalism had become the most potent challenge to their authority in the subcontinent, and, even if fuelled by Soviet propaganda, it was a challenge that would have to be met within India, not beyond its frontiers in the manner of the Great Game.

Twenty years after the establishment of the Soviet Union, the Russians and the British were once more allies with America against a renewed German bid for ascendancy in Eurasia. As its defeat was followed both by British withdrawal from India and by effective Soviet control of eastern Europe, the Soviet Union became unquestionably the greatest single power in Eurasia, with far more capacity to influence events throughout the continent than either the British or Russian governments had possessed in the nineteenth century. Yet it was soon apparent that even the Soviet government's freedom to exercise its power was restricted, this time by challenges from America and, later,

China. A 'Cold War' ensued for political ascendancy, not just in Eurasia but in the world as a whole.

The old phrase 'Great Game' has been used here because it conveys the sense of excitement and adventure with which contemporary observers invested international rivalries, just as 'Cold War' expresses the contrasting grimness and disillusionment with which comparable events are regarded in the second half of the twentieth century. From the point of view of the weaker governments whose alignment could affect the issue, the Cold War has been conducted by methods similar to those employed in the Great Game, although the 'civilizing missions' to which they have been incidentally subjected have changed in character. For 'Great Game' and 'Cold War' are simply different names for what is broadly the same immemorial phenomenon: the rivalry resulting from the urge of powerful governments to reduce relatively weak states – especially those whose control by another powerful government might constitute a threat – to some form of dependence, ranging from mildly restrictive economic ties to outright annexation. The troublesome term 'imperialism' is as appropriate as any for this urge. Although its selective and emotional use in political debate has made it a word most scholars would prefer to discard, no obvious alternative has emerged, and it seems reasonable to employ it at least in the present neutral and universal sense. It is far from clear, however, why imperialism and imperialist rivalry should be recurrent themes throughout international history. Nor is it clear why their general form should be so predictable despite the frequent emergence of new interpretations of world politics and new modes of economic and military power. The following general impressions of Russian and British behaviour during the Great Game may be thought relevant to this wider question, and to the associated question of the recurrence of war in imperialist rivalry.

In the first place, attempts to classify British and Russian behaviour towards one another as aggressive or defensive, and so decide which was responding defensively to the other's aggression, would seem pointless. Much of their rivalry was conducted by warning signals which may be loosely called aggressive in that any expression of resentment, from a sharply worded note to a movement of troops or ships, implied an ultimate willingness to fight if the causes of resentment mounted rather than declined. Yet it is clear that members of either government making the signals thought of them, at the same time, as defensive; they were warning that they felt their empire in Asia to be threatened either immediately or in the long term. 'Aggressive' and 'defensive' were not mutually exclusive terms in this context. Aggressive signalling was a normal feature of each government's defensive system. So was imperialism. A preoccupation with security in the broadest sense of the term – greater security for their frontiers and communications and, to a lesser extent, for their foreign markets and sources of raw materials – explains the cases of aggressive British and Russian conduct towards neighbouring governments as well as towards one another. Although political leaders often speak of security as if it were a goal which should reassure the outside world as to their intentions, its pursuit has rarely been a conservative and stabilizing factor in international politics, and its potentially dynamic and dangerous effects are well illustrated by the Great Game.

Political instability and military weakness in the areas bordering both empires excited the natural potential of British and Russian leaders for imagining future dangers and the changes by which they might be anticipated. The most obvious danger to imagine about neighbours like the Ottoman Empire and Persia, Sind and the Panjāb, Afghanistan and the khanates, Tibet and China, was that the rival empire might somehow try to dominate them; the most obvious change to imagine in view of their relative weakness was the assertion of one's own dominance in anticipation. Both governments had sufficient power to be at least tempted to bid for greater security through limiting or even destroying the independence of their neighbours, and improvements in weapons and in economic and organizational efficiency meant that their power was always on the increase during the nineteenth century. Aggressive behaviour in pursuit of greater security was an outstanding feature of the Great Game; but it has characterized most of the principal international rivalries before and since. Imaginative thinking about possible dangers to their state is normal in political leaders; uncertainty as to the future policies and alignments of immediate neighbours is normal in most areas and in most periods, and has been central to these imaginative exercises; a greatly uneven distribution of power as between states is also normal, and means that there have always been some leaders who can reasonably believe they have it in their power to remove the uncertainty on their borders, and with it the imagined threats to their security. In so far as the imagined opportunities have normally been taken, the Great Game may appear an altogether typical case of international discord.

Secondly, the role of war in the Great Game suggests that it was a normal but unnecessary accompaniment of the imperialist rivalry. There was only one war between the Russians and the British, and, while their wars with neighbours were more frequent, they occasioned a great deal of hesitancy and doubt. British and Russian restraint in respect of one another was due partly to the absence in either capital of political leaders addicted to wanton conquest, partly to the uneasy awareness of British and Russian leaders alike after the Crimean War of how difficult it was for them to mobilize their potentially vast resources for all-out war, and partly to the political geography of Eurasia which made it easier to strike indirect blows by intimidating governments in the lands between their empires. But their preference for the intimidation of weaker neighbours does not in itself explain the greater frequency of wars with them, because their preference was at the same time for less costly and risky ways of warning them to conform to the defence requirements of the neighbouring empire. Moreover, the rulers with whom they had to contend, though often of a very warlike disposition indeed, knew only too well that the cost of defeat by the British or the Russians would be dismemberment or even annexation, and they too hesitated to take to the battlefield if a bargain could be struck or a tacit understanding reached.

British relations with the Indian princely states, with Nepal after 1816, with Afghanistan in the later reign of Dost Muḥammad and again in the reign of Abdur Rahman were examples, in which the weaker government accepted, tacitly or by treaty, limitations on its freedom of action abroad without losing control of its internal affairs. So were Russian relations with the Ottoman Empire in the 1830s and 1840s, with Persia after 1828, and eventually with Khīva and Bukhārā. That such relationships could be sustained over long periods suggests that the all-round preference for avoiding war was a reasonable aspiration. Yet in all the cases cited mutual restraint was realized only after the experience of war, which seems to have been almost as normal a preliminary to this sort of relationship as to the numerous other cases of actual conquest.

The explanation seems to lie in the difficulty of establishing relative bargaining strengths in nineteenth-century Asia without recourse to war. None of the governments involved in the Great Game would have disputed that, in a continent of such unequal powers, concessions in the form of tribute, trading facilities, diplomatic restrictions and the like could be honourably made to obviously more imposing neighbours. Imperialism was to that extent an accepted fact of life, and did not necessarily entail war. But just how much in the way of such concessions a more powerful neighbour could reasonably demand depended on the degree of dominance it could exert, and it was never easy to assess this without war. No government would have disputed that war was indeed the only clearcut way to test relative bargaining strengths when negotiation foundered – more sophisticated devices like arbitration presupposed a measure of indifference to the result rare in this context. The test was likely to be invoked particularly when the distribution of power was undergoing rapid change of a kind difficult to calculate, as it was during the nineteenth century in both Europe and Asia.

In Europe, a series of wars was fought between 1859 and 1871 through failure to agree how much diplomatic weight should be allowed to the revived power of France and Prussia. In Asia, the uncertainties were greater and more persistent. The Chinese, Persian and Ottoman rulers were not inclined to admit the new Russian and British predominance as a fact without the test of war, and lesser Asian rulers, accustomed to coping with imperial neighbours by a mixture of deference and defiance, were uncertain how far they could carry their resistance to the newcomers. And they had good grounds for questioning the real power of the British and the Russians in Asian conditions. Not only did their rivalry mean that they could be played off one against the other, but the severe logistical problems confronting their commanders meant that their notable advantages in equipment and organization were an unreliable indicator. Asian governments could quite rationally choose war in the hope of at least forcing the British or the Russians to acknowledge that their margin of superiority was less than they had assumed and to scale down their pretensions accordingly. A peaceful relationship reflecting an inequality of power but marked by mutual restraint was therefore possible, but only if each government could convince the other that the status it was implicitly claiming within the Eurasian international system could be sustained if put to the test of war. War was the cost of failing to carry conviction, or of making the future conditions of peace look the less desirable option. The mixed fortunes of the Russians and the British in their Asian wars showed how real were the uncertainties that somehow had to be dispelled, and, given the obsession on all sides with security, it is not surprising that war was thought on occasions to be a less risky way of dispelling them than a doubtful bargain.

In so far as war was regarded as a second-best alternative in the Great Game, it may be said, therefore, to have resulted from avoidable but quite normal failures in diplomacy. Often the personal remoteness of the protagonists, whether through distance or cultural disparity or both, made exceptional calls on the skills and imagination essential to diplomacy, but otherwise, in respect of its wars as well as of its imperialism, the Great Game constituted a typical enough episode in international history. One group or other of the political leaders and their agents responsible for diplomatic relations in Asia was almost bound occasionally to misunderstand the temperament and the thinking of those whom they were trying to impress with their bargaining strength, to exaggerate its effect, and hence to miscalculate what was attainable without fighting. This has commonly been a prelude to war before and since, and the history of the twentieth century continues to provide examples. What makes for diplomatic success or failure remains imperfectly understood. This makes it all the more curious that diplomatic history, the record of human attempts to wield power abroad without bloodshed, should have become one of the least fashionable studies in a world professedly dedicated to reducing the incidence of war.

Further reading

This section is intended mainly for readers to whom the foregoing account has served as an introduction. The works selected, together with their references and bibliographies, will equip them to investigate questions which I have neglected, or where my answers have failed to satisfy. As befits a general work of this kind, footnotes have been used only to give the source of quotations. I have, therefore, taken the opportunity here to acknowledge my debt to those books and articles which I have found most convincing or challenging and on which I have particularly relied in selecting material. The authors must not, of course, be assumed to share the interpretation in support of which I have used their findings, and they may well not agree with the judgments their writings have stimulated me to form.

GENERAL

D. K. Fieldhouse, *Economics and Empire, 1830–1914* (London, Weidenfeld and Nicolson, 1973) includes a summary of Russian and British expansion in Asia by way of illustrating an important thesis about the nature of imperialism. M. S. Anderson, *The Eastern Question, 1774–1923: a Study in International Relations* (London, Macmillan, 1966) is excellent for Russian and British policies towards the Ottoman Empire. The main trends in Russian policy as a whole are conveniently summarized by Barbara Jelavich in *A Century of Russian Foreign Policy, 1814–1914* (Philadelphia and New York, Lippincott, 1964) and various aspects of its formulation and conduct are discussed by the distinguished contributors to *Russian Foreign Policy: Essays in Historical Perspective*, ed. by Ivo J. Lederer (New Haven and London, Yale University Press, 1962). Good general accounts of Russian involvement in Asia include Baymirza Hayit, *Turkestan zwischen Russland und China* (Amsterdam, Philo Press, 1971); Otto Hoetzch, *Russland in Asien: Geschichte einer Expansion* (Stuttgart, Deutsche Verlags-Anstalt, 1966); Richard Pierce, *Russian Central*

Asia, 1867–1917 (Berkeley and Los Angeles, University of California Press, 1960); and Geoffrey Wheeler, *The Modern History of Soviet Central Asia* (London, Weidenfeld and Nicolson, 1964). The best survey of British foreign policy is Kenneth Bourne, *The Foreign Policy of Victorian England, 1830–1902* (Oxford, Clarendon Press, 1970), and D. C. M. Platt elucidates an important theme in *Finance, Trade and Politics: British Foreign Policy, 1815–1914* (Oxford, Clarendon Press, 1968). Recurrent British involvement in central Asia is well described by W. K. Fraser-Tytler, *Afghanistan: a Study of Political Developments in Central and Southern Asia*, 3rd ed. (London, Oxford University Press, 1967), and, more briefly, by Pierce G. Fredericks, *The Sepoy and the Cossack* (London, W. H. Allen, 1973). Dorothy Woodman, *Himalayan Frontiers: a Political Review of British, Chinese, Indian and Russian Rivalries* (London, Barrie and Rockliff, The Cresset Press, 1969) is useful for the historical geography of boundary issues.

1. THE RISE OF RUSSIAN AND BRITISH POWER IN EURASIA

The strengths and weaknesses of China around 1800 are conveniently summarized in Frederick Wakeman's essay 'High Ch'ing, 1683–1839' in *Modern East Asia: Essays in Interpretation*, ed. by James B. Crowley (New York, Harcourt, Brace and World Inc., 1970), 1–28. For Russian attitudes to China in this period, I found Clifford M. Foust, *Muscovite and Mandarin: Russia's Trade with China and its Setting, 1727–1805* (Chapel Hill, University of North Carolina Press, 1969) particularly useful. David M. Lang, *The Last Years of the Georgian Monarchy, 1658–1832* (New York, Columbia University Press, 1957) is the essential work in English for the annexation of Georgia. Standard works on the East India Company in these years are C. H. Philips, *The East India Company, 1784–1834* (Manchester, Manchester University Press, 1940) and Holden Furber, *John Company at Work: a Study of European Expansion in India in the late Eighteenth Century* (Cambridge, Mass., Harvard University Press, 1948). In *Charles Grant and British Rule in India* (London, Allen and Unwin, 1962), Ainslie T. Embree examines the career of a leading opponent within the Company of expansionist policies. The people and events through which British paramountcy in the sub-continent was established are vividly described by Edward Thompson, *The Making of the Indian Princes* (London, Oxford University Press, 1943), and the roles of some remarkable private traders, diplomats and soldiers are skilfully portrayed in such books as Pamela Nightingale, *Trade and Empire in Western India, 1784–1806* (Cambridge, University Press, 1970), K. N. Panikkar, *British Diplomacy in North India: a Study of the Delhi Residency, 1803–57* (New Delhi, Associated Publishing House, 1968), and John Pemble, *The Invasion of Nepal: John Company at War* (Oxford, Clarendon Press, 1971). Napoleon I's diplomacy in respect of western Asia and India is explored by Vernon J. Puryear, *Napoleon and the Dardanelles* (Berkeley, University of California Press, 1951) and by S. P. Sen, *The French in India, 1763–1816* (Calcutta, Firma K. L. Mukhopadhyay, 1958). Edward Ingram studies the various British military and diplomatic activities at the turn of the century in 'A preview of the Great Game in Asia', *Middle Eastern Studies* 9 (1973).

2. BRITISH LEADERS TAKE ALARM, 1828–33

Two classics of diplomatic history, C. K. Webster, *The Foreign Policy of Castlereagh, 1815–1822*, 2nd ed. (London, Bell, 1934) and H. W. V. Temperley, *The Foreign Policy of Canning, 1822–1827* (London, Bell, 1925) should be read for British policy in relation to Europe. Patricia Grimsted has written a valuable study of *The Foreign Ministers of Alexander I: Political Attitudes and the Conduct of Russian Diplomacy, 1801–1825* (Berkeley and Los Angeles, University of California Press, 1969). British relations with Persia are best explored in the work of J. B. Kelly, *Britain and the Persian Gulf, 1795–1880* (London, Oxford University Press, 1968), and Marvin L. Enter has written an interesting account of *Russo-Persian Commercial Relations, 1828–1914* (Gainesville, Florida, University of Florida Press, 1965), especially useful for the commercial consequences of the treaty of Turkomānchāy. M. E. Yapp deals with the problem of 'The control of the Persian mission, 1822–1836', *University of Birmingham Historical Journal* 7 (1959–60), 164–70. The slaughter by a Persian mob of the Russian envoy and his staff in 1829 has attracted much attention because the murdered diplomat was the writer Alexander Griboyedov, and the circumstances of his death disputed: David M. Lang, 'Griboedov's last years in Persia', *American Slavic and East European Review* 7 (1948), 317–39, D. P. Costello, 'The murder of Griboedov', *Oxford Slavonic Papers* 8 (1958), 66–89, and S. V. Shostakovich, *Diplomaticheskaya deyatel'nost' A. S. Griboedova* (Moscow, 1960) are among the contributions to this debate. John S. Curtiss, *The Russian Army under Nicholas I, 1825–1855* (Durham, N. C., Duke University Press, 1965), William E. D. Allen and Paul Muratoff, *Caucasian Battlefields: a History of the Wars on the Turco-Caucasian Border, 1828–1921* (Cambridge, University Press, 1953), and John F. Baddeley, *The Russian Conquest of the Caucasus* (London, 1908) are excellent guides to Russia's wars in western Asia, and there is 'An enquiry into the outbreak of the second Russo-Persian war, 1826–8' by P. W. Avery in C. E. Bosworth (ed.), *Iran and Islam: in Memory of Vladimir Minorsky* (Edinburgh, University Press, 1971). A. V. Fadeyev, *Rossiya i vostochnii krizis 20kh godov XIX veka* (Moscow, 1958) and C. W. Crawley, *The Question of Greek Independence, 1821–1833* (Cambridge, University Press, 1930) are important works on Russian and British diplomacy during the Greek revolt. John H. Gleason, *The Genesis of Russophobia in Great Britain: a Study of the Interaction of Policy and Opinion* (Cambridge, Mass., Harvard University Press, 1950) is the essential work for the campaign by Urquhart and others to spread belief in a Russian danger. Earlier and later British attitudes to Russia are explained by M. S. Anderson, *Britain's Discovery of Russia, 1553–1815* (London, Macmillan, 1958) and by V. K. Chavda, *India, Britain, Russia: a Study in British Opinion (1838–1878)* (Delhi, Sterling Publishers, 1967). The puzzle of the emperor Paul's Indian expedition is examined by J. Lee Shneidman, 'The proposed invasion of India by Russia and France in 1801', *Journal of Indian History* 35 (1957), 167–75, and by John W. Strong, 'Russia's plans for an invasion of India in 1801', *Canadian Slavonic Papers* 7 (1965), 114–26; Norman E. Saul offers a sympathetic study of the emperor's motivation in foreign affairs generally in *Russia and the Mediterranean, 1797–1807* (Chicago, University of Chicago Press, 1970). For the conversion of British leaders to belief in a Russian threat I used particularly the books by J. B. Kelly and John H. Gleason already mentioned, and the early chapters of another excellent work, J. A. Norris, *The First Afghan War, 1838–1842* (Cambridge, University Press, 1967). Sir Charles Webster, *The Foreign Policy of Palmerston, 1830–1841*, 2 vols (London, Bell, 1951) is a valuable study, which does not, however, venture much east of the Ottoman Empire. Donald Southgate places Palmerston's Russian policy in its more appropriate Eurasian setting in *'The Most English Minister . . .': the Policies and Politics of Palmerston* (London, Macmillan, 1966), and a definitive biography of Palmerston is expected soon from Kenneth Bourne. M. Vereté has found interesting material about 'Palmerston and the Levant crisis, 1832', *Journal of Modern History* 24 (1952), 143–51.

3. PALMERSTON'S COUNTER-OFFENSIVE, 1833–41

This may be studied in the books by J. B. Kelly, J. A. Norris and Sir Charles Webster. Special aspects of his policy are dealt with by Vernon J. Puryear, *International Economics and Diplomacy in the Near East: a Study of British Commercial Policy in the Levant, 1834–1853* (Stanford, Stanford University Press, 1935) and Frank E. Bailey, *British Policy and the Turkish Reform Movement: a Study in Anglo-Turkish Relations, 1826–1853* (Cambridge, Mass., Harvard University Press, 1942), who describe British economic strategy abroad and regard it as central to an understanding of British foreign policy; by C. J. Bartlett, who explains the role of the navy in *Great Britain and Sea Power, 1815–1853* (Oxford, Clarendon Press, 1963); by Halford L. Hoskins, who examines the attempts to explore and protect the various *British Routes to India* (New York, Longman, 1928); and by Stevan K. Pavlowitch, *Anglo-Russian Rivalry in Serbia, 1837–39: the Mission of Colonel Hodges* (Paris and The Hague, Mouton, 1961) and Robert A. Huttenback, *British Relations with Sind, 1799–1843: an Anatomy of Imperialism* (Berkeley and Los Angeles, University of California Press, 1962), providing good local case-studies of British policy in action. H. W. C. Davis's famous Raleigh Lecture, 'The Great Game in Asia, 1800–1844', *Proceedings of the British Academy* 12 (1926), 227–56, is a brilliant sketch of the work of British agents beyond the Indian frontier, but just how uncertain our knowledge of their activities remains is shown in an important progress report by Gerald Morgan, who exposes the fable of Captain Dalgetty's intelligence school in 'Myth and reality in the Great Game', *Asian Affairs* 60 (1973), 55–65. The background to Sino-British conflict in these years may be studied in such works as Michael Greenberg, *British Trade and the Opening of China, 1800–42* (Cambridge,

University Press, 1951); H. P. Chang, *Commissioner Lin and the Opium War* (Cambridge, Mass., Harvard University Press, 1964); and Arthur Waley, *The Opium War through Chinese Eyes* (London, Allen and Unwin, 1958). Philip E. Mosely made convincing use of Russian archival material to explain Nicholas I's policy in the 1830s, and I have followed the interpretation he put forward in *Russian Diplomacy and the Opening of the Eastern Question in 1838 and 1839* (Cambridge, Mass., Harvard University Press, 1934), and in his article 'Russian policy in Asia, 1838–9', *Slavonic and East European Review* 14 (1936), 670–81. Russia's traditional frontier policies in Asia are the subject of an important case-study by Alton S. Donnelly, *The Russian Conquest of Bashkiria, 1552–1740* (New Haven and London, Yale University Press, 1968). In his discussion of Soviet claims advanced in 1945 and after, 'Russia and the Turkish Straits: a revaluation of the origins of the problem', *World Politics* 14 (1961–2), 605–32, J. C. Hurewitz conveniently summarizes the controversies surrounding Hünkâr Iskelesi and earlier treaties.

4. THE BRITISH AND THE RUSSIANS LOSE CONTROL, 1841–53

Kenneth Bourne's important study, *Britain and the Balance of Power in North America, 1815–1908* (London, Longman, 1967) explains the other and equally crucial 'Great Game' in which the British were involved. Nicholas I's efforts to reach a permanent understanding with the British in Eurasia are described sympathetically by Vernon J. Puryear in *England, Russia and the Straits Question, 1844–1856* (Berkeley, University of California Press, 1931). His view that the British government of the day entered into binding commitments subsequently violated in 1853–4 was disputed by, among others, Gavin B. Henderson in 'The Seymour conversations, 1853', included in the collection of his essays, *Crimean War Diplomacy* (Glasgow, Jackson, 1947), 1–14. G. H. Bolsover has clearly traced in these and other negotiations the emperor's changing ideas as to a redistribution of power and territory should the Ottoman Empire collapse: 'Nicholas I and the partition of Turkey', *Slavonic and East European Review* 27 (1948), 115–45. Contrasting interpretations of the 1849 crisis may be found in V. J. Puryear's book and in Harold Temperley, *England and the Near East: the Crimea* (London, Longman, 1936), one of the best accounts of the war's background and certainly the most colourful and enjoyable. For the annexation of Sind there is H. T. Lambrick, *Sir Charles Napier and Sind* (Oxford, Clarendon Press, 1952), as well as the book by Robert A. Huttenback already mentioned, while for the annexation of the Panjāb there is Bikrama Jit Hasrat, *Anglo-Sikh Relations, 1799–1849: a Reappraisal of the Rise and Fall of the Sikhs* (Hoshiarpur, Panjāb, 1968). Selection from the literature on the immediate origins of the Crimean War is difficult, but some books are particularly useful in viewing the war as an aspect of Russo-British rivalry. Important works by Puryear, Henderson and Temperley have already been noted. A. M. Zayonchkovsky, *Vostochnaya Voyna*, 4 vols (St Petersburg, 1908–13), is especially valuable for printing over four hundred documents to illustrate Russian policy, while an official Russian account, prepared in 1863 and attributed to Jomini, was published in English as a *Diplomatic Study of the Crimean War* (London, 1882). The changing and varied reactions to the crisis of British cabinet ministers are clarified by J. B. Conacher in *The Aberdeen Coalition, 1852–1855: a Study in Mid-Nineteenth Century Party Politics* (Cambridge, University Press, 1968), and for the press's role there is Kingsley Martin's justly celebrated *The Triumph of Lord Palmerston: a Study of Public Opinion in England before the Crimean War*, 2nd ed. (London, Hutchinson, 1963). The most recent detailed examination of the whole crisis, Paul W. Schroeder's *Austria, Great Britain and the Crimean War: the Destruction of the European Concert* (Ithaca, N.Y., Cornell University Press, 1972) makes British irresponsibility a central theme, and signifies that the Crimean War is still as contentious a subject as it was in the days of Puryear and Temperley.

5. RUSSIAN LEADERS TAKE ALARM, 1853–60

Military operations in the Crimean War have proved almost as controversial as its diplomatic origins. A major Soviet work is E. V. Tarle, *Krimskaya voyna*, available as vols 8 and 9 of his *Sochineniya* (Moscow, 1959); it is critically discussed by Michael E. Shaw in 'E. V. Tarle's "Krymskaia Voina": visions and revisions', *Canadian-American Slavic Studies* 7 (1973), 188–208. British books on the war are critically discussed by Brison D. Gooch in 'The Crimean War in selected documents and secondary works since 1940', *Victorian Studies* 1 (1957), 271–9. Good introductions are provided by John S. Curtiss in chs 16 and 17 of *The Russian Army under Nicholas I, 1825–1855* (Durham, N. C., Duke University Press, 1965) and in the most recent reappraisal by Philip Warner, *The Crimean War* (London, Arthur Barker, 1972). Vols 83–5 (1943–5) of the Navy Records Society, ed. by D. Bonner-Smith and A. C. Dewar, contain official correspondence on operations in the Black Sea and the Baltic important to an understanding of British thinking about the war. J. J. Stephan discusses 'The Crimean War in the Far East', *Modern Asian Studies* 3 (1969), 257–77, and Garry J. Alder, 'India and the Crimean War', *Journal of Imperial and Commonwealth History* 2 (1973–4), 15–37; the latter article suggests how the war affected British ideas as to the vulnerability of their position in Asia and as to its potential for offensive operations. Notable interpretations of the Indian revolt of 1857 include S. N. Sen, *1857* (Delhi, 1957) and J. A. B. Palmer, *The Mutiny Outbreak at Meerut in 1857* (Cambridge, University Press, 1966). Barbara English in *John Company's Last War* (London, Collins, 1971) and Douglas Hurd in *The Arrow War: an Anglo-Chinese Confusion, 1856–1860* (London, Collins, 1968) provide lively reconstructions of the British attacks on Persia and China in the years after the Crimean War; for the overall significance of these conflicts J. B. Kelly, *Britain and the Persian Gulf, 1795–1880* (London, Oxford University Press, 1968), John K. Fairbank, *Trade and Diplomacy on the China Coast: the Opening of the Treaty Ports, 1842–1854* (Cambridge, Mass., Harvard University Press, 1953), and J. S. Gregory, *Great Britain and the Taipings*

(London, Routledge and Kegan Paul, 1969) should be used. In 'The fall of Circassia: a study in private diplomacy', *English Historical Review* 71 (1956), 401–27, P. Brock discusses how far persistent Circassian resistance to Russia between 1860 and 1864 was due to the aid and propaganda of Urquhart's British and Polish associates. For Alexander II's early policy-making I found the most convincing interpretation that of Alfred J. Rieber in the introductory essay to his edition of the letters of the emperor to Prince Baryatinsky between 1857 and 1864: *The Politics of Autocracy* (Paris and The Hague, Mouton, 1966). A. L. Popov's article 'Iz istorii zavoevaniya sredney Azii', *Istoricheskie zapiski* (1940), 198–242, includes valuable material for these years. N. A. Khalfin has written several useful works on Russian expansion in central Asia: *Tri russkie missii* (Tashkent, 1956) describes the central Asian probes by Khanykov, Ignatyev and Valikhanov, but the account of these in his *Politika Rossii v. sredney Azii, 1857–1868* (Moscow, 1960) may be preferred, as there is a good translation from the Central Asian Research Centre: *Russia's Policy in Central Asia, 1857–1868* (London, 1964), abridged, but excluding nothing of importance. M. K. Rozhkova's important study, *Ekonomicheskie svyazi Rossii so sredney Aziey 40–60-e godi XIX veka* (Moscow, 1963) examines the extent to which Russian business circles influenced official thinking on central Asia. The concessions made by the Chinese to the Russians at this time have still too much political significance for any very detached account to be expected from either country, but there are very good analyses in English from Russian and Chinese sources by R. K. I. Quested, *The Expansion of Russia in East Asia, 1857–1860* (Kuala Lumpur, University of Malaya Press, 1968), and by Masataka Banno, *China and the West, 1858–1861: the Origins of the Tsungli Yamen* (Cambridge, Mass., Harvard University Press, 1964). The origins of the forward policy as a solution to India's defence problems can be studied in H. T. Lambrick's valuable biography, *John Jacob of Jacobabad* (London, Cassell, 1960). The controversy as to how far the British could afford to intimidate China in the mercantile interest receives illuminating treatment from Nathan A. Pelcovits, *Old China Hands and the Foreign Office* (New York, King's Crown Press, 1948). For the influence of pacifist ideas on British political leaders there are G. B. Henderson's essay, 'The pacifists of the fifties', in *Crimean War Diplomacy*, and A. J. P. Taylor's brilliant survey *The Trouble Makers: Dissent over Foreign Policy, 1792–1939* (London, Hamish Hamilton, 1957). American aspirations to Asian empire are discussed in such works as Walter LaFeber, *The New Empire: an Interpretation of American Expansion, 1860–1898* (Ithaca, N.Y., Cornell University Press, 1963) and Richard W. Van Alstyne, *The United States and East Asia* (London, Thames and Hudson, 1973); those of France in John F. Cady, *The Roots of French Imperialism in Eastern Asia* (Ithaca, N.Y., Cornell University Press, 1954) and in R. Stanley Thomson, 'The diplomacy of imperialism: France and Spain in Cochin China, 1858–63', *Journal of Modern History* 12 (1940), 334–56.

Further reading

6. ALEXANDER II'S COUNTER-OFFENSIVE, 1860–78

For Russian and British diplomatic activities in Europe during the post-Crimean period the best book is W. E. Mosse, *The European Powers and the German Question, 1848–1871* (Cambridge, University Press, 1958). For the extension of Russian control over central Asia there are, apart from the works by Popov and Khalfin already mentioned, N. A. Khalfin, *Prisoedinenie sredney Azii k Rossii* (Moscow, 1965); Seymour Becker, *Russia's Protectorates in Central Asia: Bukhara and Khiva, 1865–1924* (Cambridge, Mass., Harvard University Press, 1968), whose early chapters are, perhaps, the best summary, and which has excellent bibliographical notes; Mary Holdsworth, who brings together a great deal of useful information about *Turkestan in the Nineteenth Century: a Brief History of the Khanates of Bukhara, Kokand and Khiva* (London, Central Asian Research Centre, 1959); and David Mackenzie, 'Russian expansion in central Asia (1864–1885): brutal conquest or voluntary incorporation? A review article', *Canadian Slavic Studies* 4 (1970), 721–35. David Mackenzie's important article 'Expansion in central Asia: St. Petersburg vs. the Turkestan generals (1863–1866)', *Canadian Slavic Studies* 3 (1969), 286–311, presents a challenging interpretation of the role of the 'man on the spot' which led me to recast my previous ideas while drawing conclusions different from his. The question of how far the British had reason to be disturbed by Russian advances at this and other times is discussed by A. Lobanov-Rostovsky, 'The shadow of India in Russian history', *History* 14 (1929), 217–28; by Harold T. Cheshire, 'The expansion of Imperial Russia to the Indian border', *Slavonic and East European Review* 13 (1934–5), 85–97; and by Warren B. Walsh, 'The Imperial Russian General Staff and India', *Russian Review* 16 (1957), 53–8. *For the File on Empire* (London, Macmillan, 1968) brings together many of A. P. Thornton's valuable contributions to the literature of imperialism, including four articles on British reaction to Russian activities, pp. 134–251. G. J. Alder, *British India's Northern Frontier, 1865–95: a Study in Imperial Policy* (London, Longman, 1963) is a mine of information on British military and political difficulties, and, like A. P. Thornton, discusses the attempts to negotiate some agreement with the Russian government. One man's efforts to solve the military problems arising from the Russian advance are described in an interesting article by Adrian Preston, 'Sir Charles MacGregor and the defence of India, 1857–1887', *Historical Journal* 12 (1969), 58–77. Good accounts of Russo-British rivalry over central Asia are provided by William Habberton, *Anglo-Russian Relations concerning Afghanistan, 1837–1907* (Urbana, Ill., University of Illinois Press, 1937); Mohammed Anwar Khan, *England, Russia and Central Asia* (Peshawar, 1963); and D. P. Singhal, *India and Afghanistan, 1876–1907: a Study in Diplomatic Relations* (Melbourne, University of Queensland Press, 1963).

7. THE RUSSIANS AND THE BRITISH LOSE CONFIDENCE, 1878–94

There is a prolific literature on the crisis which began in 1875, and the present state of the question is discussed by W. N. Medlicott in 'The Near Eastern crisis of 1875–78 reconsidered', *Middle Eastern Studies* 7 (1971), 105–9. Particularly valuable for viewing the crisis in its Asian as well as its European context are two classics of diplomatic history, B. H. Sumner, *Russia and the Balkans, 1870–1880* (Oxford, Clarendon Press, 1937) and W. N. Medlicott, *The Congress of Berlin and After*, 2nd ed. (London, Cass, 1963), and an interesting recent work by Ram Lakhan Shukla, *Britain, India and the Turkish Empire, 1853–1882* (New Delhi, People's Publishing House, 1973). S. Megrelidze, *Voprosy Zakavkaz'ya v istorii russko-turetskoy voyny, 1877–78 gg.* (Tiflis, 1969) is useful for the Asian sector of the war, and Dwight E. Lee, *Great Britain and the Cyprus Convention Policy of 1878* (Cambridge, Mass., Harvard University Press, 1934) is an excellent analysis of the abortive attempt to make Asiatic Turkey a British bulwark. Barbara Jelavich explains why Batum was thought to be so important in 'Great Britain and the Russian acquisition of Batum, 1878–1886', *Slavonic and East European Review* 48 (1970), 44–66. D. A. Milyutin's recorded thoughts during and after the crisis are available in his *Dnevnik*, 4 vols (Moscow, 1947–50); vols 3 and 4 deal with the years 1878–82. There are discussions of his ideas and influence by Charles Jelavich, 'The diary of D. A. Miliutin, 1878–1882', *Journal of Modern History* 26 (1954), 255–9, and by Peter Von Wahlde, 'Dmitri Miliutin: appraisals', *Canadian Slavic Studies* 3 (1969), 400–14. Another important source for Russian policy both in the Turkish crisis and in the crisis involving China is *Russia in the East, 1876–1880: the Russo-Turkish War and the Kuldja Crisis as seen through the Letters of A. G. Jomini to N. K. Giers* (Leiden, E. J. Brill, 1959), ed. by Charles and Barbara Jelavich. For the policies of both Bismarck and Gladstone I found W. N. Medlicott's interpretation in *Bismarck, Gladstone and the Concert of Europe* (London, Athlone Press, 1956) the most convincing. There is a very good study of the Russian quarrel with China by Immanuel C. Y. Hsu, *The Ili Crisis: a Study of Sino-Russian Diplomacy, 1871–1881* (Oxford, Clarendon Press, 1965); L. E. Frechtling, 'Anglo-Russian rivalry in eastern Turkistan, 1863–1881', *Journal of the Royal Central Asian Society* 26 (1939), 471–89, and V. G. Kiernan, 'Kashgar and the politics of central Asia, 1868–1878', *Cambridge Historical Journal* 11 (1955), 317–42, place China's loss and recovery of the province, which formed the background to the quarrel, in the context of the Great Game. M. N. Tikhomirov, *Prisoedinenie Merva k Rossii* (Moscow, 1960) is a good account of the events leading up to the incorporation of Merv. I was unable to consult S. Z. Martirosov, *Iz istorii anglo-russkogo sopernichestva v sredney Azii v svyazi s prisoedineniem Turkmenii k Rossii* (Ashkhabad, 1966), which places Russian conquest of the Turcomans in its international setting. Among the many books and articles dealing with the British response to Russian expansion are an interesting discussion by D. K. Ghose, *England and Afghanistan: a Phase in their Relations* (Calcutta, 1960), particularly useful for the Panjdeh crisis, and the best account of the development of Salisbury's ideas on the problem, *Persia and the Defence of India, 1884–1892: a Study in the Foreign Policy of the Third Marquis of Salisbury* (London, Athlone Press, 1959) by R. L. Greaves. Aspects of the 1885 crisis are dealt with in two recent works of much wider interest, Barbara Jelavich, *The Ottoman Empire, the Great Powers and the Straits Question, 1870–1887* (Indiana, University Press, 1973), and Agatha Ramm, *Sir Robert Morier: Envoy and Ambassador in the Age of Imperialism, 1876–1893* (London, Oxford University Press, 1973). O. Zhigalina's critical discussion of the work of R. L. Greaves, G. J. Alder and other British historians in *Arabskie Strani, Turtsiya, Iran, Afganistan: istoriya, ekonomika* (Moscow, 1973), 59–68, seems representative of the current view of Soviet historians; British policy is seen as imperialism in the guise of defence against Russia, British historians as apologists for this in the tradition of nineteenth-century alarmist literature. Colin L. Smith, *The Embassy of Sir William White at Constantinople, 1886–1891* (London, Oxford University Press, 1957) ranges more widely than the title suggests, and is a useful approach to the Mediterranean Agreements and their background. The growing difficulties of the Russian government in the years leading up to the alliance with France are explored by S. D. Skazkin, *Konets avstro-russko-germanskogo soyuza* (Moscow, 1928); by Charles Jelavich, *Tsarist Russia and Balkan Nationalism* (Berkeley and Los Angeles, University of California Press, 1958); by William L. Langer, *The Franco-Russian Alliance, 1890–1894* (Cambridge, Mass., Harvard University Press, 1929); and by Baron Boris Nolde, *L'alliance franco-russe: les origines du système diplomatique d'avant-guerre* (Paris, Droz, 1936). There are many illuminating entries about Alexander III and Giers in V. N. Lamsdorff, *Dnevnik, 1891–1892* (Moscow and Leningrad, 1934; reprinted Paris and The Hague, Mouton, 1970).

8. THE END OF THE GREAT GAME, 1894–1908

Lady Gwendolen Cecil's admirable biography of her father, *Life of Robert, Marquis of Salisbury*, 4 vols (London, Hodder and Stoughton, 1921–32) goes only as far as 1892, but Salisbury's later policy in Asia and in other parts of the world is judiciously surveyed by J. A. S. Grenville in his important work, *Lord Salisbury and Foreign Policy: the Close of the Nineteenth Century* (London, Athlone Press, 1964). For naval thinking about the Straits and other questions there is Arthur J. Marder, *The Anatomy of British Sea Power: a History of British Naval Policy in the Pre-Dreadnought Era, 1880–1905* (New York, Knopf, 1940). The Pamirs affair is discussed at length in G. J. Alder's book and in B. I. Iskandarov, *Vostochnaya Bukhara i Pamir vo vtoroy polovine XIX v.* (Dushanbe, 1962). The contribution to it and to later developments in central Asia of a prominent British agent has been brought out in a valuable study, *Macartney at Kashgar: New Light on British, Chinese and Russian Activities in Sinkiang, 1890–1918*, by C. P. Skrine and Pamela Nightingale (London, Methuen, 1973). The earlier exploits of another British agent in this area and elsewhere in Asia are described in an interesting biography, *Ney Elias: Explorer and Envoy Extraordinary in High Asia* (London, Allen and Unwin, 1971) by Gerald Morgan. There is no study of Russian policy as wide-ranging as that of J. A. S. Grenville for Great Britain, but there are some excellent books on Russian activities during these years in China and

Persia. B. A. Romanov, *Russia in Manchuria, 1892–1906* (Ann Arbor, Mich., J. W. Edwards, 1952) is a translation of the major Soviet work published in 1928. Andrew Malozemoff, *Russian Far Eastern Policy, 1881–1904, with special emphasis on the Causes of the Russo-Japanese War* (Berkeley and Los Angeles, University of California Press, 1958) and Firuz Kazemzadeh, *Russia and Britain in Persia, 1864–1914: a Study in Imperialism* (New Haven, Conn., and London, Yale University Press, 1968) are important and challenging interpretations, the latter equally valuable for Persian and British policies as well. Another work is B. Mannanov, *Iz istorii russko-iranskikh otnoshenii kontsa XIX– nachala XX v.* (Tashkent, 1964), and Marvin L. Entner's study of Russo-Persian commercial relations has already been mentioned. For Witte's policy as a whole there is Theodore Von Laue, *Sergei Witte and the Industrialisation of Russia* (New York, Columbia University Press, 1963). The imperialist activities of other powers in Asia in the 1890s are best approached by way of William L. Langer's remarkable work, *The Diplomacy of Imperialism*, 2nd ed. (New York, Knopf, 1956), dated in detail and a favourite target for revisionist articles but still a masterly survey of the decade, which no one has even attempted to surpass. I found Hilary Conroy, *The Japanese Seizure of Korea, 1868–1910: a Study of Realism and Idealism in International Relations* (Philadelphia, University of Pennsylvania Press, 1960) of great value for its discussion of imperialism in general as well as of the policies of a particular country, and the same is true of Thomas J. McCormick, *China Market: America's Quest for Informal Empire, 1893–1901* (New York, Quadrangle Books, 1970). Among the numerous other good studies of American imperialism in these years, Edward H. Zabriskie, *American-Russian Rivalry in the Far East, 1895–1914* (Philadelphia, University of Pennsylvania Press, 1946); A. Whitney Griswold, *The Far Eastern Policy of the United States* (New York, Harcourt Brace, 1938); and Howard K. Beale, *Theodore Roosevelt and the Rise of America to World Power* (Baltimore, Md, Johns Hopkins Press, 1956) are especially relevant in the context of the Great Game. The changing course of British policy at the turn of the century is dealt with in important works by George Monger, *The End of Isolation: British Foreign Policy, 1900–1907* (Edinburgh, Nelson, 1963); Zara Steiner, *The Foreign Office and Foreign Policy, 1898–1914* (Cambridge, University Press, 1969); and C. J. Lowe and M. L. Dockrill, *The Mirage of Power: vol. 1, British Foreign Policy, 1902–14* (London, Routledge and Kegan Paul, 1972). The effect of the changes on British relations with Japan are explained in Ian H. Nish's excellent study, *The Anglo-Japanese Alliance: The Diplomacy of Two Island Empires, 1894–1907* (London, Athlone Press, 1966). Contemporary analysis of Great Britain's strategic problems as an Asian land power with increasingly vulnerable frontiers is examined by W. J. McDermott, 'The immediate origins of the Committee of Imperial Defence: a reappraisal', *Canadian Journal of History* 7 (1972), 253–72; Beryl J. Williams, 'The strategic background to the Anglo-Russian entente of August 1907', *Historical Journal* 9 (1966), 360–73; Max Beloff, *Imperial Sunset, vol. 1: Britain's Liberal Empire, 1897–1921* (London, Methuen, 1969), and H. Jaeckel, *Die Nord-*

Further reading

westgrenze in der Verteidigung Indiens, *1900–1908*, und der Weg Englands zum russisch-britischen Abkommen von *1907* (Cologne, 1968). There are interesting treatments of Curzon's policy in David Dilks, *Curzon in India*, 2 vols (London, Hart-Davis, 1969–70), and in Parshotam Mehra, *The Younghusband Expedition: an Interpretation* (London, Asia Publishing House, 1968); and for the whole background to British involvement in Tibet, Alistair Lamb, *Britain and Chinese Central Asia: the Road to Lhasa, 1767 to 1905* (London, Routledge and Kegan Paul, 1960) is very good. For Japanese policy in the war of 1904–1905 I found Shumpei Okamoto, *The Japanese Oligarchy and the Russo-Japanese War* (New York and London, Columbia University Press, 1970) convincing, and John A. White has explained *The Diplomacy of the Russo-Japanese War* (Princeton, N.J., Princeton University Press, 1964). The effects of defeat and revolution on Russian policy are discussed by E. W. Edwards, 'The Far Eastern agreements of 1907', *Journal of Modern History* 26 (1954), 340–55, and by Beryl J. Williams, 'The revolution of 1905 and Russian foreign policy', in *Essays in Honour of E. H. Carr* ed. by C. Abramsky, assisted by Beryl J. Williams (London, Macmillan, 1974), 101–25. Rogers P. Churchill has written a very useful account of *The Anglo-Russian Convention of 1907* (Cedar Rapids, Torch Press, 1939). B. H. Sumner, 'Tsardom and imperialism in the Far East and Middle East, 1880–1914', *Proceedings of the British Academy* 27 (1941), 25–65 is a brilliant analysis.

Since I finished writing, the following works have become available: Michael Edwardes, *Playing the Great Game: a Victorian Cold War* (London, Hamish Hamilton, 1975), a brief and vivid account, mostly of British involvement; J. R. V. Prescott, *Map of Mainland Asia by Treaty* (Carlton, Melbourne University Press, 1975), an excellent guide to the region's changing frontiers; David MacKenzie's important biography, *The Lion of Tashkent: The Career of General M. G. Cherniaev* (Athens, Georgia, University of Georgia Press, 1974); and three useful articles: J. L. Herkless, 'Stratford, the cabinet and the outbreak of the Crimean War', *Historical Journal* 18 (1975), 497–523; Edward Ingram, 'The rules of the game: a commentary on the defence of British India, 1798–1829', *Journal of Imperial and Commonwealth History* 3 (1975), 257–79; and Peter Morris, 'The Russians in central Asia, 1870–1887', *Slavonic Review* 53 (1975), 521–38.

Index

Abbott, Capt. James, mission to Khīva, 55
'Abd ül-Ḥamid II, Sultan of Turkey (1876–1909), attitude to Great Britain, 146
Abdur Rahman, emir of Afghanistan (1880–1901), relations with British India, 141, 183
Aberdeen, 4th earl of, British foreign secretary (1828–30, 1841–6), prime minister (1852–5), 26; Turkish defeat of 1829, 30, 34; policy towards France and USA, 68, 69, 70, 71; Nicholas I's visit of 1844, 70–1, 75; Russo-Turkish crisis of 1853, 82, 83, 86, 88, 89
Abkhazia, annexed by Russia, 104
Acre, 61, 92
Adana, assigned to Muḥammad 'Alī, 34
Aden, annexed by Great Britain, 43, 58–9
Adrianople, 24, 137; treaty of, 25, 81
Aegean Sea, 70, 135
Afghanistan, 14, 20, 31, 35, 46, 52, 71, 72, 74, 171, 182; rival centres of power, 47; and Herat, 47, 97; and the Panjab, 47–8; war with British (1839–42), 43, 54–6, 62–3, 65–6, 68, 109, 126, (1878–80) 139; Russian overtures to, 51, 65, 106–7, 136, 138, 166; British support for, 97, 107–10, 121, 183; and Bukhārā, 121; Russo-British negotiations over, 127–9; frontier delimitation 144, 147; Panjdeh crisis, 144–7; Pamirs crisis, 155–6; Russian capacity to invade, 168; 1907 convention, 176
Akkerman, convention of, repudiated by Sultan Maḥmūd, 24
Ak-Mesjid (Perovsk), captured by Russians (1853), 117, 120, 129
Alai Mts, 138
Åland Islands, and Franco-British naval operations (1854), 92
Alaska, 113
Alexander I, Emperor of Russia (1801–25), 18; and Napoleon I, 13; view of Russia's interests, 19, 39; and abandonment of expedition against India (1801), 27
Alexander II, Emperor of Russia (1855–81), 94, 142–3; revised view of Russian interests, 95, 101–8, 115, 134; and treaty of Paris, 96, 131; conquests in central Asia, 116–17, 119, 121–2, 130; crisis of 1875–81, 115, 132, 135–8; assessment of foreign policy, 131, 133; assassinated, 134
Alexander III, Emperor of Russia (1881–94), 134, 154, 157, 159; Panjdeh crisis (1885), 146–7; Bulgarian crises (1885–7), 148, 149, 153; end of Three Emperors'

Alexander III—*contd*
  Alliance, 148, 149; and rival views of Giers and Katkov, 150–1; alliance negotiations with France (1891–4), 151–2; Russian penetration of China, 157–8
Alma, battle of (1854), 93
Amu Darya (Oxus) river, 35, 116, 130, 138, 147
Amur river, and Russian expansion, 104–5, 133
Andrássy, Count Gyula, Austro-Hungarian foreign minister (1871–9), and crisis of 1875–81, 131
Annam, French imperialist activity in, 113
Arabia, Muḥammad 'Alī's ambitions in, 57, 58–9, 61
Aral Sea, 117, 118
Aras river, Russo-Persian frontier (1828), 23
Ardahan, ceded to Russia (1878), 135, 138
Armenians, Turkish massacres of (1895–6), 166
Arrow, Sino-British dispute over, 43, 98–101
Arys river, 118
Auckland, 1st earl of, governor-general of India (1835–41), 50, 51, 56; war with Afghans, 54, 55, 59; and Kharg expedition, 53, 59; and Arabia, 58–9, 61; and Opium War, 59, 62
Aulie-Ata, Russians capture (1864), 118
Austria (after 1867 Austria-Hungary), 8, 33, 66, 96, 113–14, 115–53; Napoleonic Wars, 7, 13, 14; Vienna settlement, 15, 19; Greek revolt, 19; Turco-Egyptian crises, 37, 38, 52, 59, 61; Russian partition schemes, 69–70, 78, 80; extradition crisis (1849), 77; crises of 1853, 80–5, 87–8, 91; Crimean War, 93, 94, 95; Polish revolt, 115–16; Black Sea clauses, 131; crisis of 1875–81, 131–2, 135–7, 139; Dreikaiserbund, 131, 142–3, 146–7; German alliance, 140; and Gladstone, 142; Bulgarian unification, 148, 150; Mediterranean Agreements, 148–149, 153; Bosnia annexed, 177; and 1914 war, 178

Badakshān, Russo-British talks and (1869–73), 128, 130
Badmayev, Mongolian adventurer, project for Russian penetration of China, 157–8
Baghdād, 138–9; Muḥammad 'Alī's ambitions, 57–8
Baḥrayn, submits to Muḥammad 'Alī, 58, 61
Balaklava, battle of (1854), 93
Balfour, Arthur J., British prime minister (1902–5), 175; assessment of Great Britain's international position, 168, 170; Younghusband expedition, 172; Russo-Japanese war, 174
Baltic Sea, 95; in Crimean War, 92–3
Baluchistan, 28, 154, 155
Baryatinsky, Field Marshall Prince A. I., viceroy of the Caucasus; views on countering British expansion in Asia, 102–3; defeat of Shāmil, 104
Bashkirs, conquered by Russians in 18th century, 117
Battenberg, Prince Alexander von, ruler of Bulgaria (1879–86), Alexander III, enmity towards, 148
Batum, ceded to Russia (1878), 135, 138
Beirut, 61
Belgium, 162; French control of, 7; crisis over 1830 revolt, 33, 34, 35, 37, 38, 60
Bengal, 12
Bentinck, Lord William, governor-general of India (1828–35), 54; and the Indus project, 32–3
Berlin: memorandum (1876), 131–2; congress of, 137–8, 142, 148
Bertie, Francis, British diplomat, view of German threat, 177
Besika Bay, despatch of British warships to, (1849), 77, (1853), 83, (1876), 132, (1878), 136

Index

Bessarabia, ceded by Turks to Russia (1812), 15; Russian loss of southern B. (1856) and recovery, (1878), 138
Bismarck, Prince Otto von, German imperial chancellor (1871–90): crisis of 1875–81, 131; attitude to Russia, 139–40, 142, 148–9; Three Emperors' Alliance (1881), 142–3; Salisbury's overture to (1885), 146; Reinsurance Treaty (1887), 149; dismissal, 149
Black Sea, 11, 24, 25, 63, 64, 69, 70, 78, 95; entry of British and French warships (1854), 88, 89–90, 91; Crimean War, 92–3; neutralization (1856–70), 96, 102, 103, 115, 131; British threat to (1878), 136, 137, 138, 154
Boer War (1899–1902), 168; and Russian policy, 166, 169
Bolan Pass, 128; strategic value to British in India, 112, 139
Bomarsund, Franco-British bombardment (1854), 92
Bombay, 12, 14, 53, 58, 59
Bosnia, annexed by Austria (1908), 177
Bosphorus, *see* Straits
Bowring, Sir John, governor of Hong Kong (1854–9), initiates conflict with China (1856), 99–100
Boxer movement, 169; and Russian occupation of Manchuria, 173
Brest-Litovsk, treaty of (1918), 179
Bright, John, peace movement during Crimean War, 111
Bruck, Frh. Karl von, idea of Austrian empire in Asia, 113–14
Brunnov, Baron Ernst, Russian ambassador in London (1839–54), assurances about Menshikov mission, 83
Bukhārā, 31, 32, 34, 51, 121, 182; British missions to, 49, 66; Russian missions to (1858), 106–8; relations with neighbouring khanates, 107, 120–1; claim to Tashkent, 120, 122; war with Russia (1866–8), and peace terms, 123–125, 126, 128, 130; Russian protectorate, 128, 139, 140, 141, 147, 148, 183
Bulgaria, 70, 137, 142; revolt (1876), 132; and San Stefano and Berlin treaties, 135, 137; and Three Emperors' Alliance, 142; relations with Russia, 147–8, 150, 153; unification, war with Serbia (1885), 148; and Reinsurance Treaty, 149
Burma, 43, 51
Burnes, Sir Alexander: Indus expedition, 49; views on defence of India, 49, 50, 97; negotiates with Dost Muḥammad, 51
Bushire, 59; attacked by British, 98
Butenev, Count A. P., Russian ambassador at Constantinople, 44

Campbell-Bannerman, Sir Henry, British prime minister (1905–8), 175
Canada, 113; rebellion (1837), and boundary disputes with USA, 68–9
Canning, George, British foreign secretary (1807–9, 1822–7), prime minister (1827), 28, 30, 137; view of British interests, 18, 19, 25–6, 33, 39–42, 97; Russo-Persian war (1826–8), 20–2, 30, 39, 46; Greek revolt, 21–2, 23–4, 70
Canning, Sir Stratford, later Viscount de Redcliffe, British ambassador in Constantinople (1825–9, 1842–58): view of British interests in Levant, 36; extradition crisis (1849), 77; influence on Porte, 79; and 1853 crisis, 81, 84, 85
Canning, Earl, governor-general, then viceroy of India (1856–62): war with Persia declared (1856), 97
Canton, 63; *Arrow* war (1856–60), 99–100
Caspian Sea, 23, 71, 130, 157, 179
Castlereagh, Viscount, and 2nd marquis of Londonderry, British foreign secretary (1812–22), view of British interests, 18, 19, 22, 33, 39

Catherine II, Empress of Russia (1762–96), 11, 38
Caucasus, 10, 146; conquered by Russia, 11, 13, 14, 76; resistance to Russian rule, 60, 88, 102, 103, 104, 115; and Crimean War, 88, 94, 95; and 1914–18 war, 179
Cavagnari, Sir Louis, and massacre of British mission in Kābul (1879), 141
Central Asia, 34, 71, 93; weakness of Khanates, 29, 108, 120; prospects of British penetration, 29, 32–3, 48, 49, 76, 102–3, 112, 121, 153–4; early Russian contacts in, 116–17; Russian conquests, 115, 117–18, 120–5, 133; attempted British deal with Russia, 127–9
Chamberlain, Austen, British chancellor of exchequer (1903–5), view of Russo-Japanese war, 174
Chamberlain, Joseph, British colonial secretary (1895–1903): view of British interests, 167–9, 170; disillusioned with Germany, 177
Charlemagne, French warship, used in Holy Places dispute, 80
Chasseloup-Laubat, Count Prosper de, French minister of marine and colonies, and French expansion in Indo-China, 114
Chernyayev, General M. G., role in Russian conquest of central Asia, 117, 118, 119, 120, 122–4
Chernyshev, Count A. I., Russian minister of war (1827–53), and Khīva expedition (1839), 65
Chesney, Francis R., 36, 58; surveys of Euphrates route (1830–1, 1835–37), 36, 58
Chimkent, captured by Russians (1864), 118, 120, 122, 123
China, 12, 29, 178, 182, 184; international status in 1800, 7–9; commercial relations with Russia, 8–9, 10, 129, 153, 157; war with Great Britain (1839–42), 43, 53, 61, 62–3, 68, 104, (1856–60), 43, 98–101, 105, 109; territorial concessions to Russia (1858–60), 104–5; British support for, 110–111; Ili crisis (1879–81), 140, 143; Pamirs crisis, 155–6; Russo-British rivalry in, 157–8, 159; war with Japan (1894–5), 161–162; concessions scramble, 164–165, 166, 167; Boxer movement, 169, 173; and Tibet, 171–2, 176, 178; and Soviet Union, 180–1
Chinese Eastern Railway, 164–5
Chornaya, battle of the (1855), 93
Chumbi, and Lhasa convention (1904), 172
Circassians, 95; resistance to Russian rule, 60; expelled from coastal area, 104
'civilising missions': in 19th century, 28–9; in 20th century, 181
Clarendon, 4th earl of, British foreign secretary (1853–8, 1865–6, 1868–70): crisis of 1853, 82, 86, 87, 89; war with Persia (1856–7), 97–8; negotiations with Russia (1869–70), 127
Clayton–Bulwer Treaty (1850), 170–1
Cleveland, Grover, President of USA (1885–9, 1893–7), 166
Cobden, Richard, peace movement during Crimean War, 111
Cold War: controversy over origins, 3; comparison with Great Game, 181; as imperialism, 181
Conolly, Arthur, mission to Bukhārā and death, 66
Constantinople (Istanbul), 36, 38, 78, 148; threatened by Russia, 24–5, 30, 32, 51, 52, 134, 135, 136–7; threatened by Egypt, 34, 35, 38; Russo-British diplomatic rivalry, 43–6, 79, 90, 167, 172; in Russian partition schemes, 69–70; French influence, 80; conference (1876–77), 132; in British war plans, 146, 147, 154; and Reinsurance Treaty, 149
Crete, 70
Crimean War (1853–6), 1, 43, 78, 84, 87–91, 92–5, 96, 97, 99, 105, 111, 115, 117, 121, 126, 145; causes, 90–1; significance, 92–5, 183

Crowe, Eyre, British foreign office official, view of German threat, 177
Cuba, Spanish-American war (1898), 164
Currie, Sir Philip, British foreign office official, mission to Bismarck (1885), 146
Curzon, Viscount, viceroy of India (1898–1905): view of Russian expansion, 172; Tibetan expedition, 172–3
Cyprus, 70; convention (1878), 138; significance, 138–9

Dalhousie, 1st marquis of, governor-general of India (1848–56): annexation of the Panjāb, 74–5, 76; effects of westernization programme, 101
Danube river, 24, 25, 86, 88; delta ceded to Russia by Turks; (1829), 25
Dardanelles, *see* Straits
Delhi: in Indian Mutiny, 101; King of, 16, 101
Derby, 15th earl of, British foreign secretary (1866–8, 1874–8), and Turkish crisis of 1875–8, 136
Diebitsch, Field Marshall Baron Ivan von, and Balkan campaign of 1829, 24–5
Disraeli, Benjamin, British prime minister (1868, 1874–80), 141; and crisis of 1875–81, 132, 136
Dniester river, 11
Dogger Bank incident (1904), 174
Dost Muḥammad Khān, emir of Afghanistan (1834–63), 50, 128; territorial ambitions, 48–9, 52, 65, 97; negotiates with Burnes, 51; Russian overtures, 51, 65, 106–7; British invasion (1839–42), 54, 56–7; and British-Sikh wars, 75; alliance with British, 97, 107, 109, 122, 183; gains Qandahār (1855) and Herāt (1863), 97, 107
Dreikaiserbund (Three Emperors' League or Alliance): in 1870s, 131, 132, 134, 140, 142; in 1880s, 142–3, 147, 148, 149, 150; *see also* Three Emperors Alliance
Dudley, Earl of, British foreign secretary (1827–8), 26
Dufferin and Ava, 1st marquis of, viceroy of India, (1884–8), Panjdeh crisis (1885), 144
Duhamel, General, Russian envoy in Tehran, and view of Russian interests in Asia, 66
Dundas, Henry, president of (India) board of control (1793–1801), and prospect of Russian threat to India, 27
Dundas, Rear-admiral Richard, naval operations in Baltic (1855), 92–3
Dutch East Indies, 15, 112, 114, 118

East India Company (British), 46, 101, 121; leading power in India, 12–13, 16–17; Indus project, 32; annexation of Sind, 72–3; Mutiny, 101
East India Company (Dutch), 12
East India Company (French), 12
Egypt, 52, 57, 61, 62, 63; attacked by Napoleon I, 9, 27; Greek revolt and, 22; wars with sultan, 34, 35, 36, 43, 59–61, 68; Franco-British quarrels over, 60–2, 146; in Russian partition schemes, 70
Elgin, 8th earl of, and *Arrow* war, 101, 105; and Mitchell Report, 110
Ellenborough, 1st earl of, president of (India) board of control (1828–30, 1834–5, 1841, 1858), governor-general of India (1842–4), 26, 74; view of British interests in Asia, 30–3, 35, 38, 39–42, 47, 49, 50, 103, 104, 106, 126, 177; withdrawal from Afghanistan, 56; annexation of Sind, 72–3
Elliot, Capt. Charles, British superintendent of Trade at Canton (1836–41), and the Opium War (1839–42), 62
Ellis, Sir Henry, British representative in Tehran (1835–6), view of British interests, 36, 47
Elphinstone, Mountstuart, British envoy to Kābul, (1808), 28

Elphinstone, Major-General William, British commander at Kābul (1841–2), 56
Erivan, captured by Russians (1827), ceded to them by Persia (1828), 23
Erzurum, captured by Russians (1829), 24, 30
Euphrates river, suggested route to India, 36, 57–8; and railway project, 138–9
Evans, George de Lacy, writings on Russian threat to India (1828–9), 28–9, 30, 31–2, 33, 125, 130–1

Fatḥ ʿAlī Shāh of Persia (1797–1834), 46; war with Russia (1804–13), 14, (1826–8), 21, 23
Finkenstein, treaty of (1807), 14
Finland, Gulf of, 92
Fischer, Fritz, controversy over German war aims in 1914, 3
France, 96, 102, 115, 184; international status in 1800, 7–8; Napoleonic Wars, 8–10, 13–15; and India, 12; congress of Vienna, 15, 19; British view of, 18–19; Russian view of, 18–19, 44, 66, 69; Greek revolt and, 19, 20, 22; Belgian revolt and, 33; and Muḥammad ʿAlī, 37, 38, 57, 59–61: support for Ottoman Empire, 43, 52, 77; friction with British in 1840s, 68, 69, 70, 71; and Africa, 68, 118, 146, 152, 158, 166, 169; in Russian partition schemes, 69–70; Holy Places dispute, 79–80; crisis of 1853, 83, 84, 88, 89; Crimean War, 90, 92–4; and China, 98–101, 105, 158, 164; Indo-Chinese empire, 113, 114, 159; Polish revolt (1863) and, 115, 116; defeat by Prussia, 131; alliance with Russia, 150–2, 153, 162; and 1914–18 war, 179
Frere, Sir Bartle, and British forward policy, 112

Gandamak, treaty of (1879), 139, 141
Gardane, General Claude, French mission to Tehran (1807), 14
Georgia, 14, 23, 25, 88, 95; annexed by Russia (1801), 11, 15
Germany, 139, 163, 167; 1914–18 war, 3, 178, 179–80; Dreikaiserbund, 131, 142–3, 146; alliance with Austria-Hungary, 140; and Africa, 146, 149, 158, 166; British overtures, 146, 170; Bulgarian crisis, 148, 149, 150; and Franco-Russian alliance, 151–2; and imperialism, 159, 161; naval programme, 162–3; Kiaochow concession, 162–3, 165; as threat to Great Britain and Russia, 176–178; and war of 1939–45, 180
Ghazna, captured by British (1839), 54
Giers, N. K., Russian foreign minister (1882–95), 150, 151
Gladstone, William E., British prime minister (1868–74, 1880–5, 1886, 1892–4), 132, 143; attitude to peace movement, 111; Panjdeh crisis, 111, 144–6; and abrogation of Black Sea clauses, 131; and concert of Europe, 141–2; and Afghanistan, 141; and Ottoman Empire, 142; refuses support to Reuter, 156
Goderich, Viscount, British prime minister (1827), 26
Gök-Tepe, captured by Russians (1881), 143, 144
Gorchakov, Prince Alexander, Russian foreign minister (1856–82), 28; 1864 circular, 2, 72, 118–20, 121, 124, 125, 126; view of Russian interests, 102, 103; doubts about expansion in Asia, 117, 118; negotiations with Great Britain, 128, 130; crisis of 1875–81, 131, 135
Graham, Sir James, first lord of the admiralty (1852–5), 89
Grant, Charles, president of (India) board of control (1830–4), 35, 58
Granville, 2nd earl, British foreign secretary (1851–2, 1870–4, 1880–85), 99; negotiations with Russia, 127–8

Index

Great Britain: character of rivalry with Russia, 1–3, 5–6, 181–5; enhanced power 1800–20, 8–10, 11–17; reactions to Russian expansion, 18, 20, 26–33, 35, 38–42, 68, 125–9, 136–9, 170, 175–7; cooperation with Russia, 21–2, 60–4, 70–2, 75–9, 175, 178
Great Game, character of, 1–3, 92–5, 105, 112, 158, 161; Russia's success, 173, 179; and 1907 convention, 175–6, 179; and German threat, 177–8; end of, 178, 179–180; comparison with Cold War, 181; as imperialism, 181–5; war and, 182–5
Greek revolt against Turks (1821), 19, 21–2, 30, 70
Grey, Sir Edward, British foreign secretary (1905–16), staff talks with French, 177; and Germany, 177, 178; and Russia, 178
Grey, 2nd earl, British prime minister (1830–4), 26, 33, 34
Gromchevsky, Col., Pamirs expedition (1889), 155
Gros, Baron, and *Arrow* war, 100
Guam, ceded to USA by Spain (1898), 164
Guizot, François, French foreign minister (1840–7), 62
Gyantse, Lhasa convention and, 172

Habsburg Empire, *see* Austria
Haines, Capt, Stafford, negotiations with Aden (1838), 58–9
Hamilton, Lord George, secretary of state for India (1895–1903), view of British interests, 170
Hardinge, Charles, British ambassador in St Petersburg (1904–6), permanent under-secretary at foreign office (1906–10), view of German threat, 177
Hardinge, Sir Henry (later Lord), governor-general of India (1844–8), war with the Panjāb, 74
Hari-Rud river, 147
Hastings, 1st marquis of (until 1817 2nd earl of Moira), governor-general of India (1813–23), 119; conquest of Pindaris and Marathas, 16, 27
Hawaii, annexed by USA (1898), 163–4
Haydarābād (Sind), 51
Haydarābād, Nizām of: treaty with British East India Company, 13
Haydar ʿAlī, ruler of Mysore (1762–82), 12
Haymerle, Frh. H. von, Austro-Hungarian foreign minister (1879–81), view of Gladstone, 142
Hay-Pauncefote Treaty (1901), 171, 176
Hennell, Capt. Samuel, British influence in Persian Gulf, 59
Herat, 14, 178; Persian designs on, 47–9, 50, 51, 52, 55, 65, 66, 96–8, 107; strategic value, 47, 105, 112, 130; Dost Muḥammad and, 48, 97, 107; relations with British, 55, 108; Russian mission, 106–7; Panjdeh crisis and, 144–146
Herzegovina: revolt (1875), 131; annexed by Austria (1908), 177
Hobhouse, Sir John, president of (India) board of control (1835–41, 1846–52), 59; and annexation of Aden, 58
Hodges, Col., mission to Serbia, 52
Holland, French control of, 7, 15; Belgian revolt, 33, 37
Holy Places dispute, 79–80, 81, 85, 86
Hong Kong, 99; ceded to Great Britain (1842), 43, 63
Huc, Abbé, memo. on French interests in Asia, 113
Hungary, Russian intervention (1849), 77
Hünkâr Iskelesi, treaty of (1833), 34, 38, 41, 43–4, 45, 51, 59, 60, 64, 78, 82

Ibrahim Pasha, 61; victory at Nezib, 59
Ignatyev, Count N. P., Russian ambassador in Constantinople (1864–77): view of Indian

Ignatyev, Count N. P.—*contd*
    Mutiny, 103; negotiations with China, 105; mission to central Asia, 106-8, 117, 120; crisis of 1875-81, 132, 135, 137, 148
Ili river, 117; Sino-Russian crisis (1879-81), 140, 143
Imeret'i, 15
Imperialism: Great Game and Cold War as examples of, 2, 181-5; universality of, 2, 181; annexation and, 75-6; novel features in 1890s, 158-61; war and, 182-5
India, 28, 47; British conquest, 10, 11-17, 118, 120, 121; Russian threat, 27-33, 35-6, 38-42, 48-9, 93, 95, 96, 98, 103, 130, 136, 138, 145, 147, 149, 153-4, 155, 168, 175; British views on defence of, 49-50, 54, 55-6, 109-11; 1857 revolt, 43, 100, 101, 103, 106-7, 109, 114; routes to, 57; Nicholas I and, 64-5; vulnerability, 101, 147, 168-9; and British alliance with Japan, 174-175; German and Turkish threat, 179; nationalism in, 180
Indus river, 14, 31, 35, 47, 73, 86, 110; Ellenborough's project, 32-33, 47, 49, 50
Inkerman, battle of (1854), 93
Iran, *see* Persia
Ireland, 9
Irtysh river, 117
Isfahān, 98
Italy, 33, 69, 159; French revolutionary wars, 7, 8; Mediterranean Agreements, 148-9
Ito Hirobumi, Japanese statesman, 173
Izvolsky, A. P., Russian foreign minister (1905-10), 175

Jacob, John, British agent in Sind (1843-58), forward policy, 112, 128, 139
Jalālābād, 139
Japan, 157; aims in 1930s, 3; Perry expedition, 113, 163; response to western penetration, 114, 161; war with Russia, 153, 173-5; war with China, 161-2; character of imperialism, 162; and Korea, 161-2, 165; alliance with Great Britain, 171, 174-5; agreement with Russia, 175
Jardine, William, and Sino-British trade and the Opium War, 62, 110
Java, captured by British (1811), 15
Jefferson, Thomas, President of USA (1801-9), view of American prospects in Asia, 113

Kābul, 28, 31, 32, 49, 52, 109, 129; strategic importance, 47; Russo-British rivalry at, 51, 63, 65, 71, 106-7, 136, 138, 139, 166, 172; in wars with British, 54, 55, 56-7
Kalat, 128, 154; British treaty with Khan of, 139
Kamchatka, and Crimean War, 105
Kars, 23; captured by Russia (1828), 24; (1855), 92, 94; (1877), 135; ceded to Russia by the Turks (1878), 135, 138
Kārūn river; in Perso-British war (1856-7), 98; opened to foreign trade, 157
Kashgar: Russian mission to, 106, 108; strategic importance, 122, 129-30, 136; Ya'qūb Bey and Russo-British rivalry, 129; China regains control of, 140
Kashmir, 129
Katkov, M. N., Russian journalist, influence on Russian policy, 150-1
Kaufman, General K. P., Russian governor-general of Turkistān (1867-82), 124, 130
Kazakhs, 65; conquered by Russians, 71, 117
Khanykov, N. V., expedition to Khurāsān (1858), 106-7, 108, 117
Kharg, British occupations of, 53, 58-9, 98
Khīva, 32, 36, 51, 116, 121, 182; Russian expeditions against (1839), 54-5, 65-6, (1873), 128, 129, 130; Russian treaties with,

71–2, 130; Russian mission to (1858), 106–7; and neighbouring Khanates, 120; as Russian protectorate, 139, 140, 141, 147, 148, 183; and Merv, 143–4

Khojand, annexed by Russia (1866), 124, 125

Khokand, 107, 119, 120, 121, 182; importance to Russia, 116, 129; and Tashkent, 118, 120, 122; and neighbouring Khanates, 120; conflict with Russia, 123, 126; treaty with Russia, 124–5, 128, 130; annexed by Russia (1876), 138

Khokand Line, 118

Khurāsān, 146, 156; Russian mission to (1858), 106–7

Khyber Pass, 47, 139, 141

Kiaochow, leased to Germany (1898), 162–3; Russian reaction, 164

Konya, battle of (1832), 34

Korea, 144, 157; rivalry of Japanese, Chinese and Russians, 161–2, 165, 173–4; Japanese secure control of, 175

Kovalevsky, E. P., head of Asian dept at Russian foreign ministry (1856–61), view of British expansion in Asia, 105, 108

Kronstadt, 93; visit of French fleet (1891), 151

Kruger telegram, 166

Kryzhanovsky, General N. A., Russian governor of Orenburg (1865–81), 123

Kuban river, 11

Kulja, occupied by Russians (1871), 129

Kyakhta, treaty of (1727), 8

Lahore, 32; treaty of (1846), 74, 108

Lansdowne, 5th marquis of, British foreign secretary (1900–5): view of British interests, 167, 170; Hay–Pauncefote Treaty, 170–1; Japanese alliance, 171, 174; settlement with France, 171, 174; Russo-Japanese war, 174

Lawrence, Sir John, chief commissioner for the Panjāb (1853–9),

viceroy of India (1863–9), 128, 129; masterly inactivity, 109–10, 112, 126, 127; proposes inviolable line, 127

Layard, Sir A. H., British ambassador in Constantinople (1877–80), 138–9, 142

Lebanon, revolt against Egyptian rule, 61

Leiningen, Count, Austrian mission to Constantinople (1853), 81

Lhasa, occupied by British, convention of, 172–3; and 1907 convention, 176; Russian influence, 178

Liaotung peninsula: Japan forced to retrocede, 162, 164, 165; Russian lease of, 165; Japanese lease of, 175

Lisbon, 22

Livadia, treaty of (1879), 140, 143

Lodge, Henry Cabot, and American expansion, 164

Louis-Philippe, King of the French (1830–48), and Belgian revolt, 33; and Muḥammad 'Alī, 59

Low Countries, see Belgium, Holland

Lytton, 1st earl of, viceroy of India (1876–80), war with Afghanistan, 139, 141

MacDonald, Col., British representative in Tehran, 21, 32

McKinley, William B., President of the USA (1897–1901), 163

Macnaghten, Sir William, 54, 66; assassinated at Kābul, 56

McNeill, Sir John, British representative in Tehran (1836–42), 47; views on Indian defence, 49–50; and siege of Herat, 53

Madras, 12

Mahan, Capt. A. T., and American expansion, 160, 162, 164

Maḥmūd II, sultan of Turkey (1808–39): Greek revolt, 22–4; Muḥammad 'Alī and, 34, 35, 36, 37, 45, 58, 59; and Russia, 24–5, 34, 38, 43–6; and Great Britain, 34, 38, 44–6

Maine, boundary dispute, 69

Malcolm, Sir John, governor of Bombay (1827–30), 32, 49; missions to Persia, 27; view of Russian threat to India, 27, 28–9, 30, 72, 120; *History of Persia*, 28

Mallet, Louis, British foreign office official, view of German threat, 177

Malmesbury, 3rd earl of, British foreign secretary (1852, 1858–9), 99

Manchuria, 162; Russian ambitions in, 164–5, 173; and Russo-Japanese agreement (1907), 175

Marathas, British wars with, 12–13, 16

Marmara, Sea of, 135

Mauritius, 14

Mayo, 6th earl of, viceroy of India (1869–72), 129; views on Russo-British spheres in Asia, 128

Mecca, 58

Medina, 58

Mediterranean Agreements (1887), 148–9

Meerut, mutiny (1857), 101

Menshikov, Prince A. S., Russian mission to Constantinople (1853), 81, 82, 83, 85, 87, 115

Merv: importance of, 130, 136, 143; annexed by Russia, 144, 145

Metcalfe, Sir Charles, views on defence of India, 49

Metternich, Prince Clemens, Austrian foreign minister (1809–48) and chancellor (1821–48), 18, 38, 52, 59; Vienna settlement, 15; Russian partition proposals and, 70

Mexico, 69, 113

Miloš, Prince, ruler of Serbia (1813–39), mission of Col. Hodges, 52

Milyutin, Count D. A., Russian minister of war (1861–81), war in Caucasus, 104; views on Russian expansion in Asia, 116, 117–18, 120; military reforms, 131; Russo-Turkish war (1877–87), 136–7; and Germany, 140

Mingrelia, annexed by Russia, 104

Minto, 1st earl of, governor-general of India (1807–13), measures to defend India, 13–15

Minto, 2nd earl of, first lord of the admiralty (1835–41), 61

Mitchell Report on Sino-British trade, 110

Moldavia, *see* Principalities

Moluccas, captured by British (1810), 15

Mongolia, 104; Russian ambitions in, 165, 178; and Russo-Japanese agreement (1907), 175

Mongols, 10

Montenegro, crisis over (1852–3), 80–1; and crisis of 1875–81, 132, 135

Moscow–Tashkent Company, 123

Mughal Empire, decline of, 12, 16

Muḥammad Akbar Khān, negotiates with Macnaghten, 56

Muḥammad 'Alī, ruler of Egypt (1806–47), 45, 46, 51, 52; wars with sultan, 34, 35, 36, 37, 57, 59–61, 70, 85; and British routes to India, 57–8; expansion in Arabia, 57, 58, 59

Muḥammad Shāh, of Persia (1834–48), 57; designs on Herat, 47–9, 51, 52, 53, 65

Muhammarah, Perso-British war (1856–7), 98

Münchengratz, convention of (1833), 38, 64

Muravyov, Count N. N., governor-general of eastern Siberia: view of British threat, 104, 110; founds Vladivostok, 105

Muravyov, General N. N., captures Kars (1855), 94

Murray, Hon. Charles, British representative in Tehran (1854–7), dispute with Shah, 97–8

Muẓaffar al-Dīn, emir of Bukhārā (1860–85): negotiates with Ignatyev, 107–8; war with Russia, 123–4

Muẓaffar al-Dīn Shāh, of Persia (1896–1907), 165

Muzart Pass, 143

Mysore, conquered by British, 12–13

Nādir Shāh, of Persia (1736–47), 46

Nakhchivān, ceded to Russia (1828), 23

Nanking, treaty of (1842), 43, 63; British merchants disappointed, 98–9, 110
Napier, Commodore Sir Charles, naval actions in eastern Mediterranean, 61; in Baltic, 92–3
Napier, General Sir Charles, conquest of Sind, 73, 76
Napoleon I, Emperor of the French (1804–15), 179; debate about ambitions, 3; French expansion in Europe, 7–8, 13, 17; ambitions in Asia, 9, 13–14, 17, 20, 27
Napoleon III, Emperor of the French (1852–70), 9; Holy Places dispute, crisis of 1853, 79–80, 83, 91; Indo-China, 113–14; Polish revolt, 116; defeat at Sedan, 131
Navarino, battle of (1827), 22, 23, 26
Nepal, relationship with British India, 16, 51–2, 183
Nerchinsk, treaty of (1689), 8
Nesselrode, Count K. R., Russian foreign minister (1822–56), 102; assessment of Palmerston's policies, 65, 66, 75; 1844 memo, 71; and Vienna Note, 86
Nezib, battle of (1839), 59
Nicholas I, Emperor of Russia (1825–55), 52, 57, 117; view of Russian interests, 19, 39, 40, 41, 63–7, 94, 95–6, 101; Greek revolt, 21–4; cooperation with British, 21–2, 60–1, 64, 70–2; and Persia, 22–3, 39, 65; war with Turks (1828–9), 23–5, 39; policy towards Ottoman Empire, 25, 39, 44, 63–4, 65, 69–70, 78–9, 134; and Muḥammad ʿAlī, 34, 37, 38, 60–1, 63; and Austria, 38, 64, 66, 69–70, 80, 81; treaty of Hünkâr Iskelesi, 44, 60, 78; Khīva expedition (1839), 65–6; 1844 talks with British, 70–2, 75–6, 78; extradition crisis (1849), 77; crisis of 1853, 79–84, 86, 87; Crimean war, 88, 89–90; death, 95; expansion in east Asia, 104–5
Nicholas II, Emperor of Russia (1894–1917), 166, 171, 174; visit to Great Britain (1896), 153, 167; policy towards Japan, 164, 173–175; and German threat, 177–8
Nicholas, Grand Duke, 136
Nicolson, Arthur, British ambassador in St Petersburg (1906–10), 177
Niger river, and Franco-British dispute, 166
Nikolayevsk, 105
Nile river, and Franco-British crisis, 166, 167, 169

Ochakov, 27
Olmütz, conference at (1853), 87
Opium War (1839–42), 43, 53, 61, 62–3, 68, 104
Orenburg, 65; Orenburg–Tashkent railway, 153, 168
Orlov, Count A. F., negotiates treaty of Hünkâr Iskelesi, 44
Ottoman Empire, 8, 10, 29, 51, 103, 182, 184; war with Russia (18th century), 10–11, (1806–12), 14–15, (1828–9), 24–6, 28, 39, 40, (1853–6), 87–91, 94, 95, 96, (1877–8), 132, 134–5; Napoleonic Wars, 13, 14–15; Greek revolt, 19, 21–2; disintegration expected, 30, 34–5, 64, 65, 66, 69, 70–1, 78, 80, 82, 132, 167; war with Egypt (1831–3), 34–7, (1839–40), 59–62; and Russo-British rivalry in 1830s, 43–6, 51; extradition crisis (1849), 77; crises of 1852–3, 80–7; massacre of Armenians, 166, 167
Outram, General Sir James, expedition against Persia (1856–7), 98
Oxus river, see Amu Darya

Palestine, 80
Palmerston, 3rd viscount, British foreign secretary (1830–4, 1835–41, 1848–51), home secretary (1852–5), prime minister (1855–8, 1859–65), 26, 137; view of British interests, 33–8, 39–42, 103, 104, 126, 177; and France, 33, 52, 59–62, 68, 69; moves to counter Russia, 35–8, 43–5, 50–5, 94; and Ottoman Empire, 34–8, 43–46, 52, 59–62, 77, 79, 82, 83, 86,

Palmerston—*contd*
  89–90; and Metternich, 38, 52, 59; and Persia, 46–9, 53, 96–8, 109; and Afghanistan, 50–1, 54, 56, 97, 109; and Muḥammad 'Alī, 58–61; cooperation with Russia, 60–1, 64, 70, 71, 127; and China, 62–3, 96, 98–100; and USA, 68–9

Pamirs, 130; crisis, 155–6

Panama scandal, 151

Panjāb, 32, 47, 73, 107, 110, 182; British alliance, 14, 48–9, 50; annexed by British, 43, 72, 74–7, 108, 119; and Sind, 48, 50–1; after death of Ranjit Singh, 55, 74, 121; wars with British, 73–4

Panjdeh crisis (1885), 143, 144–7, 148, 155, 156

Paris, treaty of (1856), 43, 96, 115

Parkes, Harry, British consul at Canton, and *Arrow* crisis (1856), 99

Paskevich, Field-Marshal I. F., 31; and Russo-Persian War (1826–8), 23; and Russo-Turkish war (1828–29), 24

Paul, Emperor of Russia (1796–1801): withdrawal from Second Coalition, 8; project for invasion of India, 27, 40–1

Pechihli, Gulf of, 100

Peel, Sir Robert, British prime minister (1834–5, 1841–6), 28, 30, 56, 68; and conversations with Nicholas I (1844), 70–1, 75–6; 'uncontrollable principle' speech (Sind), 72–3, 119, 120; Panjāb war, 74

Pei-ho river, 98, 100

Peking, 157, 165, 172; occupied by British and French (1860), 100–101; treaty of (1860), 105, 122, 129; siege of legations, 169

Perovsky, Count V. A., governor of Orenburg (1833–42, 1851–7), 117; Khīva expedition (1839), 65

Perry, Commodore Matthew, 113

Persia, 10, 11, 29, 31, 35, 62, 63, 71, 102, 103, 147, 182, 184; French alliance (1807), 14; war with Russia (1804–13), 14–15, (1826–28), 20–3, 25, 28, 39, 40; British treaties, 20–1, 27; war with British, 43, 96–8, 100, 103, 109; designs on Herat, 46–9, 52, 53, 55, 96–8, 107; and Russo-British rivalry, 106–7, 112, 127, 153, 155; 156–7, 158, 159, 165–6; and 1907 convention, 176, 178

Peshawar, 31, 50, 110; annexed by Panjāb, 48, 54; Dost Muḥammad's plans to regain, 51, 75, 107

Peter I, Emperor of Russia (1683–1725), 29, 85

Philippines, annexed by USA (1898), 163–4

Piedmont, 92

Pindaris, 16

Pitt, William (The Younger), British prime minister (1783–1801, 1804–1806), 27

Plevna, siege of (1877), 134–5

Poland, 8, 10, 11, 15, 19, 27; resistance to Russian rule, 33, 34, 77, 102, 125; failure of international protest (1863), 115, 116, 117

Pollock, General Sir George, Kābul expedition (1842), 56

Ponsonby, 2nd baron (from 1839, 1st viscount), British ambassador in Constantinople (1832–7), 38, 44–45, 61

Port Arthur: leased to Russia, 165; captured by Japanese, 174

Port Hamilton, 144

Portugal, 22, 33, 34, 60, 99; empire in Asia, 12, 112, in Africa, 158

Pottinger, Lt. Eldred, and siege of Herat, 53

Pottinger, Sir Henry, British agent in Sind (1836–40), envoy to China (1841–3): Baluchistan mission, 28; treaties with Sind, 50–1; treaty of Nanking, 63

Pozzo di Borgo, Count, Russian, ambassador in London (1835–39), 66

Principalities of Moldavia and Wallachia, 70, 77; and treaty of Adrianople (1829), 25; occupied by Russia (1853), 81, 82, 83, 85, 90; occupied by Austria (1854), 94

Prussia, 8, 33, 92, 94, 116, 126, 131, 184; and Napoleonic Wars, 7, 13; and congress of Vienna, 15, 19; and Ottoman Empire, 61, 84
Putyatin, Admiral E. V., negotiations with China, 105

Qandahār, 47, 48, 51, 65, 106, 141; occupied by British (1839), 54, (1878) 139, by Dost Muḥammad (1855), 97
Quakers: peace societies, 111; delegation to Nicholas I, 111
Quarterly Review, 125–6
Quetta, 112, 139, 144

Ranjit Singh, ruler of the Panjāb (1799–1839): alliance with British, 32, 48–9, 54, 121–2; consequences of death, 55, 56, 74
Rawlinson, Sir Henry, writings on British policy in Asia, 125–6 138, 139
Reichstadt agreement (1876), 132
Reinsurance Treaty (1887), 149, 150
Réunion, 14
Reuter, Baron Julius de, and Persian concession, 156
Reutern, Count M. K., Russian finance minister (1862–78), opposes expansion in central Asia, 117
Revel, 93
Rhodes, island, 70
Roberts, General Sir Frederick, and 2nd Afghan war, 141
Roebuck, J. A., British radical M.P., and debate on Sind, 73–4
Romanovsky, General D. I., and war against Bukhārā, 124
Roosevelt, Theodore, President of USA (1901–9), Asst. Secretary of the Navy (1897–8), 164
Rumania, 135
Russell, Lord John, British prime minister (1846–52), 65–6; foreign secretary (1852–3, 1859–65), 68; crisis of 1853, 82, 86, 89; approach to Russia, 127
Russia: character of rivalry with Great Britain, 1–3, 5–6, 181–5; enhanced power 1800–20, 10–11, 15–17; reactions to British activity in Asia, 63–7, 70–2, 75–9, 102–6, 111–12, 121; cooperation with Great Britain, 21–2, 60–4, 70–2, 75–9, 175, 178

Saburov, P. A., Russian ambassador in Berlin (1879–84), 140
Saigon, attacked by French, 113
St Petersburg, treaty of (1881), 143
Salisbury, 3rd marquis of, British prime minister (1885–6, 1886–92, 1895–1902), foreign secretary (1878–80, 1885–6, 1887–92, 1895–1900), secretary of state for India (1866–7, 1874–8): crisis of 1875–81, 132, 136, 137, 139, 142; and Straits, 138, 147, 153, 167; Panjdeh crisis (1885), 145–6, 147; extension of British influence in Asia, 154–5; and Persia, 156–7, 159, 165–6; and China, 158, 159, 166; and partitioning of world, 158, 167; and crises of 1890s, 166–7, 169–70; cabinet doubts about policy, 168, 169–70; retirement, 170; comparison with Lansdowne's policy, 170
Samarqand, captured and annexed by Russia, 124, 125
Samoa, 163
Sandeman, Sir Robert, British agent in Baluchistan (1877–92), 154
San Stefano, treaty of (1878), 135, 136, 137
Sazonov, S. D., Russian foreign minister (1910–16), 178
Schmoller, Gustav, German economist, prophetic view of world politics, 160
Sedan, 131
Selborne, earl of, first lord of the admiralty (1900–5): and Russo-Japanese war, 174; and Tirpitz's naval programme, 177
Semipalatinsk 117
Seoul, 161
Serbia, 70; autonomy recognized, 25; Hodges mission, 52; and crisis of

Serbia—*contd*
1875–81, 132, 135; war with Bulgaria, 148; and 1914–18 war, 178
Sevastopol, 89, 131, 136; siege, capture, 92, 93, 94
Seward, William H., arguments for American expansion, 113, 114
Seymour, Sir Hamilton, British ambassador in St Petersburg (1851–54), conversations with Nicholas I, 81
Shāh Shujāʿ, Afghan ruler (1803–9, 1839–42), and British invasion of 1839, 54, 55, 56
Shakespear, Capt. Richmond, release of Russian slaves from Khīva, 55
Shāmil, imām of Daghestan and war against Russia in Caucasus, 104
Shantung, 162; murder of German missionaries in (1897), 163
Shēr ʿAlī, emir of Afghanistan (1863–79), 130; and Badakshān 128; relations with British India, 129; and British invasion (1878), 139
Shimonoseki, treaty of, 164
Shuvalov, Count Peter A., Russian ambassador in London (1874–9): special mission about Khīva expedition, 130; and 1877–8 war, 135
Siam, crisis of 1893, 155
Siberia, early Russian expansion, 8–9, 10
Sidon, 61
Sikhs, 49, 50, 51, 56
Sikkim, 172
Simonich, Count, Russian representative in Tehran: and Persian designs on Herat, 47, 53; recalled, 65; view of British threat, 66
Sind, 47, 55, 57, 112, 121, 182; French and Persian overtures, 14; threat from Panjāb, 48, 50; British treaties, 50–1, 54, 123; annexed by British, 43, 72–3, 75, 76, 108, 119
Sinkiang, Russian activities in, 178
Sinop, Turkish defeat (1853), its significance, 88–9, 91

Sīstān, 176; Khanykov's expedition (1858), 106; British railway project, 155
Skobelev, General M. D., defeats Tekke Turcomans, 143
Social Darwinism, and imperialist attitudes, 159–61, 162–3
Solomon, King of Imeretʿi, struggle against Russia, 15
South Manchurian Railway, 165
Soviet Union: view of world politics, 180; and Second World War, 180; and Cold War, 180–1
Spain, 60, 69; intervention in (1823), 19; empire in Asia, 112; war with USA, 164
Stoddart, Col. Charles, and ultimatum to Persia (1838), 53; death at Bukhārā, 66
Stoletov, General N. G., mission to Kābul (1878), 136,139
Stopford, Admiral Sir Robert, attack on Acre (1840), 61
Straits, 26, 30, 57, 63, 70, 71, 134, 142; treaty of Adrianople, 25; treaty of Hünkâr Iskelesi, 43–4; 1841 convention, 60–2, 66, 77, 80; 1849 crisis, 77; crises of 1852–3, 80, 88; crisis of 1875–81, 136–7, 138; Panjdeh crisis, 146; Reinsurance Treaty, 149; change in British policy, 153–4, 167, 168; Izvolsky and, 175
Sudan, 146
Suez, and British route to India, 57, 58, 138
Sukhozanet, General N. O., Russian war minister (1855–61), view of British threat, 102
Sutlej river, 16, 17, 27, 48, 49, 56, 74
Suvorov, Field-Marshal Alexander, 8
Suzak, captured by Russians (1864), 118
Svaneti, annexed by Russia, 104
Sveaborg, Franco–British bombardment, 92–3
Sweden, 8, 10, 93, 94
Switzerland, 8
Syr-Darʿya river, 117
Syria, and Muḥammad ʿAlī, 34, 35, 45, 57–61

Tabriz, captured by Russians (1827), 23
Taiping rebellion, 99, 111
Taku, and *Arrow* war, 100
Talki Pass, 143
Talleyrand, Prince, 15
Tashkent, 120, 143, 144, 153; attacked by Chernyayev, 118, 122–3, 127; Russian policy towards, 122; annexed by Russia, 124, 125
Taylor, A. J. P., controversy over Hitler's foreign policy, 3
Tbilisi (Tiflis), 11, 143, 144
Tehran, 14, 21, 23, 35, 36; status of British mission, 46–7; Russo-British rivalry at, 63, 65, 156–7
Tekes valley, 143
Tekke Turcomans, defeat Russians, 140, 141; power destroyed by Russians, 143
Temperley, H. W. V., view of Turkish policy in 1853, 84
Thiers, Adolphe, 61–2
Three Emperors' Alliance (1881), 142–3, 148, 150
Tibet, 182; Younghusband expedition, 171–3; 1907 convention, 176; Russian ambitions, 178
Tien-shan mts, 140
Tientsin, treaty of (1858), 43, 100; British merchants and, 110
Tilsit, treaty of (1807), 13, 14
Times, The, view of crisis of 1853, 86, 89
Tirpitz, Admiral Alfred von, 162–3
Todd, Major d'Arcy, breach with Herat government, 55
Totleben, Count E. I., defence of Sevastopol, 93; advice to Alexander II in 1878, 136–7
Toulon, visit of Russian fleet (1893), 151
Tourane, 113
Trans-Siberian Railway, 157, 158, 161, 164, 173
Trebizond, 24
Triple Alliance (1882), 149, 150, 151, 152, 153, 170
Tripoli, 80
Trucial coast, 59
Tsushima Straits, battle of (1905), 175

Turkey, *see* Ottoman Empire
Turkistān, town of, captured by Russians (18-64), 118
Turkistān, governorate-general established, 124
Turkomānchāy, treaty of (1828), 23, 156
Tyre, 61

United States of America, 3, 111, 118, 158; relations with Great Britain, 68–9, 70, 71, 96, 166, 170–1; and China, 100; views of expansion in Asia, 112–13, 114, 159, 161, 163–4; Civil War, 114, 121, 126; annexes Hawaii and Philippines, 163–4; and 1914–18 war, 179; and 1941–45 war, 180; and Cold War, 180–1
Urquhart, David: writings on Russian threat, 41, 45; and 'Vixen' affair, 60; and Caucasus after 1856, 103
Ussuri river, 105
Ust-Urt plateau, 130

Valikhanov, Capt. Chokan, mission to Kashgar (1858–9), 108, 117
Varna, captured by Russians (1828), 24
Verevkin, Col. N. A., and Khokand Line (1864), 118
Vernoye, captured by Russians (1854), 117
Vienna, 16; congress of, 19, 33
Vienna Note, 84, 85, 86, 87
Vitkevich, Capt., 66; mission to Kābul, 51, 65
Vixen incident (1836), 60
Vladivostok, 105, 144
Volga river, 116, 130
Vyshnegradsky, I. A., Russian finance minister (1887–92), 154

Wahhābi, 58
Wake island, 164
Wallachia, *see* Principalities
Wellesley, Marquis, governor-general of India (1798–1805), 16, 27, 121; conquest of Mysore, 12–13
Wellington, Duke of, British prime minister (1828–30), 28, 34; view

Wellington, Duke of—*contd*
 of Russian expansion, 26, 30–3, 35, 38, 39–42, 126, 177
Willcock, Sir Henry, memo on British interests in Asia, 35–6
William II, German Emperor (1888–1918), 9; Reinsurance Treaty not renewed, 149; and social Darwinist attitudes, 162–3; and Kiaochow lease, 162–3, 164; and Kruger telegram, 166
William IV, King of Great Britain (1830–7), 32
Wilson, Sir Robert, view of Russian threat, 28
Witte, Sergei, Russian finance minister (1892–1903), and economic imperialism, 154, 159, 165; and Persia, 155, 157, 165–6; and China, 155, 157–8; and Japan, 164–5
Wolff, Sir Henry Drummond, British minister in Tehran (1888–91), 156–7

Wood, Sir Charles, president of (India) board of control (1852–5), view of crisis of 1853, 89
Wood, Richard, British agent in Syria (1832–3, 1835–6), 61
Wynn, C. W. Williams, president of (Indian) control (1822–7), and Russo-Persian war, 21

Yaʿqūb Bey, ruler of Kashgar, relations with Russia and Great Britain, 129
Yarkand, 128
Yellow Sea, 165
Younghusband, Capt. Francis, Pamirs expedition, 155; Tibetan expedition, 171–3
Yüan Shi-k'ai, and Chinese influence in Korea, 161

Zarafshān river, 124
Zulfiqar, 146–7

For Product Safety Concerns and Information please contact our EU
representative GPSR@taylorandfrancis.com
Taylor & Francis Verlag GmbH, Kaufingerstraße 24, 80331 München, Germany

www.ingramcontent.com/pod-product-compliance
Lightning Source LLC
Chambersburg PA
CBHW061443300426
44114CB00014B/1815